Climbing & Hiking in Ecuador

THE BRADT STORY

In 1974, my (former) husband George and I spent three days sitting on a river barge in Bolivia writing our first guide for like-minded travellers: *Backpacking along Ancient Ways in Peru and Bolivia*. The 'little yellow book', as it became known, is now in its sixth edition and continues to sell to travellers throughout the world. Since 1980, with the establishment of Bradt Publications, I have continued to publish guides for the discerning traveller, covering more than 100 countries and all six continents, and winning the 1997 *Sunday Times* Small Publisher of the Year Award; *Climbing & Hiking in Ecuador* (4th edition) is the 136th Bradt guide to be published.

The company continues to develop new titles and new series, but in the forefront of my mind there remains our original ethos – responsible travel with an emphasis on the culture and natural history of the region. I hope that you will get the most out of your trip, and perhaps have the opportunity to give something in return.

Travel guides are by their nature continuously evolving. If you experience anything which you would like to share with us, or if you have any amendments to make to this guide, please write; all your letters are read and passed on to the author. Most importantly, do remember to travel with an open mind and to respect the customs of your hosts – it will add immeasurably to your enjoyment.

Happy travelling!

Hilary Bradt

Hilary Bradt

41 Nortoft Road, Chalfont St Peter, Bucks, SL9 0LA, England
Tel/fax: 01494 873478 Email: bradtpublications@compuserve.com

Climbing & Hiking in

Ecuador

4th Edition

Rob Rachowiecki
Mark Thurber
Betsy Wagenhauser

Bradt Publications, UK
The Globe Pequot Press Inc, USA

First edition published in 1984 by Bradt Publications.
This fourth edition published in 1997 by Bradt Publications,
41 Nortoft Road, Chalfont St Peter, Bucks SL9 0LA, England.
Published in the USA by The Globe Pequot Press Inc, 6 Business Park Road,
PO Box 833, Old Saybrook, Connecticut 06475-0833.

The author and publishers have made every effort to ensure the accuracy of the
information in this book at the time of going to press. However, they cannot accept any
responsibility for any loss, injury or inconvenience resulting
from the use of information contained in this guide.

British Library Cataloguing in Publication Data
A catalogue record for this book is available from the British Library
ISBN 1 898323 54 2

Library of Congress Cataloging-in-Publication Data
Rachowiecki, Rob, 1954-
    Climbing & hiking in Ecuador / Rob Rachowiecki, Mark Thurber,
Betsy Wagenhauser. – 4th ed.
        p. cm.
    Rev. ed. of: Climbing and hiking in Ecuador. c1984
    Includes index.
    ISBN 1-898323-54-2
    1. Mountaineering–Ecuador–Guidebooks. 2. Hiking—Ecuador—
Guidebooks. 3. Ecuador–Guidebooks. I. Thurber, Mark. II. Title.
        GV199.44.E2R33   1997
918.6604'74—dc21   97-22963
                                                        CIP

Cover photographs
Front: Antisana from Cotopaxi (Bob Lancaster, High Places)
Back: Cofan Indian (Hilary Bradt)
Engravings From *Travels Amongst the Great Andes of the Equator* by Edward
Whymper, originally published in 1891 by John Murray
Maps *Inside covers*: Steve Munns *Others*: Mark Thurber, Hans van Well

Typeset from the author's disc by Patti Taylor, London NW10 1JR
Printed and bound in Great Britain by The Guernsey Press Co Ltd

CONTENTS

MAPS

ABOUT THE AUTHORS

Mark Thurber has been living in Ecuador for the past three years but periodically visits his home in the Pacific Northwest, USA, when it is not raining. When not rambling in the mountains of Ecuador and Peru he splits his time between guiding and working as an environmental consultant in the Oriente of Ecuador.

After several years living in South America, including a long stint in Ecuador, Englishman Rob Rachowiecki moved to Arizona where he now lives with his American wife and three children. He returns to Ecuador and Peru every year both as a tour leader for Wilderness Travel, the adventure travel company, and to research his other popular travel guidebooks.

Betsy Wagenhauser is an experienced climber. She set up and ran for several years the South American Explorers Club in Quito, during which time she updated the second edition of this guide. She now lives in Central Asia.

Readers' comments can be sent directly to either of the authors by email. Rob Rachowiecki: RobRachow@aol.com and Mark Thurber: sun@ecnet.ec.

DANGER: TOURISTS

Tourism need not be a destructive force for tribal peoples but unfortunately it frequently is. We at Bradt Publications totally support the initiative of the charity Survival in protecting the rights of tribal peoples:

Recognize land rights
  Obtain permission to enter
  Pay properly
  Behave as if on private property

Respect tribal peoples
  Don't demean, degrade, insult or patronize

Don't bring in disease
  Diseases such as colds can kill tribal peoples
  AIDS is a killer

Survival (11-15 Emerald Street, London WC1N 3QL, England; tel: 0171 242 1441; fax: 0171 242 1771; email: survival@gn.apc.org) is a worldwide organization supporting tribal peoples. It stands for their right to decide their own future and helps them protect their lives, lands and human rights.

ACKNOWLEDGEMENTS TO THE FOURTH EDITION

A generous thank-you to all the outdoor enthusiasts who helped update the book for the fourth edition. Jane Letham was singularly of greatest help in this project, both accompanying me on numerous hikes and editing the new figures and text. Rosa Calahorrano scanned all of the new maps and diagrams, added text and was extremely patient with numerous changes. Thai Verzone sketched the peaks and also provided invaluable information on many of the climbing routes. Peace Corps volunteer and climbing partner John Clark wrote the section on the new Reserva Ecológica Mache-Chindul and provided important information on other routes. Woulter Devriendt took time from his banking career and often acted as driver and negotiator on outings in the *páramo*. Peter Ayarza, Jorge Ayarza, Jon McClurg, Nina Binder, Will Surber, Jay Graham, Catherine Hubler, Peter Hibbs, David Naish, Michael Johnson, Rowhan Marshall, Martin Leitz, Chris Canaday, Sven Claeys, Logan Ward, Valerie Hahn, Jason Haberstadt, Susan Kirinich, Yossi Brian, Stefanie Prügel, Willy Navarette, Thomas Burg, Mark James, David Douglas, Charles Erhart, Stan Lanzano, Clive Cutler, Michele Leonard, Brian Collins, Clay Roscoe and Janet Scheile are among the many climbing and hiking partners and acquaintances who helped in revising this edition.

The staff and written resources at the South American Explorers Club in Quito were essential to this update; particular thanks to club managers Damaris Carlisle and Sheila Corwin. An inspiring group of college students from the Costa Rica Outward Bound School walked with me from Atillo to Achupallas and then on to Ingapirca. Thanks to the numerous GAP and Inti Travel groups that tolerated my note-taking while guiding. David Gayton and Jean Brown from Safari provided a good photo of Chimborazo. Fausto Lopez of Fundación Ecológica Arco Iris helped with updates on the Parque Nacional Podocarpus. Dr Marcos Serrano and the rest of the San Gabriel climbing club helped with logistical information. James Attwood and Piet Sabbe wrote the section on the Golondrinas area and Richard Parsons wrote the section on the Tandayapa area. Juan Diego Dominguez helped update the section on Parque Nacional Cajas. Michele Kirby and Andy Hammerman of the Black Sheep Inn provided much of the information for the Chugchilán area. Peace Corps volunteer Shane McCarthy wrote updates on Parque Nacional Sangay. Luis Martinez from INEFAN provided excellent information on walks in Reserva Ecológica Cayambe-Coca. David Parión draws me back to Oyacachi again and again with his enthusiasm and love of the Reserva Ecológica Cayambe-Coca. Don Francisco Chimbo is an inspiration to me as I grow older – he is still hacking his way through the jungles of Sumaco in his 60s.

Finally, many thanks to Rob Rachowiecki and Hilary Bradt for giving me the opportunity to contribute to the text and an incentive to stride out into the hills of the Ecuadorian Andes.

Mark Thurber

Introduction

WHY ECUADOR?

Though one of the smallest countries in South America, Ecuador offers an incredible diversity of scenery, wildlife and people. The mountaineer and adventurous traveller have a choice of the ice-clad Andes, tropical rainforest, mountain trails leading to Inca ruins, and quiet beaches; all these attractions lie within a day's journey of Quito, the capital city. This accessibility makes Ecuador an attractive destination for climbers and hikers of all abilities, and avoids the long approaches and expedition planning often necessary in other high mountain ranges.

Mountaineers find Ecuador well suited as a high-altitude training ground. There are many technically straightforward ascents of 5,000m peaks. Climbers can gain technical experience in the lower ranges of Europe and North America and then learn about how the body functions at high altitudes in the Ecuadorian Andes. A combination of these abilities will produce climbers ready to challenge some of the world's most difficult high peaks.

Superb mountain scenery is only one of Ecuador's attractions. It has some of the best beaches in South America, colourful indigenous markets and plenty of wildlife, especially birds. Come and see for yourself.

PREFACE TO THE FOURTH EDITION

A concerted effort has been made to update and correct descriptions of hikes and climbs for the fourth edition by making numerous field visits. As with any outdoor guide, it is a labour of love for the authors and the publisher. We rely on readers to point out changes in routes and errors, and to give us new ideas for future editions. Everyone who takes the time to send a letter or email to us at Bradt with careful comments makes the next edition more understandable to future travellers to Ecuador. We appreciate all your feedback.

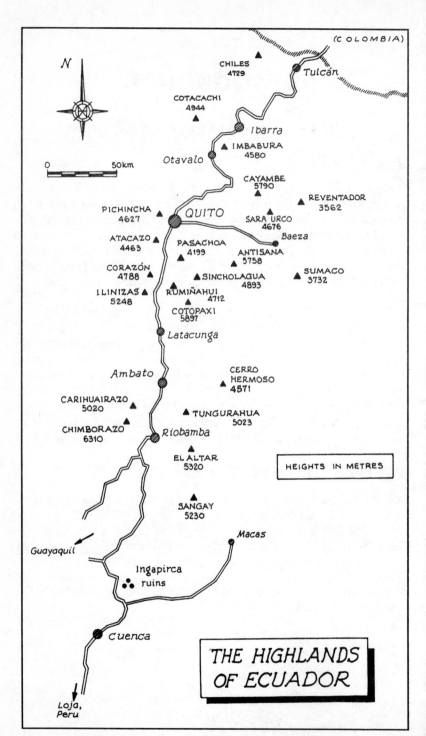

N

0   50km

(COLOMBIA)

CHILES
4729

Tulcán

COTACACHI
4944

Ibarra

IMBABURA
4580

Otavalo

CAYAMBE
5790

REVENTADOR
3562

PICHINCHA
4627

QUITO

SARA URCO
4676

Baeza

ATACAZO
4463

PASACHOA
4199

ANTISANA
5758

CORAZÓN
4788

SINCHOLAGUA
4893

SUMACO
3732

ILINIZAS
5248

RUMIÑAHUI   4712

COTOPAXI
5897

Latacunga

CERRO
HERMOSO
4571

Ambato

CARIHUAIRAZO
5020

TUNGURAHUA
5023

CHIMBORAZO
6310

Riobamba

EL ALTAR
5320

HEIGHTS IN METRES

SANGAY
5230

Macas

Guayaquil

Ingapirca
ruins

Cuenca

THE HIGHLANDS
OF ECUADOR

Loja,
Peru

Chapter One

General Information

'A traveler. I love his title. A traveler is to be reverenced as such. His profession is the best symbol of our life. Going from–toward; it is the history of every one of us.'

Henry David Thoreau

ECUADOR: THE FACTS

Size
283,520km² (second smallest republic in South America)
685km from north to south.

Population
12,000,000 (1998 estimate)
40% indigenous, 40% *mestizo*, 10% European, 10% others
48% of the population live on the coastal plain, 47% in the Andean sierra and 5% in the eastern lowlands (the Oriente).
Population growth 2.9% per annum
Population density 42 per km² (highest in South America)

Main towns
Quito The capital, in the highlands. Population 1,200,000.
Guayaquil Largest city and main port. Population 1,600,000.
Cuenca Main town of southern highlands. Population 200,000.

History
1527   First Spanish contact; Pizarro's men land at Esmeraldas, in northern Ecuador.
1535   Incorporated into the viceroyalty of Peru; Ecuador is known as the Audiencia de Quito.
1822   Ecuador gains independence from Spain after the battle of Pichincha, May 24, under the leadership of Mariscal Sucre. Incorporated into Gran Colombia.
1830   Becomes fully independent under first president, Juan Flores.
1942   War with Peru; much of the Ecuadorian Amazon lost to Peru but Ecuador still claims this region.

1979   First democratic elections in seven years.
1995   President Abdala Bucaram elected.
1997   Bucaram outsted by congress and replaced by President Fabian
        Alarcon.

Weather

Quito Rainy season: September–May; average annual rainfall 1,270mm.
Mean temperature 13°C; average high temperature 22°C, average low
temperature 7°C. *Guayaquil* Rainy season: December–May. Average high
temperature 32°C, average low temperature 20°C.

Holidays

January 1	New Year's Day
Movable	Epiphany
Movable	Carnival (Monday and Tuesday before Lent)
Movable	Holy Thursday, Good Friday, Holy Saturday, Easter Sunday
May 1	Labour Day
May 24	Battle of Pichincha
July 24	Bolívar's Birthday
August 10	Quito Independence Day
October 9	Guayaquil Independence Day
October 12	Columbus Day
November 1	All Saints' Day
November 2	All Souls' Day
November 3	Cuenca Independence Day
December 6	Foundation of Quito
December 24-25	Christmas

GEOGRAPHY

Geographically, Ecuador is one of the most varied countries in the world,
despite its small size: 283,520km², only a little larger than Great Britain.

The Andean range is at its narrowest here and divides the country into
three distinct regions. To the east of the Central Sierra lies the tropical
rainforest of the upper Amazon basin (known as the Oriente) and to the
west are the more accessible but equally hot and humid coastal lowlands.
It is barely 200km from the western lowlands to the eastern jungle, yet
within this narrow area are found peaks to 6,310m forming two major
cordilleras or mountain ranges.

The two *cordilleras* run north–south and are 40 to 60km apart. Between
them lies the fertile Central Valley which is about 400km long and contains
Quito and most of Ecuador's major cities as well as almost half of the
country's inhabitants. It is this Central Valley that was called 'The Avenue
of the Volcanoes' by the famous German explorer and scientist, Alexander
von Humboldt, who visited Ecuador in 1802.

CLIMATE

Most descriptions of Ecuador's climate agree that its most reliable aspect is its unreliability. Unfortunately, this really seems to be the case, so it is difficult to give foolproof advice on the best months in which to visit. However, some generalizations are possible.

In common with other tropical countries, Ecuador does not experience the four seasons known in temperate parts of the world. Instead there are wet and dry seasons. Despite its small size, Ecuador has several distinct climatic zones with wet and dry periods varying from area to area.

The coastal areas are influenced by the cold Humboldt current which flows up from the south Pacific, but during December a warm current from the north, seasonably called 'El Niño' (the Christ Child), predominates. This marks the beginning of the coastal rainy season. The northern coast is wet from January to June and dryish for the rest of the year, while further south the coast experiences a shorter wet season and in the dry season, from May to December, it is much drier than in the north. The effects of 'El Niño' are not yet fully understood, and in some years there are devastating floods in the coastal lowlands during the wet season.

Inland, the climate is completely different. It rains most of the time in the Oriente though some months are a little less wet than others, depending on the area. The weather in the mountains varies from east to west. The eastern mountains, especially Antisana, El Altar and Sangay, and to a lesser extent Cayambe and Tungurahua, are influenced by air from the Amazonian lowlands. The wettest months are June through August. December and January are when the highest number of successful ascents have been made on the difficult El Altar. Ecuadorian climbers favour February for climbing Antisana, and October through January are suggested for Cayambe.

The situation is reversed in the western mountains. Here, the dry season is late June through early September, with a short dry spell in December and early January. The wettest months are February to May with April being the wettest of all. Edward Whymper claims to have spent 78 days in the vicinity of Iliniza during February to April of 1880 '... yet we did not see the whole of the mountain on any single occasion'. During the dry season temperatures tend to be very low at night and high winds can be a problem, particularly in August. The weather in October and November tends to be variable. Snow build-up during these months sometimes provides quite good snow conditions for the short December–January season.

The temperature variation is mainly influenced by altitude. From sea level to about 900m it is hot with an average temperature of 26°–28°C. The warm zone is from 900m to 2,000m with an average temperature range of 20°–26°C. From 2,000m to 3,000m it is quite cold with an average of 12°–20°C. (Remember that average includes warm afternoons and freezing nights.) Above 3,000m is the *páramo,* with temperatures averaging from 0° to 12°C, and above the lowest snowline at about 4,500m the mean temperature stays below freezing, although the strong sun sometimes makes it feel much warmer.

There have been noticeable recent changes in the world's climatic patterns and Ecuador has been experiencing a period of relative drought compared with a century ago (although this is difficult to believe when you are caught in a torrential Ecuadorian downpour). This has also contributed to the receding glaciers on Ecuador's mountains. Some people also claim that sunspot and other solar activity affects the climate in a seven-to-eleven-year cycle. Certainly, a year of greater precipitation is experienced at irregular intervals. Although proper detailed records have been kept only since about the 1960s, it is known that the periods 1965, 1972–73, 1975–76 and 1982–83 have been particularly wet. This cycle is said to be wet to begin with and drier in later years; the drier years mean a significant reduction or disappearance of glaciers. In 1981, the last year of the most recent cycle, many mountains which have permanent glaciers shown on the IGM maps were completely bare of snow. Examples include Iliniza Norte and Sincholagua. After the wet years of 1982–83 more snow and ice were again found on these peaks but the last few years have been considerably drier, as evidenced by the glacial recession on most of the peaks.

Not only is there variation in the climate from year to year, but the daily weather is also highly unpredictable. There is a local saying that in the mountains all four seasons can be experienced in one day. As Michaux notes in his *Ecuador: A Travel Journal* (1928):

> 'Morning summer.
> Noon springtime. The sky is beginning to get overcast.
> 4 p.m. rain. Freshness.
> A night cold and luminous like winter.
> For this reason clothing is a problem if you must be out for more than a few hours.
> You watch the accursed setting forth, armed with straw hat, canvas, furpiece, and umbrella.'

It is amazing and confusing that so much variation can be found in such a small area. With windows of good weather and seasonal variations, climbing any given mountain in any given month is feasible. However, as a general rule, December and January are the best months to be in the Ecuadorian mountains and March to May the worst. If you're there in June through September, avoid the east and climb in the west. In October through February concentrate on the east. Cotopaxi lies in a strange dry micro-climate of its own and can be climbed during most of the year.

GEOLOGY

Tectonically, Ecuador is similar to other countries around the 'Pacific Ring of Fire'. A dense oceanic plate (Nazca Plate) is subducting under a less dense continental plate (South American Plate). The collision of the two plates has resulted in the uplift of the Ecuadorian Andes and partial melting of the mantle below the South American Plate. The melts or magmas forming at the base of the South American Plate migrate along weaknesses in the earth's crust, eventually erupting on the surface to form volcanoes. Consequently the landscape of Ecuador is quite dynamic, with numerous eruptions and earthquakes as well as lahars (volcanic mud flows) and landslides all constantly reforming the geography. These geological events have also caused a tremendous amount of destruction and loss of human life throughout the history of Ecuador.

The core of the Sierra was first uplifted in the Palaeozoic era, 230 million years ago, and divides the drainages of the Oriente and the coast. The visually dominant geological features in the Sierra are the short-lived (in geological time) volcanoes represented mostly as the numerous eroded volcanic edifices. An example of one of these extinct volcanoes is the craggy peak of Cerro Imbabura near the town of Otavalo. There are eight active volcanoes towering above the landscape, occasionally throwing out ash and lava flows to counteract the erosive work of lahars, glaciers and rivers. Cotopaxi (5,897m) is a classic and famous example of an active cone-shaped volcano.

The Sierra is really two geologically distinct mountain ranges: the Cordillera Real (eastern range) and the Cordillera Occidental (western range). A system of generally north–south trending valleys (the Central Valley or Valley of the Volcanoes) separates these two ranges in the northern part of the country. These valleys are down-dropped blocks or grabens and are filled with a thick layer of sediments and volcanic ash, which makes for very fertile soil.

The metamorphic basement rocks of the Cordillera Real are older (Palaeozoic era) and consist mainly of high-grade metamorphic rocks like gneisses and mica-schists. These rocks were once buried deeply in the crust and exposed to high pressures and temperatures, but now are being uplifted towards the surface. However, basement rocks are generally not exposed in the Sierra because they are covered by a thick layer of volcanic material. They can be observed in the 'fold and thrust belt' on the eastern slope of the Andes (first you need to cut through the thick cloudforest to actually see the rock!). The alpine-looking Cerro Sara Urco is made of this hard crystalline rock and so is good for rock climbing.

The basement rocks of the Cordillera Occidental are volcanic units from the Cretaceous to Upper Tertiary ages that probably developed originally in the form of an 'island arc' (like Japan) and were subsequently sutured on to the South American Plate. Intense volcanic activity has also covered the basement rocks in the Cordillera Occidental but interesting outcrops of bedrock (such as quartzite and conglomerates) can be observed in the river valleys cutting down the western slope (eg: Angamarca).

The coast is a 'fore-arc sedimentary basin' but is probably underlain by oceanic crust of the Mesozoic age – a piece of the ocean crust that was sutured on to the South American Plate that is now covered by sediments. The geography here consists of a wide hilly terrain drained mostly by the Río Guayas and Río Esmeraldas. There is a low coastal range (about 600m high) which was uplifted in the Neogene era (2 to 22 million years ago) and which harbours some interesting coastal forest. Parque Nacional Machalilla and Reserva Ecológica Mache-Chindul protect some of the remnant forests in this range.

The Oriente is a 'back-arc sedimentary basin'. Sediments eroded from the Sierra have been transported by rivers and deposited in this basin for millions of years. The transition zone between the eastern slope of the Sierra and the Oriente is faulted and folded, resulting in several small cordilleras and a hilly geomorphology. These largely unvisited ridges and peaks on the eastern slope of the Sierra extend into the Oriente (eg: Cordillera de Los Guacamayos or Vieja Cordillera de Cutucú). There are also several anomalous volcanoes completely separated from the Sierra that poke up through the jungle in the Oriente. The most important are Volcán Reventador (3,562m) and Volcán Sumaco (3,732m), both of which are active and relatively inaccessible.

Farther east in the Oriente the sediments are more flat lying and less deformed. This area was once a shallow inland sea that harboured swampy vegetation. As the organic material was buried and heated it was converted to oil and natural gas which has been trapped in fold axes and faults. Texaco discovered this oil near Lago Agrio in the late 1960s – an event which has radically changed the environment of the Oriente. Towns, an infrastructure of roads and oil pipelines, and an alarmingly high rate of deforestation have resulted in profound changes to the ecosystem.

NATURAL HISTORY

The great variety of habitats in a country which rises from ocean to snow peaks and drops back to tropical rainforest ensures an abundance of wildlife. The best-known wildlife reserve is the Galápagos Islands; the plants and animals found there are fully described in several good guidebooks. The mainland, on the other hand, is a relatively unstudied naturalist's paradise. Since there are no comprehensive field guides to the flora and fauna, Ecuador offers wonderful opportunities for study for a field researcher but many frustrations for the ordinary traveller who has difficulty in identifying this bewildering wildlife.

Although Ecuador lies in the heart of the tropics you wouldn't call the natural history of the highlands tropical. Indeed, the vegetation here has been compared to that of the arctic tundra. This is because altitude as well as latitude has an important influence on the flora and fauna of an area. Pioneer work on this concept was done in Ecuador in 1802 by the German scientist Alexander von Humboldt. He related ecology to altitude and recognized three major ecological zones: lowland (hot), central (temperate), and highland (cold). This last is said to begin at about 3,200m and continue to the glaciated mountain tops. It can be sub-divided into the snow region above about 4,700m, where insects and birds are occasionally seen, and the area below the permanent snowline which is known as the *páramo*.

The *páramo* is a highly specialized zone unique to tropical America, and found only from the highlands of Costa Rica at 10° north down to northern Peru at 10° south. Similarly elevated areas in other parts of the world differ in their climates and evolutionary history. Most of the hikes and climbs in this book will pass through the *páramo*, so this section concentrates on highland ecology rather than giving space to the overwhelmingly diverse flora and fauna of low-lying areas which deserve a book to themselves. (See *Further Reading* for suggested books on the subject.)

Páramo weather is typically cold and wet, with frequent rain often replaced by moist mists and clouds. Snow falls occasionally and strong winds are common. Night-time temperatures are below freezing and glaring sunlight can be a hazard during short spells of fine weather. In short, conditions are harsh, and comparatively few animals are seen. Plants, on the other hand, have adapted well to this difficult environment and as a result the vegetation looks strange and interesting.

Flora

The Andean flora has evolved over many millions of years of uplift of the range. Thus the vegetation has had adequate time slowly to modify itself. The major adaptations have been the formation of smaller and thicker leaves which are less susceptible to frost; the development of curved leaves with thick waxy skins to reflect or absorb extreme solar radiation during cloudless days; the growth of a fine hairy 'down' as insulation on the plant's surface; the arrangement of leaves into a rosette pattern to prevent them shading one another during photosynthesis and to protect the delicate centre; and the progressive compacting of the plants until they grow close to the ground where the temperature is more constant and there is protection from the wind. Thus many *páramo* plants are characteristically small and compact, some resembling a hard, waxy, green carpet. There are exceptions to this however, including the giant *frailejones* and the *puyas*.

Giant espeletia, locally known as *frailejones*, are a weird sight as they float into view in a typical *páramo* mist. They are high enough to resemble human beings – hence the name *frailejones,* which means greyfriars. Despite their size they retain certain features of other *páramo* vegetation, such as downy hairs for insulation. Espeletia belong to the daisy family, and are an unmistakable feature of the northern *páramo* of Ecuador, particularly in the region of El Angel.

Further south the *páramo* is rather drier and here we often find the *puyas*, members of the bromeliad family which replace the *frailejones* of the wetter north. The *puyas* are some of the least understood of the *páramo* plants, having very few of the normal characteristics of the plants found here. They are very large (reaching a height of over 8m in Peru) and have no typical downy insulation. Their leaves, though still in a rosette pattern, are

During Whymper's visit he observed a condor hunt. A horse carcass was used to entice the birds to the ground.

not small and compact but long and spiky and grow on top of a short trunk instead of at ground level.

Another attractive plant of the dry southern *páramo* is the *chuquiragua*. In some ways it resembles a tall thistle topped with orange flowerheads and with stems densely covered with tough spiky leaves. This plant has medicinal properties and is used locally to soothe coughs, and for liver and kidney problems.

Apart from the flowering plants there is a great variety of other vegetation found in this zone. Everywhere you go you will encounter a spiky, resistant tussock grass (*ichu*) which grows in clumps and makes walking rather uncomfortable. In the lower *páramo* (below 4,000m) dense thickets of small trees may be seen. These are often of the rose family and a particularly common tree is the *quinua* (*Polylepis sp*), locally known as *el colorado* (the red one) because its bark is a dull reddish colour. If you push your way into one of these thickets, which are common in the *páramos* of Las Cajas in the south of Ecuador, you will observe a variety of lichens, mosses, epiphytes and fungi.

Fauna

Animals have not adapted themselves quite as well as plants to this harsh environment and are never plentiful. You are most likely to see birds, toads and rabbits.

The most exciting bird species is the Andean condor (*Vultur gryphus*). This is the largest flying bird in the world. With its three-metre wingspan and effortless flight it is indeed magnificent – particularly from a distance. Close up, its vicious hooked beak and its uncompromisingly hard eye set in a revoltingly bare and wrinkled pink head identify it as a carrion eater. Often it soars hundreds of metres in the air and its huge size is difficult to appreciate unless there is another bird close by for comparison. It is best identified by its flat, gliding flight with 'fingered' wingtips (formed by spread primary feathers), silvery patches on the upper surface of its wings and a white neck ruff. The rest of the body is black. Condors are becoming much rarer now than in the days of Whymper, who wrote after his visit in 1880 '... we commonly saw a dozen on the wing at the same time'. Good condor spotting areas include El Altar and Parque Nacional Cotopaxi, while the largest population is reported to be found in the Antisana area. Nineteen have been counted there. The crags of Pasochoa Reserve, only 20km south of the capital, support a pair of nesting condors that are sometimes spotted by climbing up to the *páramo*.

Smaller birds of prey are also seen in the *páramo*. The black-chested buzzard-eagle (*Geranoaetus melanoleucus*) is quite common, especially in the Papallacta area. At 58cm in length it is one of the largest of the Ecuadorian hawks (though small compared to the 108cm of the condor). It is identified by a very short, dark, wedge-shaped tail, a white belly finely barred with black, and blackish sides of head and breast. The throat is almost white. The most common hawk is the variable (or puna) hawk (*Buteo poecilochrous*) which is limited to the open *páramo*. Measuring 52cm in length, its most distinctive feature is a white tail with a black band near the end. As its name suggests its plumage varies; it is usually light bellied and brown backed. The fairly small (44cm) cinereous harrier (*Circus cinereus*) is sometimes seen. It is mostly grey with a white rump and belly barred with brown. Finally, the distinctive carunculated caracara (*Phalcoboenus carunculatus*), with its bright orange-red facial skin and legs, white belly and black above, is also sighted here.

One of the most common *páramo* birds is the Andean lapwing (*Vanellus resplendens*). It is unmistakable with its harsh noisy call and its brown/white/black striped wing pattern, particularly noticeable in flight. Of the ducks, the speckled teal (*Anas flavirostris*) with its blue-grey bill and brown head is the most common. Lago Limpiopungo in Parque Nacional Cotopaxi is a good place for both these species, as well as for the yellow-billed pintail (*Anas georgica*), the Andean gull (*Larus serranus*) and the American coot (*Fulica americana*).

If you wake up in your tent during the dark early hours of the morning to hear a weird whizzing sound like a lost UFO, don't be too alarmed. It's probably a cordillera snipe, also known as the Andean snipe (*Chubbia jamesoni*). They often fly at night and produce this strange drumming noise with their outer wing feathers. Another night flier in the *páramo* is the owl. You may catch sight of the great horned owl (*Bubo virgianus*) or even the well-known barn owl (*Tyto alba*). More frequently seen is the short-eared owl (*Asio flammeus*), because it hunts during the day.

Of the small birds found in the *páramo*, the most easily identifiable are the hummingbirds, at least 126 species of which have been listed as occurring in Ecuador alone. The Andean hillstar (*Oreotrochilus estella*) is one of the most common found at high altitudes. I've often been amazed to see one come humming past my tent at a snowline camp at 4,700m. This tiny bundle of life survives the intense night-time cold by lowering its metabolism by as much as 95% and entering an almost lifeless state, similar to hibernation. Its body temperature drops dramatically; one researcher measured a decrease from 39.5°C to 14.4°C overnight. The bird passes the night in a protected crevice or overhang and regains its day-time temperature in the morning sun with no ill effects. Hummingbirds are the smallest birds in the world and the most manoeuvrable. The Andean hillstar, at 13cm in length, is comparatively big; the short-tailed woodstar (*Myrmia micrura*), which is common on the coast, is a mere 7cm in length and this includes the needle-like bill. Hummingbirds' wings beat in a shallow figure of eight instead of the normal up and down; this, combined with a 'humming' 80-beat-a-second wingspeed, enables them to hover and even fly backwards; speeds of up to 110km per hour have been recorded.

Swallows are frequently sighted in the *páramo*; look particularly for the brown-bellied swallow (*Notiochelidon murina*) and the blue-and-white swallow (*N. cyanoleuca*); both are common. The thrushes are represented by the great thrush (*Turdus fuscater*); the only pipit found is the *páramo* pipit (*Anthus bogotensis*). Other small species tend to come under the category of 'small brown birds'; of these the cinclodes are the easiest to recognize, with their distinctive white eye stripe. The stout-billed and the bar-winged cinclodes (*C. excelsior* and *C. fuscus*) are among the commonest of all *páramo* birds.

Good places for highland ornithology are the Papallacta area and Parque Nacional Cotopaxi. Don't forget that this is a harsh environment so you won't see birds flocking in their hundreds. In the Cotopaxi park station there is a small museum which displays several dozen species of stuffed *páramo* birds; this should help you with identification.

Looking groundwards instead of skywards you'll frequently find another animal in the *páramo*: the toad. At this altitude they usually belong to the *Atelopodidae* family and may be recognized by their lethargic movements and diurnal activity. They are particularly active after a heavy rain. On one walk in Parque Nacional Cotopaxi I saw literally hundreds of *Atelopus ignescens* toads almost falling over one another. They are jet black with bright orange bellies and are locally known as the jambato toad. In the more southerly *páramos* these black toads are less common and are replaced by more ordinary-looking green examples of the same genus.

When talking of wildlife, it is the mammals which tend most to arouse the general observer's excitement and curiosity. Interesting and strange species live on the *páramo*, but most, unfortunately, are extremely rare and difficult to observe. The first species you will see will be rabbits (*Sylvilagus spp*) which need no description. Semi-wild horses and cattle range in the highlands, but llamas, perhaps the animals most closely associated with the Andean mountains and their people, are found only in domestic situations. An experimental herd can be seen in Parque Nacional Cotopaxi.

Three species of deer are found in the highlands. The familiar white-tailed deer (*Odocoileus virginianus*) occurs at various altitudes and is seen fairly often in Parque Nacional Cotopaxi. Two smaller species are infrequently observed. Between 3,000m and 4,000m one may see the small brocket deer (*Mazama rufina rufina*). It is about 50cm tall and of a rusty-brown colour with a blackish face. Its horns are limited to tiny 8cm-long prongs. One of the smallest and rarest deer in the world is the dwarf Andean *pudu* (*Pudu mephistophiles*) which averages under 35cm in height. It is light greyish brown and lives in high scrub over 3,000m, usually in the Eastern Cordillera.

Both felines and canines are represented in the *páramo*. The American lion or puma (*Felis concolor*) has been observed around 4,000m, and the erroneously named Andean wolf (*Dusicyon culpaeus*), which is in fact a fox, is also occasionally seen.

The largest Ecuadorian land mammals are the tapirs. The mountain or woolly tapir (*Tapirus pinchaque*) is one of the rarest South American animals, and inhabits the high cloudforests and *páramo* of the Eastern Cordillera from 1,500m to 4,000m. It is comparatively common in the Papallacta and Sangay regions, but is extremely difficult to sight because it spends most of its time in thick cover. Its heavy brown body, relatively short legs, large ears and emphatically elongated nose make it unmistakable – if you ever see it! You're more likely to find its tracks, four toes in front and three on the rear foot.

Finally, the smallest bear in the world may be seen in the *páramo* by the extremely lucky and very patient observer. *Tremarctos ornatus*, the Andean spectacled bear, is extremely versatile and has been observed from just above Peru's desert coast to *páramo* at over 4,000m. It is called 'spectacled' because of the irregular light-coloured eye patches on its otherwise almost black hair. In Ecuador it has been sighted on both the outside slopes of the Western and Eastern Cordilleras and, as with the woolly tapir, the Papallacta region is favoured.

HISTORY

Very little is known of the earliest history of the area. In the early 1400s at least six linguistic groups were recognized in the highlands alone (the Pasto, Cara, Panzaleo, Puruhá, Cañari and Palta) and by the middle of the century the Caras had gained a dominant position. They overpowered a minor tribe, the Quitus (hence Quito), forming the kingdom of the Shyris which was the major presence in the area at the time of Inca expansion from the south. Despite several years of resistance, the Shyris and nearby lesser groups were integrated into the Inca empire by about 1490.

In 1525 the Inca Huayna Capac died, dividing his empire between two sons. Atahualpa, of Shyri descent on his mother's side, became ruler of the northern part of the empire, whilst Huáscar received the rest. Violent civil war between the two brothers followed and Atahualpa won. Thus when the Spanish conquest began in 1532 the Inca Empire had been severely weakened by civil war. Atahualpa was captured and, although he paid a huge ransom in gold and silver for his release, he was murdered by Pizarro and the Inca Empire effectively came to an end.

In 1534 Sebastián de Benalcázar founded Quito on the ruins of the old Shyri city. After the success of the Spanish conquest the area became known as the Audiencia de Quito, and (except for a period of six years) remained under the viceroy of Peru until 1740 when it became part of the Viceroyalty of Nueva Granada. The 16th to 18th centuries were characterized by peaceful colonialism. Agriculture was developed, the indigenous people were exploited, and Spain profited.

By the 19th century, in common with other parts of South America, a strong independence movement had developed. From 1809 several unsuccessful attempts were made at independence but it was not until May

24, 1822 that Mariscal Sucre finally defeated the royalist forces at the Battle of Pichincha. Although free of the Spanish, the area now became part of Gran Colombia and it was over eight more years before Ecuador became completely independent under the leadership of the first president, General Juan José Flores.

The rest of the 19th century was a continuous struggle between conservatives and liberals. By the end of the 1800s Ecuador was under the military rule of General Eloy Alfaro and much of the 20th century has seen a succession of unstable military governments. A civilian leader, President Jaime Roldós, was elected in 1979 and after his untimely death in an air accident was succeeded in 1981 by his vice-president, Osvaldo Hurtado Larrea. The country has continued to elect civilian governments democratically, with León Febres Cordero serving from 1984 to 1988, Rodrigo Borja Cevellos in office from 1988 to 1992, and Sixto Durán Ballén from 1992 to 1996. The populist Abdala Bucaram was elected to the office of president to serve through 2000, but lasted in office only a few months before being ousted by a congressional vote in early 1997. Congress claimed that Bucaram was mentally unfit to lead the country. The current president is Fabian Alarcon.

PEOPLE

A census held in 1990 revealed that Ecuador's population had reached 10,400,000; by 1998 it was estimated at 12,000,000, approximately ten times the number of indigenous people estimated to have been living in the area at the time of the Spanish conquest. The population density of about 42 per km² is the highest in South America.

About 40% of the population are indigenous and an equal number are *mestizos* (mixed Spanish and indigenous stock). About 15% are white and the remainder black or Asian.

The majority of the indigenous people are Quechua speaking and live in the highlands; they are the direct descendants of the inhabitants of the Inca Empire. There are also several small groups living in the lowlands and speaking their own distinct languages. These tribes include, among others, the Quechua, Shuar (Jívaro), Achuar, Huaorani, Cofán, Secoya, Siona and Zaparo of the Oriente and the Chachi, Awá and Colorado of the coastal plain. The highland indigenous people are often bilingual, although Spanish is a second language and not much used in remote areas. Until land reforms of the 1960s the majority of the Quechuas were little more than slaves to the big *hacienda* owners. Nowadays they are developing cooperatives and own land but nevertheless live at a subsistence level in many cases.

Some groups, notably the Otavaleños and to a lesser extent the Salasacas and Cañaris, have developed a reputation as excellent weavers and craftsmen (and women) and their goods are in great demand. After some time in Ecuador you will notice the different styles of clothing that individual groups traditionally wear. The Otavalo men are characterized by their white, calf-length trousers, rope sandals, grey or blue ponchos, and long single braid of hair. The women wear a colourfully embroidered blouse and a bulky gold-coloured necklace. The Salasaca men wear distinctive broad-brimmed white hats, white shirts and black ponchos. The indigenous people of the Saquisilí area are most often seen wearing red ponchos and little felt 'pork-pie' hats.

Another interesting and attractive feature of indigenous life is the fiestas which often celebrate church holidays. One of my favourites is that of All Souls' Day (November 2) when throngs of people visit cemeteries to pay their respects to the dead. Everyone does this, from rich Quiteños to poor *campesinos* (peasants), but the cemeteries near the indigenous villages are the most colourful. Here, hundreds of people show up in their best clothes and leave wreaths and flowers on the graves. To ensure that their departed friends and relatives also enjoy the day the people bring food and drink and leave some in remembrance and offering. The majority of the food and drink is, of course, consumed by the indigenous people themselves and the atmosphere is generally festive rather than sombre.

MOUNTAINEERING: A HISTORICAL VIEW

Despite some legends, there is no evidence, as found in more southerly countries, of any mountain ascents by the local indigenous people prior to the arrival of the Spanish conquistadors. The Spanish contented themselves with noting major volcanic activity in their journals, their first records being of the eruptions of Cotopaxi and Tungurahua in 1534. The earliest recorded ascent is that of the Ecuadorian[1] José Toribio Ortiguera, who reached the crater of Pichincha in 1582. There is a disputed record of an ascent of Pichincha by Padre Juan Romero in 1660, the same year that a major eruption buried Quito in 40cm of volcanic ash, but generally speaking during the first two centuries of Spanish occupation there was little interest in geographical aspects. The windfall of a treasure-laden Inca civilization was something the Spaniards wished to exploit themselves, so all foreign visitors, including natural historians or explorers, were regarded with suspicion. It was not until well into the 18th century that a European scientific expedition was first permitted to make a serious attempt at mapping and exploring Ecuador and this led to an awakening of interest in the mountains of the country.

By the beginning of the 18th century it had been established that the world was round, but controversy still raged over the concept of polar flattening. In an attempt to settle the issue, the French Académie des Sciences organized expeditions to the Arctic and the Equator. At this time Africa

---

[1] I use 'Ecuadorian' for convenience here and later in the chapter although the country was not known by that name until 1830.

was still the 'dark continent', Indonesia was little known, and the Amazon basin was virtually unexplored. Consequently Ecuador, with its capital just 25km south of the Equator, was the obvious venue for such an expedition. This took place from 1736 to 1744 and was led by the Frenchman Charles-Marie de La Condamine, accompanied by two countrymen, two Spaniards and an Ecuadorian. Surveying was undertaken, and their calculations of the distance from the Equator to the North Pole became the basis of the metric system of weights and measures. The flora, fauna, geology and geography were also studied. The explorers were very interested in the highlands, and during the course of their investigations concluded that Chimborazo (6,310m) was the highest peak in the world – a belief which existed until the 1820s. They made the first serious attempt to scale this mountain, reaching an altitude of about 4,750m. The less important peaks of Pichincha (4,776m) and Corazón (4,788m) were successfully climbed and most of the major peaks were surveyed.

The expedition's surveys and measurements started a series of disputes which have not been resolved to this day. For example, Cotopaxi, Ecuador's second highest peak, was measured at 5,751m by La Condamine's expedition. Succeeding expeditions turned in considerably higher measurements: 5,753m by Humboldt in 1802, 5,978m by Whymper in 1880, 5,940m by Martínez in 1906; the highest of all, 6,005m, was published by Arthur Eichler in his *Ecuador – Snow Peaks and Jungles* (1970) and is the only figure over 6,000m. The height most generally accepted today is 5,897m, as surveyed by the Instituto Geográfico Militar in 1972. Nevertheless many recent sources are still unable to agree on the correct elevation. The same perplexing situation exists with other peaks (see *Appendix Two*).

After the departure of the French expedition, the 18th century saw no more major exploration of the Ecuadorian mountains. It was not until 1802 that an expedition led by the famous German scientist and explorer Baron Alexander von Humboldt reawakened interest in the Ecuadorian highlands. Von Humboldt visited and studied various peaks, including Cotopaxi, Pichincha, Antisana and El Altar, but it is for his research on and attempted ascent of Chimborazo that his expedition is particularly remembered by mountaineers. Accompanied by the Frenchman Aimé Bonpland and the Ecuadorian Carlos Montúfar, he identified many plants including some new species, as well as noting barometric data during his attempted ascent of the southern flanks of the mountain. He made a sectional sketch map of Chimborazo which shows the plant species, various geographical landmarks, the expedition's penetration beyond the snowline and finally, high above the surrounding *páramo*, includes the comment, '*Crevasse qui empêcha les voyageurs d'atteindre la cime*' (crevasse which prevents travellers from reaching the summit). This indicates the point at about 5,875m where Humboldt and his companions, suffering from high-altitude sickness, with cracked and bleeding lips and badly sun-burned faces, were forced to turn back. This attempt is particularly noteworthy since, despite their failure to gain the summit, they did reach the highest point so far attained by Western man.

Since Chimborazo was still considered the highest mountain in the world, other attempts on its summit soon followed. The Venezuelan liberator of the Andean countries, Simón Bolívar, climbed to the snowline in 1822 and nine years later Bolívar's colonel, the French agronomist Joseph Boussingault, managed to reach about 6,000m on Chimborazo's southern slopes, again increasing the altitude so far attained by Western explorers. Boussingault also made several attempts on other peaks, but without notable success.

President Gabriel García Moreno, a much criticized and despotic ruler, was nevertheless the first Ecuadorian leader to take an active interest in the environment. He enacted several conservationist laws and in 1844 climbed to the crater of Pichincha. In succeeding years several European expeditions arrived. Around 1847 the almost forgotten Italian traveller Gaetano Osculati spent a year in Ecuador, and although he made no attempts to climb any of its peaks he left us with some interesting paintings and drawings of Ecuadorian mountains. 1849 saw the first recorded expedition to the highly active volcano Sangay (5,230m) where the Frenchman Sebastian Wisse counted 267 strong explosions in one hour. During the 1850s and 1860s several expeditions from various nations visited Ecuador but achieved little, and it was not until 1872 that the next major breakthrough in Ecuadorian mountaineering occurred.

In this year the German Wilhelm Reiss, accompanied by the Colombian Angel M Escobar, succeeded in reaching the 5,897m summit of Cotopaxi by climbing the southeastern flank, rather than the northern route which has since become accepted as the normal route. The following year another German, Alfonso Stübel, accompanied by four Ecuadorians, Eusebio Rodriguez, Melchor Páez, Vicente Ramón and Rafael Jantui, reached the summit via the same route, making Cotopaxi the first major peak to have been climbed by Ecuadorians. The two Germans then joined forces and in 1873 made the first ascent of the active volcano Tungurahua (5,023m), as well as attempts on other summits.

A disastrous volcanic eruption on June 26 1877 left the slopes of Cotopaxi bare of ice and snow, and several climbers took advantage of this situation and climbed the volcano by the northeast side. Then a remarkable expedition in 1880, led by the renowned English climber Edward Whymper, succeeded in reaching the summit and spending a night by Cotopaxi's crater. Whymper had already established his reputation as a climber by making the first ascent of the Matterhorn, at one time deemed to be impossible. His Ecuadorian expedition must surely rate as one of the most successful mountaineering expeditions ever undertaken. With the Italian cousins Louis and Jean-Antoine Carrel, Whymper proceeded not only to climb Cotopaxi but also to make the first ascent of Chimborazo, a climb which raised a storm of disbelief and protest. To quell his critics Whymper repeated the climb later in 1880 accompanied by two Ecuadorians: David Beltrán and Francisco Campaña. Ecuador's third highest peak, Cayambe (5,790m), and Antisana (5,758m), the fourth highest, also fell to the ice axes of Whymper and the Carrels, as did Iliniza Sur (5,248m), Carihuairazo (5,020m), Sincholagua (4,893m), Cotacachi (4,944m) and Sara Urco (4,670m). In addition to these eight first ascents, several other climbs were made by this expedition including Corazón and Pichincha. There was also an unsuccessful attempt on El Altar (5,320m), which is Ecuador's most technical snow peak and which was not climbed until 1963. Edward Whymper is remembered in Ecuador to this day; there is a street named after him in Quito and the country's highest mountaineers' refuge, the new and well-equipped hut at 5,000m on Chimborazo's eastern slopes, has been named Refugio Whymper.

After Whymper's memorable exploits no important expeditions occurred until the 20th century. Whereas the 19th century had seen many important European expeditions to the Ecuadorian Andes, the 20th century saw an awakening of interest in mountaineering by national climbers. The father of Ecuadorian mountaineering is Nicolás Martínez who in the first decades of this century succeeded in making many notable ascents. In 1900 Martínez climbed Tungurahua (5,023m), and in succeeding years climbed this peak several more times. His interest in mountaineering awakened, Martínez made first Ecuadorian ascents of many major peaks: Antisana in 1904, a failed attempt on Cayambe in 1905, and successful climbs of Cotopaxi and Chimborazo in 1906. Succeeding years saw various successes and failures in Martínez's climbing career. A particularly noteworthy ascent was that of Iliniza Norte in 1912; this 5,126m peak is the only one of Ecuador's ten 5,000m peaks which was first climbed by an Ecuadorian.

World War I and its aftermath left little time or money for new foreign expeditions to Ecuador and it was not until 1929 that a United States expedition, led by Robert T Moore, achieved the first ascent of Sangay (5,230m). This, the most continuously active volcano in Latin America, was experiencing a rare period of tranquillity at the time. Moore's expedition also made various other notable climbs, including the first US ascent of Chimborazo.

By 1929 all but one of the major Ecuadorian peaks (the ten over 5,000m) had been conquered. The exception was El Altar (5,320m), Ecuador's fifth highest peak, which was not climbed until 1963 when an Italian Alpine Club expedition led by Marino Tremonti succeeded in reaching the summit. In the intervening years many repeat ascents of the major peaks were made by climbers of various nationalities and several minor peaks were conquered for the first time. These included Cerro Hermoso (4,571m) by four Germans in 1941 and Quilindaña (4,878m) by a large party of Ecuadorians, Colombians, French and Italians in 1952.

The 1960s and 1970s saw a new approach to mountaineering in Ecuador. With Tremonti's first ascent of El Altar in 1963 all the major peaks had been climbed and emphasis was laid on climbing new routes and lower summits of the more important mountains. El Altar's eight other virgin peaks provided great impetus and excitement to Ecuadorian mountaineering as, one by one, they were climbed between 1965 and 1979 by climbers of various nationalities, including three first ascents by Ecuadorian climbers. During these decades Ecuadorian mountaineers were consistently in the forefront of finding new climbs, such as the second and third summits of Antisana, new routes on Cayambe and Iliniza Sur, the Central Summit on Chimborazo, the first ascents of the minor peaks of Achipungo and Ayapungo, and many others too numerous to mention. In connection with these new climbs the names of the Ecuadorians Bernardo Beate, Marco Cruz, Milton Moreno, Ramiro Navarrete, Romulo Pazmiño, the Reinoso brothers, Santiago Rivadeneira, Hugo Torres, Iván Rojas, American James Desrossiers and Frenchman Joseph Bergé will long be remembered. Many of these and other Ecuadorian climbers have also made notable ascents in different parts of the world. Mention should also be made of Fabián Zurita who, perhaps more than any other Ecuadorian, has brought the mountains of Ecuador closer to its people through his frequent and non-technical articles in the Ecuadorian press.

In the 1960s it was realized that mountaineering in Ecuador was economically important as a tourist asset and refuges were constructed to accommodate visiting foreign as well as national climbers. The first of these was the now badly damaged Fabian Zurita refuge built in 1964 at 4,900m on the northwest slopes of Chimborazo. Since then, several more mountain huts have been built; some are extremely basic and others very comfortable.

Today, with its network of climbing huts and their easy accessibility, Ecuador has become an important mountaineering centre. For professionals and experts it still provides the opportunity for good new routes but it is of particular interest to intermediate climbers who wish to experience the excitement of high-altitude ascents. It is also very useful as a high-altitude training ground for climbers wishing to test and improve their skills before attempting ascents in the difficult mountains of the more southern Andes.

Chapter Two

Preparations

'A journey is a person in itself; no two are alike. And all plans, safeguards, policies and coercion are fruitless. We find after years of struggle that we do not take a trip; a trip takes us.'

John Steinbeck

GETTING THERE

From Europe, there are direct flights on major airlines, but these are expensive. Discounted tickets are often available. In London try Imaginative Traveller (tel: 0181 742 3045) or Journey Latin America (JLA) (tel: 0181 747 3108) who are the experts in arranging discount fares for this part of the world and are pleased to answer unusual travel queries from their customers. In Quito, Ecuaviajes (tel: 593 2 501 913) or Ecuagal (tel: 593 2 229 579) are great at finding the cheapest way to travel from Ecuador to other parts of the world.

From North America there are inexpensive flights with some of the Latin American carriers. Try Eco-Travel Services (tel: 1-800-655-4053) or Council Travel (tel: (212) 661 1414/50; 0800 226 8624; fax: (212) 972 3231). if you are a student. You can also get a cheap excursion ticket from Miami. Ecuador is well placed for overland journeys from either Colombia in the north or Peru in the south, so look out for cheap flights to those destinations. Bear in mind that there is a 10% tax on air tickets bought in Ecuador and a US$25 departure tax (payable in cash dollars, sucres or travellers cheques) from the airport for international flights.

From Australia, Aerolíneas Argentinas has flights from Sydney to Buenos Aires, where a connection can be made to Ecuador.

Finally, passenger and cargo ships call at Guayaquil from all over the world – but sea voyages are often more expensive than flights.

DOCUMENTS

All visitors need a passport valid for at least six months and a tourist card which is valid for up to 90 days and is available from any port of entry. You are legally required to be able to show evidence of 'sufficient funds' (as much as US$20 per day) and an exit ticket out of the country, although this is rarely asked for, particularly if you are travelling overland. An MCO (Miscellaneous Charges Order) from any IATA airline is often adequate. Your tourist card is easily renewed at the Department of Immigration in Quito at Av Amazonas 3149 and in other major cities, but tourists are allowed a maximum of only 90 days in any one calendar year. Obtaining permission for a longer stay is relatively easy. Tourist visas can be renewed after the maximum 90-day stay has expired for a fee of US$12 per 30-day extension. Normally only three extensions (for a total of another 90 days) are granted. Technically the fee is a fine paid in advance to Immigration for overstaying the 'official' 90-day tourist visa. Under no circumstances should you allow your visa to expire while you are in the country. On-the-spot police checks are frequent and a trip to jail is possible. Usually the staff at the South American Explorers Club in Quito (tel/fax: 593 2566 076) can give you advice on how to extend your stay in Ecuador.

WHAT TO TAKE

In the words of Edward Whymper: 'It is indeed true that nearly everything may be obtained in Ecuador. It is also true that we often had great difficulty in obtaining anything.' Although climbing and backpacking equipment is available for sale and hire, it is usually very expensive and often inadequate. If you're large then you'll have difficulty in finding clothing, and particularly footwear, to fit you since Ecuadorians are generally small. It is best to bring what you need with you. It is easy enough to find storage facilities for your excess gear whilst you are hiking or climbing.

The following checklist reflects the fact that, while you may be a mountaineer one day, you'll be just a tourist the next. We have included everything we consider useful but doubtless some people's needs will differ from ours.

Backpack Bear in mind that an external frame pack, while very comfortable, is awkward if hitchhiking and liable to break during the rough treatment it will receive on planes, buses and trucks. External frame packs tend to snag on everything from hotel doors to tropical vegetation and to throw the climber off balance; an internal frame or frameless pack hugs the body better. Buy as large a pack as you can carry – when the weather's terrible and your hands are cold it's easier to stuff a sopping wet tent and gear into a large pack than to struggle with a small one which held everything so snugly when you were warm and dry in your hotel.

Sleeping bag It gets cold – but not very cold. Even when mountaineering high above the snowline temperatures below -10°C are not very common, so you don't need the most expensive sleeping bag. A medium-weight one is adequate, especially if combined with a bivouac sac (waterproof sleeping bag cover) or a down jacket. If you plan on doing a lot of backpacking then you should consider a bag with artificial filling because it will stay fairly warm when wet, whereas a soggy down bag is almost useless. At present artificial fillings are cheaper than down, though heavier and bulkier, but lighter new materials are constantly being developed.

Mattress This is essential. Any closed cell (ensolite type) foam pad will do. I use a cheap light one which works as well as more expensive ones for insulation (which is the most important thing), although for comfort you may want a more elaborate one such as a Thermarest, which is a combination air mattress/foam pad.

Tent You can manage without a tent if you climb only the major peaks as good mountain refuges are available. If planning extended hikes or climbs, however, you'll need a tent which is waterproof and withstands buffeting by high winds, although some climbers make do with bivouac sacs instead. I used a single-walled Gore-Tex tent for two years and it stayed more or less dry, even in all-night epic rainstorms. Gore-Tex is unique in that it 'breathes', so there is less problem of condensation. All tent seams must be carefully waterproofed with seam-sealer before leaving home.

Stove Four of Ecuador's climbers' huts have kitchens equipped with stoves, but if you plan trips away from the huts you'll need a stove as there is little firewood in the highlands. The best stove for high altitudes is the American MSR XGK which runs on paraffin (kerosene, sold as 'Kerex' in Ecuador), white gas (which is becoming easier to find in Ecuador), and even car or aviation fuel. The drawback to this excellent stove is its cost and the difficulty of obtaining it in the UK. In this country the best alternative is probably the Optimus 96 which burns paraffin. Another very good stove is the Bleuet Gaz 200 which operates on gas cartridges which are obtainable in Ecuador as well as in Europe and the USA. If you use this stove don't litter the mountains with 'dead' cartridges, and remember that you may not carry them on aeroplanes.

Cooking utensils and cutlery Bring your own or buy them in Ecuador; the locals use cheap, lightweight pans which are available in any town. Aluminium spoons and plastic cups are also easily found. For larger groups the weight of a pressure cooker is offset by the need to carry less fuel. You can also cook dry beans, potatoes or rice quickly, thus saving money on instant meals. They are also great for 'steam washing' dishes on a cold evening.

Water bottle I carry one or two light plastic one-litre water bottles and a two-gallon water bag (which weighs 4oz/113g and packs smaller than my fist) for carrying water to campsites.

Light Being on the Equator means you can be sure of one thing: 12 hours of darkness. So you'll be needing light more than in the northern summers. Torches (flashlights) and batteries are usually available throughout Ecuador, as are candles. Slow-burning candles are particularly useful but cannot be bought in Ecuador. For large groups you can bring a lantern to fit Bleuet gaz cartridges.

Food With a little imagination you can find plenty of food in Ecuador's stores suitable for backpacking and climbing. Freeze-dried food is virtually unobtainable but you can use noodles, dried soups, chocolate, raisins, nuts, oatmeal, powdered juices, dried milk, cheese, crackers, biscuits, salami, cans of fish and peanut butter. Some of the large supermarkets like Supermaxi and Mi Comisario have the same selection as you will find in the States.

Footwear You can climb most peaks with heavy hiking boots, although double climbing boots are warmer. Medium-weight hiking boots are adequate for all the hikes and some of the lesser peaks; you'll need good Vibram soles. EBs and similar rock-climbing boots with smooth rubber soles are useless. Ex-army jungle boots are the best footwear for jungle and lowland trips. By far the most common footwear for walking in Ecuador are knee-high rubber boots (*botas para agua*), equivalent to British wellingtons. These are especially good for jungle and swampy *páramo* excursions. Once you get used to them they keep your feet cosy and dry, but beware of blisters (tape your feet or wear extra socks) and the lack of ankle support. Venus brand is considered one of the best. Field scientists who have been in Ecuador for a few years have even been seen practising *salsa* in them! Also bring a pair of light shoes, sneakers or sandals for sitting around camp and walking in cities, and some rubber thongs (flip-flops) for use in dubious hotel bathrooms.

All footwear stops at English size 9–10 (43 metric) in Ecuador. This includes socks, so larger people should bring spares. Heavy woollen socks are best for keeping feet warm, and cotton and nylon liners help prevent blisters.

Clothing Thermal underwear (both top and bottom) can be slept in and keeps you warm at high altitudes. Jeans are useless in the mountains as they bind on your legs when climbing and offer no insulation when wet. They are also too hot to wear in the sun, heavy to carry, hard to wash, and take ages to dry. (Despite this, they're the *gringo* item most frequently stolen from washing lines.) For climbers, woollen mountaineering trousers are excellent, or a pair of fibrepile or fleece trousers combined with rain pants (waterproof overtrousers) to keep out the wind. One or two pairs of lightweight slacks are good for town and lowland use. Shorts are not worn in the towns but are comfortable for lower hikes in remote regions and for visits to coast, rivers and hot pools.

Bring at least one light long-sleeved shirt to protect against the intense tropical sun. You can buy thick woollen sweaters (even large sizes) cheaply in the indigenous markets, so think twice about carrying sweaters from home. Fleece pullovers or jackets stay warm when wet, dry quickly, and are lighter than wool. Bring your usual assortment of T-shirts etc, and one warm wool shirt.

Without a doubt, a down jacket (or one with artificial filling) is the single most useful clothing item. Even if you're not planning any high-altitude mountaineering it's useful for the hikes which go over 4,000m and at night when it's very cold.

Raingear is essential as it can rain even during the 'dry' season. Nylon ponchos are better than nothing but are a problem in the wind. A rain jacket and separate trousers are better. Gore-Tex is expensive but it works – this waterproof material allows sweat to evaporate so you don't get wet from perspiration.

A hat is essential for mountaineering and high-altitude hikes. Up to 40% of your body heat can escape from your exposed head and neck so it really helps to keep warm if you wear a wool hat or, better still, a balaclava which also protects your face and neck. A wide-brimmed sunhat is good for calm, sunny days and in the lowlands. Two pairs of gloves are needed by mountaineers: a light inner pair and a heavy wool outer mitt. Hikers will get by with one warm pair. Also bring swimwear. All trousers should have deep pockets, preferably secured with buttons, zipper, or velcro (see *Security*), and they're handy in shirts (and skirts) as well. You may have to add them yourself.

Mountaineering equipment Rope, ice axe, climbing harness and crampons are the basic necessities for snow climbs – often you can get by with nothing else. A second tool (ice hammer) is useful for some mountains (as detailed in the text). Protection may be needed for less experienced climbers, particularly whilst descending and for crevasse rescue. Two long ice screws and two snow stakes (with their respective slings and carabiners) will normally suffice. Make prussiks in case you fall into a crevasse. A helmet is always a good idea. A bivi-sac is worth throwing into your pack just in case... A mountaineers' headlamp is needed for the pre-dawn departures which are standard features of most snow climbs. Bring one from home as Ecuadorian ones are too heavy. Alkaline batteries are available in most cities. Buy extra if you are depending on local batteries. Lithium batteries, which can last for 60 hours of continuous use, are available at a few photo-developing shops in Quito.

Glacier cream (not ordinary suntan lotion), lipsalve and climbers' goggles are essential – the power of the Equatorial sun bouncing off glaciers at 6,000m will astound you. A friend of mine became snow-blind while wearing ordinary sunglasses.

Footpaths in Ecuador are not signposted or marked in any way, so a compass is essential for following directions particularly when hiking cross-country. Bring marker flags or wands (which can be made from sticks and strips of plastic from plastic bags). Gaiters and good climbers' gloves should be packed. Other useful but not essential items are ski poles and an altimeter.

Miscellaneous useful items   Pocket torch (flashlight) with spare bulbs and batteries; travel alarm clock; Swiss-Army-style penknife; sewing kit (including large needles and thick thread for heavy repairs); scissors; a few metres of cord (for clothes-lines, emergency repairs, spare shoelaces, tent guys, etc); spare glasses; sunglasses; binoculars; camera; plenty of film. A compass is more than useful, it is essential. In very remote areas a GPS would also be handy.

Plastic bags (including large bin liners to cover backpacks at night); flat rubber universal bath plug; soap for clothes and body (in a soap dish); shampoo; toothbrush, toothpaste and dental floss (great for emergency repairs); towel; toilet paper (rarely found in cheaper hotel and restaurant lavatories); earplugs for noisy hotels and buses; insect repellent; suntan lotion; handcream.

Pens and pencils; address book; notebook for journal and letter writing; paperback book (easily exchanged with other travellers when you've finished); pocket Spanish-English dictionary; waterproof matches or cigarette lighter; waterproofing for boots; small padlock (for cheap hotel rooms or locking gear in storage); a large lightweight nylon bag for leaving gear in storage; medicine kit (see *Health*).

MONEY

The Ecuadorian currency is the sucre. The rate of exchange in September 1997 was 4,100 sucres to the US dollar, but the sucre is rapidly depreciating against the dollar. There is a plan to create a new currency and link it to the US dollar in 1997 when the exchange rate hits 4,000 sucres to 1 US dollar.

The pound sterling, the German mark and the French or Swiss franc can normally be changed in Quito but the US dollar is the most readily accepted currency, especially outside the capital. There is normally little difference in exchange rates between dollar travellers cheques and cash, and converting cheques to cash dollars is easily done. There are slight variations in exchange rates between different banks and *casas de cambio* (exchange houses) so it pays to shop around if exchanging a lot of money. Rodrigo Paz, a *casa de cambio* which has several branches, including the main one at Amazonas 370 in Quito, usually gives a good rate. Exchange facilities are available at the airport seven days a week, or try the Hotel Colón. There is a small, but illegal, black market in operation. The exchange rate will not be much better, so stick with the official *cambios*.

Travellers cheques are the most convenient and safe way of carrying large amounts of money. Guard against robbery by dividing your travellers cheques and keeping them in different places, and be conscientious about recording each cheque cashed so that if the worst happens you can get a quick refund. Be careful which travellers cheques you buy. American Express are recommended; in the event of loss or theft refunds can normally be arranged within 48 hours if you report the loss promptly and back up your claim with a police report (easily obtained), the receipts to show you paid for the cheques, and personal identification (passport). Other companies are less efficient.

If you run out of money it is relatively simple to have more sent from home. Unlike most Latin American countries, Ecuador will pay you all your money in US dollars. All you need to do is pick a Quito bank which will co-operate with your bank at home (eg: Lloyds Bank, Banco del Guayaquil, Banco del Pacífico) and ask family or bank manager to deposit the money in your name in the Ecuadorian bank you have chosen. If you use telex your money can arrive in 72 hours if there are no hitches or holidays; usually it takes four to five days.

Credit cards

Credit cards may be used to obtain cash. The easiest way is to buy American Express travellers cheques with your AMEX card, although you must have an account at home from which the money can be drawn. The charge is 1%, and the entire process takes about ten minutes. In Quito, the American Express office is at Ecuadorian Tours, Amazonas 339 and Washington. With MasterCard or Visa you may get a cash advance, but this is given in sucres. Banco del Pacífico is the MasterCard representative, Filanbanco handles Visa credit cards and Banco del Guayaquil on Colón at Reina Victoria in Quito will handle Visa transactions. The limit on how much you withdraw is set by your Visa account but, because of an increase in fraud in South America, cash advances equivalent to US$1,500 or more are often automatically blocked. In this case you must call your credit card company to remove the block.

Budgeting

Ecuador, still one of the cheapest countries in Latin America, is no longer the ridiculous bargain of years past. Increased petrol prices, now roughly linked to US prices, and a higher standard of living in the capital city have forced costs up. The classic bare-bones budget is now up to US$13, in the city with cheap accommodation at about US$6 a day. In rural areas, basic accommodation can be had for as little as US$2 a night and an overall daily cost of US$8 is possible if you want to scrape along.

If you expect to spend much time climbing or hiking in established parks and reserves you'll also spend more money. Park entry fees have shot up drastically. In the highlands, park fees are US$10 and coastal parks charge US$20. (See complete list on page 47.) In addition, the refuges at Cotopaxi and Cayambe now charge US$10 per night. The Chimborazo refuge is still US$5 but the price is expected to go up.

If you're broke and desperate (Rob has been down to his last US$50 in the world a few times in South America), don't give up. You can always sell your climbing and backpacking gear easily. The same applies to your camera or cassette recorder or whatever. Used but good equipment can often be sold for its original price – even more if you're a shrewd businessman or a smooth hustler, depending on your point of view. A good place to advertise is in budget hotels (see *Accommodation* in *Chapter Three*). You can also approach climbers you meet on the mountains or go to climbing clubs. Another way of making money is by teaching English. This will at least leave your weekends free to hike and climb, and you'll still have the gear to do it with. There are several language schools and the turnover is high. You don't need experience, just act schoolteacherish!

INSURANCE

Carrying AMEX travellers cheques insures your money but you should get comprehensive travel insurance against theft, accident and illness. Most travel agents will advise you of available policies but shop around and read the small print carefully. Often you'll find that certain activities, including mountaineering, aren't covered. In the UK, the British Mountaineering Council can supply a comprehensive and not too expensive climbers' insurance policy. This is available to members only. Write to the BMC Insurance Department, Crawford House, Precinct Centre, Booth Street East, Manchester M13 9R2, and ask for Expedition Remote Area forms. The insurance company, after hearing your plans, will offer a policy to suit your needs.

In addition to hospital coverage, you should consider a policy which includes evacuation to your home country if you become seriously ill or injured.

PHOTOGRAPHY

This is worth thinking about before you go. Cameras are expensive in Ecuador so bring all the equipment you'll need. Film prices are reasonable, and certainly less expensive than in most Latin American countries. The choice of film is limited and my personal favourite, Kodachrome 64, is not available in Ecuador. (If you're hoping to publish anything on your return, remember that a few magazine editors won't consider anything but Kodachrome.) Slide films which are available are Ektachrome, Fujichrome and Agfachrome. High speed Ektachrome 400 is good for the jungle, which is always darker than you'd expect. Kodacolor print film and most black and white film is easily found but always check the expiry date; I've seen professional-looking camera stores selling film which is two years out of date. Film processing is sometimes shoddy and Kodachrome cannot be developed in Ecuador.

Shadows in the tropics are very dark and come out almost black in photographs. A bright cloudy day is therefore often better for photography than a very sunny one. Taking shots in open shade or using fill-in flash will help. The best time for photography is when the sun is low: the first two hours after dawn and the last two before sunset. At high altitudes a haze can spoil your pictures; using a UV filter will improve them.

The people of Ecuador are both picturesque and varied. From the handsomely uniformed presidential guard to a charmingly grubby indigenous child – the possibilities of 'people pictures' are endless. However, most people resent having a camera thrust into their faces without so much as a 'by your leave'. Indigenous people in markets will often proudly turn their backs on pushy photographers. You should ask for permission with a smile or a joke, and if this is refused don't become offended. Some people are fed up at seeing their pictures in magazines or on postcards – they realize that someone must be making money at their expense. Others are still superstitious about bad luck being brought on them by cameras. Carrying a cheap Polaroid is one way of gaining people's confidence – you can give them one photo whilst shooting more for yourself with your better camera. Sometimes a 'tip' is asked for. Taking photos from a discreet distance with a telephoto lens is another possibility. Be aware and sensitive of people's feelings; it is never worth upsetting someone for a good photograph.

HEALTH
Written in collaboration with Dr Jane Wilson-Howarth

Before you go
Inoculations
Though not required by law, normal precautions for tropical travel should be taken. Vaccinations against typhoid and poliomyelitis are strongly advised, as is a yellow fever immunization if you are visiting the Oriente. A cholera inoculation is no longer recommended even though there was an epidemic in Peru and Ecuador in the early 1990s. This shot is only about 50% effective and your best defence is to avoid uncooked food (especially seafood), salads, ice-cream and unboiled water. While the epidemic has long since passed, the bacteria are now present throughout South America. Cholera is not passed by casual contact; it is contracted by eating or drinking contaminated food or water. The disease can be easily treated, but can kill within 24 hours if not treated.

Smallpox has been eradicated worldwide and inoculations are no longer required.

A full course of the necessary inoculations with boosters can take six weeks or more so be sure to see your doctor well before departure. Carry, and keep up to date, your international vaccination card.

There is now an effective (ten-year protection) inoculation, Havrix, against hepatitis A. This replaces the far less effective gamma globulin, although the latter is cheaper so may be preferable for a short, low-risk visit. Hepatitis, like travellers' diarrhoea, is caused by eating contaminated food or water: salads, uncooked or unpeeled fruit and unboiled drinks. Infection risks are minimized by using bottled drinks, washing your hands before eating and especially after using public toilets.

The incidence of dog bites has increased in the last few years, and the possibility of contracting rabies or tetanus from the most innocuous of bites cannot be overestimated. For many victims who choose to go home for treatment, it's an abrupt end to a great holiday. An effective though costly rabies vaccine, the human diploid vaccine, consists of a series of injections given over a two- month period. Then, if bitten, you require only a simple follow-up shot for complete protection. The serum and other vaccines are readily available at Vos Andes Hospital in Quito. When making the decision on whether to terminate your trip after a suspect bite, bear in mind that the rabies virus migrates slowly along the nerves from the site of the bite to the brain. If the bite is on the face, it should be attended to immediately, but a reaction could take six weeks if the bite was on a finger, or several months if on the foot. Once the disease reaches the brain it is invariably fatal but before that it is treatable. So if you are bitten on a leg you could risk the wait until you get home (if only a matter of a few weeks) before having the injections.

Malaria

If you're planning a visit to a lowland area anti-malaria pills are recommended since the disease is on the increase in Latin America. If you stay above 2,500m you aren't at risk since malarial mosquitoes don't usually fly this high. In the Oriente, locals say that you're safe at 1,000m. Pills must be taken from one week before you enter a malaria area until six weeks after you leave. Check the dose carefully as it varies with the brand. Until recently, chloroquine (Aralen) was the drug of choice, but chloroquine-resistant strains of malaria are now present in Ecuador. The new drug Mefloquine (Lariam) is now preferred. In the UK phone the Malaria Reference Laboratory (0171 636 7921) for the latest tape-recorded recommendations. In the US, contact the Centers for Disease Control (CDC) in Atlanta, Georgia (tel: 404 332 4559). You must also avoid getting bitten by the night-feeding anopheles mosquito by wearing long-sleeved shirts and long trousers from dusk until dawn, using frequent applications of insect repellent, and sleeping under a mosquito net. If you buy insect repellent remember that the active ingredient is diethyl-metatoluamide (or DEET). Some repellents contain less than 10% of this and others over 90% so check the composition of the repellent before you buy. I find that the rub-on lotions are the most effective, and the pump sprays (use environmentally friendly ones) are useful for your clothes. Be careful, though, since these may erode some plastics and man-made fibres.

Fitness

If you are planning a short, intensive trip and hope to climb several major peaks you should carry out regular pre-departure exercises such as swimming, running, cycling or whatever you prefer. If planning a longer trip then doing some of the Quito area day hikes will help get you into shape.

In Ecuador
The drastic change of diet you will experience during your stay means you'll probably be ill at least once. Stomach upsets are almost unavoidable but this is nothing to worry about. Diarrhoea is the most common ailment; drink plenty of fluids, rest, eat bland foods such as dry biscuits, crackers, bread, boiled rice, etc, and the condition will normally clear up in about 24 hours. Many travellers find that eating yoghurt (commercially available and pasteurized) helps the digestive system adapt more quickly to the new bacteria being introduced into the diet.

Symptoms and remedies for other travellers' maladies are easily found elsewhere, so I am concentrating on the more specialized area of mountain health. If you fall very ill, see a doctor. Many Ecuadorian doctors speak English, have been educated in the US, and are very good. Your embassy or hotel can recommend one. Metropolitano is one of the best hospitals in Quito – the staff is professional and most of the specialists have had some training and experience abroad.

Many prescription-only medicines are available in Ecuadorian pharmacies at a much lower cost than in the US or Europe and are sold 'over the counter' without a prescription. These include a variety of antibiotics, cold medicines, pain relievers, etc. The availability of certain medications within the country may make it much easier to put together a decent first-aid kit at a much lower price (see page 35). However, exercise extreme caution if trying to treat yourself without the benefit of medical opinion.

Mountain health
Hiking and climbing in the Ecuadorian countryside is more likely to keep you healthy than to make you ill. However, conditions can be extreme and perhaps disastrous for the uninitiated. The major medical problems you may be faced with can be classed in four groups: those caused by cold, heat, altitude and injury. This section is designed to help you recognize and deal with these problems.

Hypothermia
Often known as 'exposure', this insidious killer occurs when the body loses heat faster than it can produce it. Medically it exists when rectal temperature falls below 35°C or 95°F. Heat loss leading to hypothermia often occurs when the temperature is well above freezing, and is caused primarily by wet clothing and by the removal of body heat by the wind, especially from the head and neck which can lose up to 40% of body heat (though this is partly through heat loss by breathing).

Prevention is better than cure. Put on rain gear as soon as it begins to rain and not after you're soaking wet. Wear several layers of clothing which can be removed to regulate your temperature; one very thick layer may cause you to get wet through perspiration. If you do get wet remember to wear a windproof layer; at least your wet clothes will stay a little warmer. Cotton clothes (eg: jeans) lose 90% of their insulating properties when wet, whilst wool loses only 50%. Artificial fleece is also a good wet insulator and has the added advantage of drying much more quickly than wool. Remember to keep your head and neck warm. Exposed hands should be covered – use spare socks in an emergency.

If you take the above precautions you are unlikely to get hypothermia but lack of judgement or an accident can soon change a normal situation into a dangerous one. The hypothermia victim will begin to feel tired and start shivering uncontrollably. At this stage you can still prevent hypothermia by getting out of the wind and rain and wearing more dry clothes (camping, getting into a dry sleeping bag, and eating some warm food). If this is not done, the person affected will begin to lose co-ordination, have difficulty in speaking and show a lack of judgment. By this stage victims are in serious trouble as they can't get themselves warm and must be rewarmed by their friends. Climbing into a cold sleeping bag is inadequate as the victim won't have enough body heat to warm the bag. The bag must be warmed. The best way is for someone to share the victim's sleeping bag after first removing wet clothing. If you're alone, try to make a hot water bottle with your canteen and drink small quantities of warm liquids. The final stage of hypothermia is a lapse into irrationality and incoherence, with hallucinations and disorientation, and a slow irregular pulse. Often the sufferer then feels warm and comfortable and is unaware of the danger. The skin becomes blue and cold, and drowsiness and dilation of the pupils follow. Then come unconsciousness and death. The whole process can take as little as two hours. The combination of cold, wet and windy weather is common in the Ecuadorian highlands, so be prepared; even on a day hike carry hat, gloves, wind and rain jacket, and a spare warm sweater.

Frostbite

This occurs when any part of the body becomes frozen. Backpackers are less likely to experience it but snow and ice climbers are possible candidates. The usual ways of getting frostbite are by exposing or wetting skin or by cutting off blood circulation to the extremities. These problems can be avoided by always wearing gloves and a balaclava helmet in extremely cold conditions. The nose and cheeks are more difficult to protect. A scarf or handkerchief wrapped bandit style around the face will help, as will rewarming your nose with your hand at frequent intervals. (Rubbing snow on to the area, the traditional 'cure', is actually dangerous.) Ensure good blood circulation in your feet by not lacing boots and crampon straps too tightly. Keep your socks dry and unwrinkled. Bear in mind that exposed flesh will freeze more rapidly in windy conditions (the 'wind chill factor') and, because of lack of oxygen to the body tissues, the higher you are the higher the risk.

Some people are more susceptible to frostbite than others, including smokers: if you smoke a cigarette when extremities are frozen or thawing, you are more likely to experience permanent damage. Also susceptible are people weakened by hypothermia, exhaustion, drugs, alcohol, injury or blood loss. Frostbite is liable to recur in those areas of the body which have been previously frozen.

The first symptom is pain. Warm and protect the area with extra clothing or by putting in a warm place (eg: warm your face with your hands or put your hands in your groin). Restore circulation to your feet by stamping them and loosening your laces. The pain may often increase in intensity during the first minutes of rewarming but this will soon disappear. If the pain disappears without rewarming and numbness takes its place, then the problem is getting serious. The area becomes whitish and hard. Even at this late stage a small frostbitten area can be rewarmed without damage. If your feet are involved then they could be rewarmed on a friend's belly or armpit.

If a whole finger or toe (or larger area) becomes deeply frostbitten then the situation is grave. This is because rewarming the part will cause it to become extremely delicate and sensitive so it cannot be used at all for several weeks. For this reason a badly frostbitten climber should be taken to hospital to be rewarmed. Once a part has been frostbitten it can remain that way for several days without much more damage and so climbers with severe frostbite should be evacuated under their own steam as soon as possible. This is entirely feasible in Ecuador as most climbing areas are within a couple of days of Quito. Once in hospital, a badly frostbitten area must be gently thawed in water just above blood temperature or damage will result. Those who have suffered from frostbite must not ascend again for several months.

Heat exhaustion
A calm, sunny day in the high Andes can be extremely hot and heat problems are not uncommon, although they are more of a danger on lowland hikes. Lack of liquids aggravates this condition so drink as much as possible both before setting off on a hike or climb, and during the hike. If you are unusually tired, thirsty, giddy, suffer from cramps, and are not urinating much (less than three good-volume pees in 24 hours), you're probably suffering from heat exhaustion or dehydration. Rest in the shade and drink as much as you can. Refrain from activity till you recover.

If symptoms of heat exhaustion are ignored, more serious problems such as heat syncope and heatstroke could develop, so these warnings must be taken seriously. Ensure a high fluid intake and wear a wide-brimmed sunhat and loose, light clothes.

Sunburn

This is a major problem for climbers on snow or ice because they are unaware of the power of the Equatorial sun at 6,000m. The sun will reflect from the glacier and burn in all sorts of surprising places such as behind the ears, under the chin and in the nostrils. These areas are very sensitive and must be carefully covered with glacier cream or sunblock. Lipsalve is needed to prevent cracked and bleeding lips. Ordinary suntan lotion is helpful but normally doesn't offer enough protection for climbers on a glacier. A sun protection factor of at least 15 should be used. When making a pre-dawn departure remember to stop when the sun rises and put cream on. Reapply frequently. Good glacier cream is readily available in Ecuador, as is the heavier zinc oxide. Don't be fooled by a cloud layer; the ultraviolet rays of the sun will burn you anyway. Wear a wide-brimmed hat when possible. Backpackers should also be aware of sunburn and use plenty of suntan lotion, especially at the beginning of a trip.

Snow blindness

The only cure for this is to have your eyes completely covered for a few days – obviously inconvenient at the top of a mountain! Snow and ice climbers must use the darkest goggles available as ordinary sunglasses are inadequate.

High-altitude sickness

Until the 1960s this unpleasant and often dangerous reaction to high altitude was medically unknown in the West and climbers suffering (and dying) from it were said to be suffering from pneumonia. Recent studies have shown this not to be the case and today high-altitude sickness is recognized as a major mountaineering problem and studies are continuing to increase our knowledge of this condition.

It is known that high-altitude sickness can be divided into a) mild acute mountain sickness (AMS), which can progress to serious b) pulmonary oedema, or c) cerebral oedema (see page 33 for symptoms). All three are caused not just by lack of oxygen at high altitude, but by a too-rapid ascent to these heights. The best prevention is acclimatization which means not climbing too high too fast. It is unusual for anyone to be seriously affected at elevations around 2,850m (Quito's), so using Quito as a base for acclimatization is recommended. Spending about a week at this altitude is normally adequate acclimatization providing you do not then climb very high fast.

Research has shown that an ascent rate of about 300–500m per day is normally slow enough to prevent problems, but it is impractical to spend over a week climbing Chimborazo which, at 6,310m, is almost 3,500m above Quito. Once acclimatized in Quito, it is quite common for one-day ascents to be made with little danger. Remember that high-altitude sickness usually takes from six hours to reveal itself, so a quick ascent and descent can normally be made with few ill effects. The old maxim 'climb high and sleep low' is a good one.

Despite these reassurances, one should bear in mind that cases of high-altitude sickness can occur even if precautions are taken. Every mountaineer should be able to recognize the symptoms described below and know how they must be dealt with.

Acute mountain sickness (*soroche*) is the most common of the three variations. The symptoms are severe headache, shortness of breath, nausea, vomiting, fatigue, insomnia, loss of appetite and a rapid pulse. Irregular (Cheyne-Stokes) breathing during sleep affects some people but is relatively harmless, although disturbing to both the sleeper and his companions. The best treatment is rest and deep breathing. Analgesics may alleviate the headache (some doctors recommend non-aspirin-based ones) and Diamox can also be used as treatment as well as preventative (see below). An adequate fluid intake must be maintained. If a victim doesn't improve then a descent is called for. A climber should never force him or herself to ascend when symptoms of AMS are present as the conditions will probably worsen.

Acetazolamide or Diamox (a mild diuretic) taken for five days, beginning two to three days before the ascent, may help prevent an attack of AMS. Climbers who are short on time to acclimatize should talk with their doctor about the drug. Despite encouraging reports from several recent expeditions, it should be stressed that this drug is still not completely accepted in medical circles. Apart from the annoyance of slightly increased urination, other side-effects include increased cold sensitivity, numbness and tingling in the extremities. Missing a dose usually reduces the symptoms in the extremities.

Pulmonary oedema kills climbers in South America each year. It is a more extreme form of AMS where, in addition to the symptoms mentioned, the victim suffers from increased shortness of breath when at rest and a dry, rattling cough. As the condition worsens, frothy bloodstained sputum is produced and the victim turns blue. Fluid collects in the lungs, literally drowning the person if the condition is not recognized. Victims must immediately be assisted to a lower altitude (at least 600m lower) and taken to hospital if necessary.

Cerebral oedema is less common but equally dangerous. Here the fluid accumulates in the brain instead of the lungs and may cause permanent brain damage or death. Symptoms include an agonizing headache, giddiness, confusion, aggression and hallucinations. Anyone showing these signs must immediately be assisted to a lower altitude. Poor judgement is also one of the symptoms so strong persuasion (or force!) may have to be used to evacuate the victim.

Finally, remember that not everyone is prone to AMS but that youth and fitness make no difference. It is important for the less affected members of a climbing party to keep their eyes on climbers who may be trying to push themselves beyond sensible limits. Climbers are often so determined to reach a summit that they can jeopardize the whole expedition by trying to cover up an attack of AMS. Being affected by high-altitude sickness is not a sign of inherent weakness. It often takes more courage to stop, rest and acclimatize further than it does to keep pushing dangerously closer to an attack of pulmonary oedema.

Accidents
These can vary from a simple twisted ankle or sprained knee on a hiking trail to multiple injuries caused by a major climbing fall. The most important advice here is never to hike or climb alone.

If a person is injured on a trail or route which is frequently travelled then it is best to wait for help or rescue. The partner should stay with the victim and ensure that the injured party is as warm, comfortable and reassured as possible. If you are climbing an unusual route or hiking cross-country then waiting for help may be pointless. If you go for help make sure that you will be able to find the victim again – leave wands or markers and arrange a whistle or flashlight signal if the victim is conscious. Don't leave injured climbers alone unless it is totally unavoidable.

All climbers should carry a booklet on the principles of first aid, particularly with reference to mountaineering injuries. The value of a course in first aid cannot be overemphasized.

Water purification
Since many diseases are caught by drinking contaminated water, it is important to sterilize your drinking supply. The simplest effective method is boiling for two minutes but this is time consuming and uses a great deal of the precious fuel you've carried. Various water-purifying tablets are available but they aren't wholly effective against everything: hepatitis, for instance. An effective method is to use a saturated iodine solution. Take a small (1oz/28g) glass bottle and put about 2–3mm of iodine crystals in it (both iodine crystals and suitable bottles can be obtained from pharmacies, or from the South American Explorers Club in Quito). Fill the bottle with water and give it a good shake for about a minute, then let the crystals settle to the bottom. The resulting saturated solution is added to a litre of water and left for 15 minutes to produce clean drinking water. The advantage of this method is that the crystals can be used and re-used hundreds of times: very few of the crystals actually dissolve and you pour only the iodine liquid into the water, leaving the crystals in the 1oz bottle for re-use. This is more effective than water purifying tablets and doesn't taste as bad. The only danger is for people who have been treated for thyroid problems and for pregnant women (whose ingestion of iodine may cause thyroid problems in their babies). Otherwise this is a safe and recommended method. Swallowing a crystal by mistake, though inadvisable, is unlikely to have the severe repercussions implied by some authors.

Medical kit

Assuming there is no doctor in your party, the following basic first-aid kit is suggested:

- antiseptic cream
- paracetamol or aspirin and more powerful analgesics (discuss with your doctor)
- oral rehydration packets
- ampicillin and tetracycline antibiotics
- throat lozenges
- ear and eye drops
- antacid tablets
- travel sickness pills
- alcohol swabs, or non-alcohol antiseptic swabs, which sting less
- water purifier
- Vaseline (useful for cracked or chapped skin), lipsalve
- foot powder
- thermometer in a case (low-reading, for hypothermia)
- surgical tape, assorted sticky plasters (Band-aids), moleskin (for blisters), gauze, bandages, butterfly closures or steristrips
- scissors
- first-aid booklet (see *Further Reading* for suggestions)

Remember that some people are allergic to apparently simple drugs like penicillin.

Chapter Three

In Ecuador

'I never travel without my diary. One should always have something sensational to read on the train.'

The Importance of Being Earnest, Oscar Wilde

ARRIVAL

Most visitors will fly into Quito International Airport. This is about 7km from the new city or 10km from the old section. Taxis into town are cheap and should charge about US$3–4 (up to US$5 if going further to the colonial section of town) during the day and about a dollar more at night. Be aware that many airport taxi drivers, in the finest spirit of capitalism, will ask as much as $20 to take you into town! Don't let yourself be taken in: there are more taxis than there are passengers to fill them, so the advantage is yours. Within the city, taxis are required by law to use meters, but fares from the airport will have to be negotiated. Those taxis waiting directly in front of the international area will be harder to bargain with than the others posted near the national section of the airport. If you don't have too much to carry, walk left from the international exit about 25m and look for a taxi there. It is normal to agree on the price beforehand. Drivers will accept cash US dollars but the airport bank is usually open for incoming international flights. If you're really broke, take a bus southbound (to your left) from outside the airport to town.

ACCOMMODATION IN QUITO

The best first-class hotel in town is the new **Oro Verde** at 12 de Octubre and Cordero, though the landmark **Hotel Colón** at Amazonas and Patria is still highly regarded. A good middle-range hotel is the **Cafe Cultura** at Robles and Reina Victoria, tel/fax: (593 2) 224 271, email: sstevens@pi-pro.ec. There are many more listed in *Ecuador & the Galapagos Islands – a travel survival kit* (Lonely Planet) or other guidebooks. Hotels and hostels tend to come in all price ranges. Family-run hotels known as *pensiones* or *residenciales* are usually good and economical.

Old town

Hotels tend to be cheaper in the old town, but there are more occurrences of theft during the day and it can be risky walking around at night. The **Grand Casino** at García Moreno 330 and Ambato is a legend fallen on hard times. Rooms with bath cost US$2.50–3, but the place is rather run down and the staff tend to be abrupt. The **Grand Casino International** around the corner is better, charging US$6 with bath. Another choice in this area is the **Grand Hotel** at Rocafuerte 1001 and Móntufar. In between the old and new sections of Quito is the **Residencial Marsella** at Los Ríos and Castro just above Parque Alameda. Rooms with shared bath are US$3–6, single/double and US$7.50 for room with private bath.

New town

There is a wealth of lodging choices in the new town, where everything seems to be happening these days. If you like the idea of staying in a house with kitchen privileges and washing facilities, a couple of good choices in the new town are **La Casona** at Andalucía 213 and Galacía, tel: 230 129, and **Casa de Eliza** at Isabel la Católica 1559 and Salazar, tel: 226 602, both charging US$6.50 per person. Both are run by friendly folk and have luggage storage available. The **Magic Bean** at Foch 681 y Juan Leon Mera, tel: 566 181, email: bhunta@ecnet.ec, offers shared accommodation for US$7, is located in the heart of the tourist district and is a good place for leaving messages and meeting friends. Recently opened is **Hostal Campo Base**, run by local climbers and located at Veintimilla 858 and Reina Victoria, tel: 224 504. Campo Base is also a restaurant with excellent food, fireplace and pictures of all the major peaks – it feels like an alpine hut. There is a message board which is useful to meet other climbers and slide shows on climbing are shown several times a month.

Accommodation is cheap all over Ecuador. You can always find a basic hotel for US$2–3 per night, and if you want something a little more luxurious than four walls and a bed you'll find plenty of reasonably priced accommodation in all the major cities.

GETTING AROUND

Quito has a slow, crowded, but cheap bus service which covers the city thoroughly. There is a new electric bus line that travels down Av 10 de Agosto to the old town which is quicker but more expensive. If you're in a hurry there are many yellow taxis which are required to use meters. Know the base rate and be sure your taxi driver starts the meter at this figure. At night and for trips outside the city, fares will have to be negotiated. In most other cities, meters are not used so fares must be agreed upon in advance.

A train service (slow but great views) runs daily from Riobamba to Durán (near Guayaquil) and on Saturdays from Quito to Riobamba. There is also a daily train from Ibarra in the north to San Lorenzo on the Pacific. See

Chapter Eight for more details.

The best way to travel in Ecuador is undoubtedly by bus. Quito's central bus terminal, the Cumandá Terminal Terrestre, is located in the old city on Av Cumandá and scores of buses leave here every day. (Be wary of pickpockets and rip-off artists.) Buses heading south on the Pan-American Highway through the 'Avenue of the Volcanoes' past Latacunga, Ambato and Riobamba are very frequent. If you can't get a direct bus to a less well-known destination, take one to the nearest big town and change; the construction of central bus stations in all major Ecuadorian cities means that if you have to change buses you don't have to go looking for out-of-the-way bus stops – all departures are usually from the same place. Some of the 'luxury' bus lines, like Sucre and Panamericana which have routes heading south to Cuenca, Guayaquil and the Peruvian border, now have terminals in the new town. Using the bus system is easy but here are some suggestions to make your journey more enjoyable:

- If you go to the offices in the Terminal Terrestre the day before your departure you can nearly always buy a seat in advance; this also means you can choose your seat number, and obviously the front means better views, more leg room, and a more exciting trip. With luck, you can get these front seats as late as an hour before departure; if travelling during long holiday weekends, however, everything may be sold out several days in advance, so book early.
- Both small microbuses (holding 22 passengers) and large coaches are used. The small buses tend to be faster and more efficient.
- The drivers and their assistants usually run around yelling out their destinations and looking for passengers. Often you will be on a bus going your way within a few minutes of arriving at the terminal.

There is a separate, interprovincial bus area for departures to the small towns around Quito. This is located in the area of Plaza La Marin, and is not really a terminal but a central location from where buses leave. It is located around the end of Av Pichincha in the old town only a few blocks from the main bus terminal, Cumandá. Plaza La Marin is also the end of the line for scores of city buses. Look for any bus that has a La Marin sign displayed in the window or as part of its route name. Buses for a few other nearby destinations, especially Machachi, leave from Villa Flora, a neighbourhood south of Quito. To get there you can catch any city bus marked 'Villa Flora' along Av 12 de Octubre south of Patria, or along Av Colombia above and west of Parque Alameda. It's called the Villa Flora bus terminal, though it is just a street where buses line up and depart for Machachi every 15 minutes.

Air transportation is growing in Ecuador and the main cities of Cuenca and Guayaquil have several inexpensive flights a day from Quito. Lesser cities often have daily flights. The major internal flight companies are TAME and SAN-SAETA.

Hitchhiking is also possible and may be the only transportation in more remote areas. Often you will be expected to pay the driver - arrange this beforehand. Free rides are more common on the major roads.

SECURITY

Rip-offs are a fact of life in Latin America, but Ecuador is safe in comparison with the worst offenders, Colombia and Peru. Nevertheless, certain precautions taken before and during the trip will make your stay a happier one.

Thieves look for easy targets. Tourists who carry a wallet or passport in a hip pocket are asking for trouble. Leave your wallet at home; it's an easy target for a pickpocket. Carrying a roll of paper money loosely wadded under a handkerchief in your front pocket is as safe a way as any of carrying your daily spending money. The rest should be hidden. Always use an inside pocket or (preferably) a body pouch to protect your valuables. A money belt is good; so is a neck pouch under your shirt or a leg pouch as available from the South American Explorers Club in Quito.

Bag snatching is another problem. Motorcyclists sometimes zoom past unsuspecting pedestrians and grab a shoulder bag or camera. If you put luggage down it can be stolen in seconds whilst your attention is diverted.

Crowded places are the haunts of thieves and pickpockets. A bustling market or an ill-lit bus station are prime venues for robbery so be particularly alert. Razor blades are sometimes used to slash baggage (including a pack on your back) for a grab-and-run raid. Don't wear expensive watches or jewellery as this also invites snatch theft.

Armed robbery is still rare in Ecuador. While Quito's old town has become notorious for pickpockets and bag snatchings, the area with the worst reputation is the coast. Guayaquil is the most dangerous, particularly the south end of town near the waterfront. Assaults along the Atacames beach in Esmeraldas have also been reported.

I've heard recent travellers' reports of an extremely insidious form of robbery. *Gringos* are offered biscuits or chocolates on a bus by seemingly friendly passengers and they wake up several hours later in an alley with just a T-shirt and a pair of trousers. One person I talked to had been unconscious for two days. Unopened packages are injected with horse tranquillizers using hypodermic syringes. So... don't take sweets from strangers.

When travelling by public transport, watch your luggage being loaded to ensure that it's not left behind, and try to keep your eye on it during stops. Don't leave valuables in vulnerable places like the easily opened outside pockets of your pack.

Beware of theft from your hotel room. Many hotels have signs that they are not responsible for theft unless valuables are placed in deposit at reception. If using cheaper hotels, you'll find you can often lock the door with your own padlock. A combination lock is more secure than a normal padlock. Some travellers carry a short length of chain for securing baggage in storage areas or on luggage racks. Camera or bag straps can be reinforced with thin chain or guitar strings to prevent slashing.

Before you leave home make a photocopy of your passport to show embassy officials should yours be stolen. Take out travellers' insurance.

When you're climbing or hiking you'll want to leave your excess luggage in a safe place. Your hotel is usually OK, but beware of other *gringos* claiming your luggage. Not all travellers are honest! Many hotels will give you a numbered receipt – this way no-one else can claim your bag. A small charge sometimes accompanies this service.

In some of the mountain *refugios* you'll be able to lock up your gear in one of the storage compartments provided, or in a spare room. Bring a small padlock for this purpose. When camping, it's best never to leave gear unattended. Some climber friends had everything but their tent stolen from the Italian base camp on El Altar whilst they were scouting Obispo. Always leave someone to guard the camp. If your entire group wants to climb, I suggest you hire a local *mulero* or muleman to look after your gear.

COMMUNICATIONS

Post
The main post office in the old town is at Calle Espejo y Calle Guayaquil. They will hold mail for you addressed Lista de Correos, Correos Central, Quito, Ecuador. In the new town, you may receive mail at the main post office located on Av Eloy Alfaro between 10 de Agosto and 9 de Octubre. Have mail addressed Lista de Correos, Correos Eloy Alfaro, Quito, Ecuador. The American Express office will also accept mail for their clients and for holders of their travellers cheques. Their postal address is Apartado 2605, Quito, Ecuador and their street address is Amazonas 339. Members of the South American Explorers Club may have their correspondence sent to the clubhouse, Apartado 21-431, Quito.

Telephones and email
Public telephones are rare in Ecuador. Many small stores will let you make a local call for 1,000 sucres. For long-distance calls, go to the telecommunications building, IETEL, at 10 de Agosto y Colon in Quito. There's one in every town. Also several North American long-distance companies now offer service from Ecuador and collect calls can be made from most hotels. Email service is available at the British Council, SAEC (members only) and some hotels.

TOURIST INFORMATION

The main tourist office in Quito is at Av Eloy Alfaro 1214 y Carlos Tobar (between Av Republica and Av Shyris), tel: 507 509. There is also a small office open in the old town at Venezuela 976, tel: 514 044. They are helpful for standard queries (museums, buses, restaurants, etc).

The South American Explorers Club

Founded in 1977 by Don Montague and Linda Rojas in Lima, Peru, this club opened a branch in Quito in 1989 to the joy of many travellers who have made use of its services over the years. It primarily functions as an information network for travellers, adventurers, scientific expeditions, etc, and provides a wealth of advice about travelling anywhere in Latin America, with an emphasis on Ecuador and Peru.

The club is an entirely member-supported, non-profit organization. Annual membership costs US$40 per person (US$60 for a couple), and includes a subscription to their excellent quarterly journal, *The South American Explorer*. In addition, members have full use of the clubhouses and their facilities (in both Quito and Lima) which include an information service and library, paperback book exchange, email service, trip reports, equipment storage, discounts on books and maps, mail service, equipment sales, and many other benefits. It's a relaxing place to have a cup of tea and chat with other members. Non-members are welcome to come by for a one-time visit, but must come up with the US$40 membership fee to take advantage of the numerous benefits. If you're in Quito, you can stop by the club at Washington 311 y Leonidas Plaza near the American Embassy, and sign up. Otherwise, you can send your US$40 and any questions you may have direct to the club at Apartado 21-431, Quito, Ecuador, tel: 593 2 225 228. The club is open 09.30 to 17.00, Monday to Friday. The club's web page is http://www.samexplo.org, which you can access with your laptop and cellular phone from the refuge at Cotopaxi!

You can also contact the Lima clubhouse, postal address: Casilla 3714, Lima 100, Peru; street address, Av Rep de Portugal 146 (Breña), tel: 51 1 425 0142; or get in touch with the US office for a free catalogue: 126 Indian Creek Rd, Ithaca NY 14850-1310; tel: (607) 277 0488. Bradt Publications can organize membership in the UK.

MAPS AND GUIDEBOOKS

All maps, ranging from Quito city plans to wall charts of Ecuador, are published by and available from the IGM (Instituto Geográfico Militar). Their offices and map sales department are on top of a hill on Av T Paz y Miño, off Av Colombia, behind the Casa de Cultura. There are very few buses up the hill but it's not a very hard walk; alternatively, a taxi will take you. A permit to enter the building is available in exchange for your passport at the main gate; it is open from 08.00 to 16.00 (without closing midday), Monday to Friday.

There is a single 1:1,000,000 chart of Ecuador or four sheets making a 1:500,000 map (the latter maps are currently out of print). Most of the highlands and some of the coast are covered by 1:50,000 topographical maps and some 1:100,000 sheets of the mountains are also available. There are 1:50,000 planometric sheets of some otherwise mapless areas. All extant maps are displayed in large folders so they can be examined before buying. Topographical sheets are available within a half hour and if they are out of stock a photocopy can be purchased. Parts of the Oriente as well as the coast and border areas are restricted and can only be purchased with special permission – they are difficult to obtain due to recent border conflicts with Peru. The 1:50,000 topographical maps are most useful for hikers and climbers. Much of the highlands has also been mapped to higher scales – 1:25,000 or even 1:10,000.

The South American Explorers Club now has an excellent collection of maps which you can use as a reference. Usually some of the more popular maps are on sale by members who have left the country. If you do not need your maps when you leave Ecuador it is a good gesture to drop them off at the club for other travellers to use.

The sketch maps supplied with this book are intended to complement rather than replace the IGM sheets, so details of the sheets needed for each hike or climb are given in the text. It is essential with almost all of the hikes to have the appropriate topographic maps.

On the international level, ITMB Publishing produces excellent maps to the continent. Their three-part map of South America is a little unwieldy but is probably the most accurate you'll find. In addition, a new 1:1,000,000 country map of Ecuador is now available and is much better than the local IGM version. These can be purchased through the South American Explorers Club, or direct from ITMB, 736A Granville Street, Vancouver BC, Canada V6Z 1G3.

The best single general guidebook to the country is *Ecuador & the Galápagos Islands – a travel survival kit,* published by Lonely Planet.

RENTING AND BUYING EQUIPMENT

There are many sports stores in Quito that have a variety of gear for hire and for sale. Most of the new equipment for sale is locally made, reasonably priced, but of lower quality than in the US or Europe. Rental items are a mixture of Ecuadorian-made products and imported equipment, most of which is sold to the shops by travellers who are either broke or tired of lugging the stuff around. The quality of rented gear is extremely variable. A friend of mine rented some locally made crampons but the front points bent downwards at his first attempt to climb a small ice wall. Ecuadorian ice axes are somewhat primitive but boots and sleeping bags are OK. For simple climbs you could get by with this rental gear but your own is obviously better.

Most of the sports stores are open Monday to Friday, from 09.00 to 13.00 and from 15.00 until 18.00, and usually on Saturday morning. Renting equipment is relatively inexpensive but a sizeable deposit is required (travellers cheques, or sometimes the return portion of your international flight coupon, will do). These outfits are also good sources for information on clubs and meetings, etc. The following is a selection of those shops which have proved to be the most reliable:

Sierra Nevada, Joaquin Pinto 637 y Amazonas Baquedano, tel/fax: 593 2 554 936, is owned and operated by Freddy Ramirez, an experienced climber who guides trips to the mountains and arranges excursions into the jungle.

Campo Abierto, Baquedano 355 y Juan Leon Mera, fax: 593 2 524 422, run by climber Ivan Rojas, rents equipment and organizes climbs.

Altamontaña Expediciones, Jorge Washington 425 y 6 de Diciembre, tel/fax: 593 2 504 773, has equipment for rent and sale with a good selection of larger-sized boots. They work with Compañia de Guías next door, a cooperative of guides specializing in mountain climbing.

Andisimo, 9 de Octubre 479 and Roca, fax 593 2 223 030, has good-quality outdoor equipment and rents climbing gear. They also organize treks and climbing tours.

Pamir, Juan Leon Mera 721 and Veintimilla, tel: 220 892; fax: 593 2 547 576, buys, sells and rents equipment and organizes trekking and climbing tours, jungle expeditions and river rafting. Owner Hugo Torres is a long-time climber and guide.

Agama Expediciones, Venezuela 1163 and Manabí, is run by Eduardo Agama, rents and sells equipment and arranges trips into the mountains.

The Explorer, Reina Victoria y Pinto, tel: 550 911, and **Los Alpes**, Reina Victoria 821 and Baquedano, tel: 565 975, both have reasonable camping equipment at cheaper prices.

Outside Quito, equipment rental is hard to come by. Surtrek has a shop in Ambato at Los Shyris 210 and Luis Cordero, tel: 03 844 448, fax: 03 844 512. In addition to renting gear they also provide accommodation and guides. Gear can be hired in Baños and rates are often cheaper than in Quito – but beware of quality. Climbing guide Willie Navarette at Cafe Higueron, Noviembre 270 and Luis Martinez, tel: 03 740 646/740 910, can give good advice.

Don't forget the noticeboards at the South American Explorers Club and also Campo Base.

CLIMBING CLUBS

The majority of climbing clubs seem to vacillate from active to dormant at any time, so it's best to check with the local equipment shops for current information. The International Andean Mountaineers Club, which for many years assisted *gringo* climbers, was operating in recent years under the name of the International Hiking and Climbing Group. At the present time, the club is dormant, but it seems to come back to life from time to time. To find out if it's once again functional, you can contact the British Embassy or the American School, Academia Cotopaxi, both of which have a high participation in the club when it is active. The other clubs are all Ecuadorian and don't often organize trips for the general public. There is a certain amount of rivalry and cliquism in these Quito clubs. They are useful as centres of information but don't expect to arrive and be taken climbing the following weekend. Most of the major colleges and universities have active mountain clubs. The best known and oldest of these is the Colegio San Gabriel group (men only), which meets at the school on Wednesdays after 20.00 at Rumipamba y Vasco, and also irregularly publishes *Montaña* magazine. The club at the Universidad La Católica sometimes has climbing films and lectures open to the general public. General meetings are held at 19.30 every Tuesday at the university. One of the greatest contributors to Ecuadorian climbing over the years is the Polytécnica Climbing Club. The group meets regularly on Wednesdays at 19.00 on the sixth floor of the Ingeneria Cívil de la Polytécnica Nacional, across the street from the Universidad La Católica on Av Isabel de la Católica.

In addition, one of the main climbing organisations in Quito is the Asociacíon de Excursionismo y Andinismo de Pichincha, comprised of amateur climbers who meet irregularly at the Complejo Deportiva de la Vicentina, Calle La Condamine and Manuel Cajías in the Vicentina section of Quito. Climbers are also beginning to gravitate towards the Campo Base restaurant where some Fridays slide shows are shown of recent ascents.

GUIDES

This book aims to get you to the top of most mountains without a guide. Many inexperienced climbers, however, will feel more confident with one to start with.

Climbing in Ecuador can be deceptive, especially to the novice mountaineer. A climb of only 8 to 10 hours to a summit nearing 6,000m may sound like a piece of cake requiring little commitment. This, however, is not necessarily true. The effects of high altitude combined with abruptly changing weather patterns and variable snow/ice conditions can put heavy demands on the most experienced of climbers. In 1992 six people perished on Chimborazo, and another ten (including three experienced Ecuadorian guides) were killed in an avalanche there in 1993, yet Chimborazo is considered a technically easy climb. Every year climbers die on Ecuadorian peaks and the hazards of embarking on a climb should not be underestimated. For these reasons, guided climbs on the major peaks may be the best alternative for some.

Choosing a guide is as important as deciding whether or not you need one. 'A little knowledge is a dangerous thing' applies unequivocally to some locals who consider themselves capable climbers on any peak after one or two ascents of minor summits. I ran into one fellow at the Cotopaxi refuge who had been hired as a guide by a couple of Americans. In a casual way, he chatted to me about the route up, wanting to know where it went exactly, and what time was I leaving, perhaps he and his 'friends' could tag along? It turned out that he had gone up Tungurahua a few times and decided he could climb anything, not to mention actually guide other people! Fortunately, the weather turned sour, and no-one got out of the hut that night. The thing to realize is you get what you pay for. Some so-called guides charge as little as US$30 per person to climb one of the major peaks, while the going rate for an experienced, professional guide is somewhere between three to four times that amount, depending on group size. The Baños area is especially notorious for inexperienced guides exaggerating their abilities and touting their services at bargain prices.

The best way to locate a reliable guide is to contact the climbing/rental shops. Many of these, as described in the previous section, are owned and operated by experienced climbing guides. You can get recommendations from other travellers or contact the South American Explorers Club which keeps updated information about local guides and guiding services.

The Ecuadorian Guide Association (ASEGUIM – Asociación Ecuatoriana de Guías de Montaña) has recently become more actively involved, attempting to 'professionalize' the guiding service by licensing their mountain guides. While most members have years of technical guiding experience, the standards are still below those expected in Europe and North America. There are now guiding/skills courses being planned and a system for routine equipment checks is being organized. Hiring a licensed guide does not guarantee expert quality; it does, however, provide a format for negotiation and registering problems, should any arise.

The Compañia de Guías, Montanismo Integral Capac Urcu, Expediciones Andinas (Riobamba), Surtrek, Pamir, Sierra Nevada, Inti Travel and Safari are guiding agencies that have good reputations. This is not an exclusive list, however – there are many other good agencies and guides working independently.

In case of an emergency, ASEGUIM organizes rescues. The guides do not charge for their time, but they do ask that their expenses (food and transport) be paid. Donations are gladly accepted. Ivan Rojas at Guías de Montaña is the current contact for the association.

INEFAN

The parks system of Ecuador recently underwent sweeping changes in administration. No longer under the direct management of MAG, the Ministry of Agriculture, Ecuador's parks and reserves are now managed by the newly formed department, Instituto Ecuatoriano Forestal y de Areas Naturales y Vida Silvestre – INEFAN. In addition to significantly raising park entrance fees for foreign visitors (nationals and residents pay a fraction of this) and establishing administrative offices in several rural areas, some new reserves have been established and other existing protected areas amplified. Amidst these changes, it is not yet clear how much impact or what specific accomplishments INEFAN will achieve. In any event, the formation of a separate parks management bureaucracy must be viewed as a step forward, and hopefully the drastic increase in fees will provide funds with which to manage and preserve Ecuador's spectacular natural areas effectively.

Protected forests

There are also over a hundred *bosques protectores* (protected forests) under the auspices of INEFAN. Some of these are privately owned and permission to visit them must be obtained by the owner. INEFAN (offices in the MAG building at Av Amazonas and Republica in Quito) now sells an excellent and inexpensive map of the park system entitled *Sistema Nacional de Áreas Protegidas del Ecuador.*

Principal park entry fees (for foreign visitors)

Some of these charges, as with the Cotacachi Reserve fee, have met with strong resistance and, in this case, the fee has been dropped. In the case of 'greater demand' areas such as Cotopaxi, Chimborazo and the Galápagos (of course!) the park charges are likely to remain at the fixed rates below. Still, be prepared to see these rates vary in implementation.

Parque Nacional Galápagos	US$80
Parque Nacional Cotopaxi	US$10
Parque Nacional Sangay	US$10
Parque Nacional Podocarpus	US$10/20*
Parque Nacional Machalilla	US$20
Parque Nacional Llanganates	US$10
Parque Nacional Sumaco-Napo Galeras	US$10
Parque Nacional Yasuní	US$20
Parque Nacional Cajas	US$10
Reserva Producción Faunistica de Chimborazo	US$10
Reserva Producción Faunistica de Cuyabeno	US$20
Reserva Ecológica Cayambe/Coca	US$10/20*
Reserva Ecológica Cotacachi/Cayapas	US$10/20*
Reserva Ecológica Antisana	US$10/20*
Reserva Ecológica Manglares Churute	US$20
Reserva Ecológica El Angel	US$10
Reserva Ecológica Limoncocha	US$20
Reserva Ecológica Manglares-Churute	US$20
Reserve Ecológica Cayapas-Mataje	US$20
Reserva Geobotanica Pululahua	US$10
Amigos de la Naturaleza – Mindo	US$4
Pasochoa – Fundación Natura	US$7

*The two prices reflect the sierra (US$10) and lowland (US$20) areas of the reserve.

Note: For simplification, dollar prices are listed here. Fees are actually fixed in sucres, so ideally it's better to pay in local currency as the cost will drop as inflation rises.

MINIMUM IMPACT

One look at the areas around base camps and huts on some of the more popular Ecuadorian volcanoes will show you that not all mountaineers are environmentally aware.

Minimum impact means that a place is unchanged by your visit: no garbage, no fire-scars or other damage, no indigenous people taught to beg by thoughtless handouts of sweets or money.

Don't litter. All your trash should be burned, carried out with you, or disposed of properly at mountain refuges. If you can bring yourself to clean up after less considerate climbers, so much the better.

When nature calls, go well away from the trail, campsite or river, and dig a hole. Bring a lightweight trowel or use your ice axe for the purpose; burn toilet paper.

Conservation in Ecuador is the responsibility of the Departamento de Áreas Naturales y Vida Silvestre, under the Ministry of Agriculture. An organization which helps to protect the country's flora and fauna is the Fundación Natura, which publishes a bi-monthly newsletter.

Don't build fires in the highlands where wood is scarce and is sometimes the only fuel for inhabitants of remote areas. Bring your stove for cooking.

Ecuador's indigenous people are proud people with their own culture and beliefs. Gratuitous present-giving tends to impose your culture on theirs, so give gifts or money only in return for their help or work. Children are especially influenced and gifts of sweets and 'school pens' will quickly establish a cycle of begging and a view that the *gringo* is simply a walking handout. If you want to do something for the village children you encounter, give a donation of supplies or money to the local school. Indiscriminate photography will often alienate you from mountain dwellers. These people, although living under extremely simple conditions, are as sensitive and

THE TOP TEN: PEAKS OVER 5,000M IN ECUADOR		
Chimborazo	6,310m	(20,703ft)
Cotopaxi	5,897m	(19,348ft)
Cayambe	5,790m	(18,997ft)
Antisana	5,758m	(18,715ft)
El Altar	5,320m	(17,455ft)
Iliniza Sur	5,248m	(17,219ft)
Sangay	5,230m	(17,160ft)
Iliniza Norte	5,126m	(16,818ft)
Tungurahua	5,023m	(16,480ft)
Carihuairazo	5,020m	(16,471ft)

intelligent as anyone else and resent being treated with arrogance by foreign visitors. Not only will a few exchanged words in greeting and a round of handshakes be more likely to get you that special photo, it will also bring you closer to experiencing a culture different from your own.

LAST WORDS ABOUT CLIMBING AND HIKING

Keep in mind that the conditions related to climbing and hiking, as detailed in this book, are *not* static. Things change constantly. Climbing routes, particularly on glaciers, will vary from season to season. Sometimes this may be a minor variation of our description, but at other times the change may be drastic enough to make the described route life-threatening. Since the last edition of this book, every major climb has seen a number of route changes. Also, we are not always right and there are often several ways to do a trek or climb.

It is always best to get recent verbal information about a route from someone who has been to your destination recently. Be a responsible climber. Go with as much information as you can get and use your experience and judgement to evaluate climbing conditions. Treks will see less variation, but water sources may come and go, again depending on the season. New roads, constantly being constructed in Ecuador, will alter, if not completely ruin, some beautiful hikes. Always carry a compass and topographic maps of the area you're venturing into. Even on lower-altitude hikes and climbs clouds can roll in and obscure the most visible landmarks. It is hoped that this guide will be a valuable tool in getting you into a variety of incredible places and on top of a number of beautiful summits, but no guidebook can replace common sense or be a substitute for experience.

A final note is that there are many possible walks and climbing routes that are not described in this or any guidebook. If you really want to do some exploring buy some maps and start walking. For most indigenous people the primary form of transportation is still on foot or horseback and there are trails everywhere. Equally, many of the less used roads are great for trekking. There are still a lot of 'undiscovered' corners of Ecuador.

MOUNTAIN BIKING IN ECUADOR

One of the reasons Ecuador is such an attractive destination for adventure is that it's small enough for even out-of-the-way places to be accessible. Hikers and climbers appreciate the speediness with which they can get off the beaten track and into the remote highlands or up to 6,000m. For this same reason, mountain biking has become increasingly popular. A short bus-ride away are trails and tracks leading up to isolated villages and natural areas of extreme beauty, all approachable by bicycle. Many of these areas are places ignored by hikers/climbers except as incidental approaches to their end destination. For the climber the reasons are obvious as he/she heads straight for the highest point without veering, and for the hiker, well, trudging along even infrequently used roads is not very appealing: most hikers choose to eschew man-made tarmac for the more rustic footpath. All of this leaves a very big area for exploring by mountain bike, especially since Ecuador seems intent on building the most roads per capita in the world! This is not to say that venturing off-road isn't possible or equally rewarding, but the plethora of access routes makes almost anything possible.

Apart from the Pan-American Highway, very few of the roads in Ecuador are paved. The rest may vary from blissfully smooth, hard-packed dirt (best avoided during the rainy season) to bone-jarring, rock-strewn, cobbled track. These serve as better choices for biking than the Pan-American which can sometimes be hair-raising (and life-threatening) due to speeding buses and recklessly driven trucks. Because of the road conditions, mountain bikes are much better suited for Andean excursions than narrow-tyre road bikes as punctures and bent rims tend to occur more frequently with less sturdier equipment.

Transport

These days, it could not be easier to transport your own bicycle by air. Airline personnel will rarely give you a second look as you approach the check-in counter lugging a cumbersome bike box. While I've heard of friends avoiding additional freight charges by holding their head the right way, generally expect to pay a reasonable fee from your home country. From the US it's about US$45 extra to ship a bicycle as accompanied baggage. Ecuadorian customs officials will usually wave you straight through inspection without any trouble.

Within Ecuador, transporting your bicycle is equally painless. Most of the inter-provincial buses have large roof racks which accommodate a variety of substantial belongings from double-bed mattresses to bundles of live sheep. An ordinary mountain bicycle is not likely to attract much attention. You may be asked to pay a little extra, but never more than the price of a passenger ticket. Be sure to remove all easily detachable objects from your bike before storing it on top. Things have a habit of disappearing.

Travelling with wheels on domestic flights requires very little effort – you can practically ride your bike on to the plane. No box is required, but it's better if you want maximum protection. If you don't have a box, at least remove the pedals and disassemble the handlebar and attach it to the crossbar with packing tape in order to prevent major damage. Be sure to call the airline office ahead to ensure there's baggage space available on the day you expect to travel. Always deflate the tyres prior to flying – unpressurized luggage-holds have a way of causing inflated tyres to explode!

Equipment

As with climbing and hiking equipment, bring what you think you'll really need from home in the way of spare parts and extra gear. As interest grows, more equipment and expertise becomes available, but the quality is not up to US and European standards. You'll at least need a spare tube, tyre pump, basic tool kit, and the minimum knowledge to keep your bicycle in a reasonable state of repair. If something really goes wrong, there are a few bicycle repair shops in Quito that can get you out of a jam. One is located on the southeast side of Parque Carolina just off Av Republica, and there are a few nestled together at the top of Av 6 de Diciembre just south of Parque El Ejido. Lightweight panniers or at least a rack for attaching a daypack are probably essential. Lastly, you'll want a reliable lock and chain for theft prevention. In the larger cities, you can generally lock up your bike outside during the day and find it still where you left it some time later. This is not true at night – bring it inside your hotel or secure it in an enclosed area of some sort. While camping out, it's best to affix your bike to some permanent object nearby. If this is not possible, lock it and consider attaching bells or other noise makers to alert you of any mischief.

At the end of your trip, you may consider selling your bike to spare the expense of packing it up and shipping it home. Secondhand mountain bikes fetch a good price in the country.

Renting bikes in-country is not accomplished easily. The towns of Baños and Otavalo are about the only two places where you can rent bikes to pedal around on your own. The cost is about US$7 per day and the equipment is usually of poor quality and inadequately maintained.

Guided trips

If you'd like to do a bike trip but find it's impractical to lug your own wheels along there are a few outfits that specialize in mountain-bike excursions ranging from one to several days. In many cases, personalized itineraries can be arranged, established itineraries have frequently scheduled departures, and generally the bikes are imported and of good quality. Guides always accompany the group, and often a support vehicle is used.

Jan the Downhill Flying Dutchman, Foch 714 y Juan Leon Mera, Quito, tel/fax: 593 2 449 568, has a special approach which is indicated in the name and popular with *gringos*. Jan specializes in downhill riding. He offers trips of one day and longer which are graded according to ability and vehicle-supported. He has good-quality bikes available, helmets and gloves, and pads for knees, shoulders and elbows. A minimum group of four costs about US$45 per person per day.

Explorbike, Calle Juan Jaramillo 910 y Hermano Miguel, Cuenca; tel: 07 883 362/831 293, operates in the Cuenca area offering one-day bike trips. Local national parks, rural communities and craftspeople are part of the scenic tour. Costs run at about US$30 per person including guide, imported bike, helmet and lunch.

On your own

Many of the approaches to the hikes and climbs described in this guide will also serve as excellent routes for mountain biking. Topographical maps of the area will (sometimes reliably) give indications of disused tracks suitable for two wheels. Locals are always free with advice; just be sure to exercise the proper amount of scepticism. The more open you are to experiencing what happens as opposed to remaining fixed on achieving a particular experience, the more you're likely to have a remarkable trip. We've included a few detailed trips to give an idea of what mountain biking in Ecuador is all about. It is not intended to be a fully fledged guide to the art of mountain biking; this is after all, a hiking/climbing guide. However, the beauty of biking cannot be ignored and perhaps a few details here will be of some value.

Salinas–Guaranda–Riobamba (2 days)

Approach From Quito, take a bus to Ambato and from there another to Guaranda, or catch a less-frequent Quito–Guaranda direct bus. Have the driver drop you at the turn-off for Chimborazo (see Climbing Chimborazo approach) at what is described as the white house (covered in graffiti).

Route Rather than following the dirt path that leads into the Chimborazo area, look opposite to the other side of the main road and you'll see a track leading off into the *páramo*. Follow this as it veers to the right, passing through several small communities. Initially the track is uncomfortably stony, but soon levels off into a nicely packed dirt road, gently rolling. Behind you, if the weather cooperates, you'll have great views of Chimborazo. When you come to a junction of the track, take the left turn to ride into Salinas. The right turn will carry you along the road towards Facundo Vela and stunning views, but you'll have to backtrack to get to Salinas. From the roadhead, without diversions, it's about a 3-hour ride to Salinas.

Salinas is a delightful village which is run as a cooperative producing salt, hard cheeses, mushrooms and other commodities. The setting is impressive, tucked under a sheer cliff face. (If you are in no hurry, you may opt to stay overnight in the cooperative hostel and partake of the guided tours available through the salt mines and cheese-making plants.) After a lunch stop in the plaza restaurant, ask for the road to Guaranda, a gentle, chiefly downhill ride. This first day is about 7 hours, including the lunch stop. There are several hostels in Guaranda, the best of which is Residencial Bolívar on Sucre y Roca Fuerte (tel: 980 547).

The next day take the old road out of Guaranda towards Riobamba. It immediately begins as a steep climb and doesn't let up until you reach the pass about 5 to 6 hours later. The road is hard-packed dirt, but can often be muddy and the weather windy at 4,000m. The views are spectacular if you can relax a moment from the exertion and have a look around. From the pass, it's about 2 hours of downhill rolling into Riobamba. The first hour is on dirt to the village of San Juan where the tarmac takes over. Watch for the cement factory where you'll take the left fork into Riobamba. It's a tough 66km ride with an altitude gain of 1,300m but the views are great and the severity of life on the *páramo* becomes a little more real.

Saquisilí–Zumbahua–Quilotoa–Sigchos (3–4 days)

Approach From Quito bus terminal get an infrequent bus direct to Saquisilí, or a more frequent bus to Latacunga from where you can catch a regular bus direct to the village. You can also have the Latacunga bus driver let you off at the Saquisilí turn-off which is about 20 minutes before reaching Latacunga. From the Pan-American Highway, it's a flat 12km ride into town on a good secondary road, but it's best avoided on chaotic market day (Thursday).

Route This first section of the ride, Saquisilí to Pujilí, covers about 19km in 2 hours along mostly good dirt roads. From the Saquisilí plaza head south on the paved road to the edge of town where you'll see several prominent signs to the Muller Ranch. Follow the signs to the right down a cobbled track for about 200m. Here you'll encounter two roads forking to the left. Take the road furthest to the right (keep right, avoid going straight into the woods) and continue until you can take a left turn past a military base. When you come into the village, you'll go left up a road just past the church. This leads to the old monastery of Tilipulo which was recently bought by a local municipality and is being restored. The caretaker, Santiago, will be happy to provide a guided tour if you request. A tip is appreciated.

From Tilipulo, continue along the road until you reach a cobbled junction where you'll head right. Cross a small river and take the dirt road up the hill to the left, avoiding the impossibly steep-looking section of the hill directly in front of you. You'll roll through a couple of small villages; in the first one take the right-hand exit, and continue on straight ahead until you hit paved road. Turn right on to the tarmac. About 200m along you'll come to a junction with a statue of a potter. Keep to the left and head into Pujilí. There is a lively market here on Sundays. With a start from Quito the same day, an overnight stop here would be just about right.

The second full section is from Pujilí to Zumbahua, beginning with 28km of uphill riding on paved road, and then a shift from tarmac to compacted dirt with continuous up and down along high *páramo* for a further 29km. This takes about 7 to 8 hours. If you're in a hurry and want to continue on through Pujilí, the best alternative is to catch a bus to Zumbahua (irregular) or hire a truck (about US$16) to carry you and your bikes up along the Zumbahua road to the Guangaje turn-off. This will cut 29km and 4 to 5 hours off the trip, making it feasible to get there from Saquisilí in one day. At the Guangaje turn-off, continue along the main road (not the turn-off) to Zumbahua, about 29km and 3 hours away.

This area is high, dusty, stark *páramo* that is stunning to behold and fascinating to the visitor for the primarily indigenous communities settled throughout the area. In many ways life here has been relatively untouched by the modern world. Zumbahua is especially appealing for its Saturday market which is considered by some to be the most traditional in the country. Much of the produce and other saleable goods arrive on the backs of llamas, transported from smaller villages higher up on the *páramo*. This and a visit to nearby Quilotoa, a volcanic crater filled by a beautiful emerald lake enhanced by several snow-capped volcanoes in the distance, are said to be the best excursions in the country.

Overnight facilities in Zumbahua are basic to say the least. The best place is up past the church, taking the track to the right up the hill. There will be a little shop on the left where you can enquire about rooms.

The following day the route carries on from Zumbahua to Quilotoa and on to Sigchos, covering a distance of about 65km. Prepare for an early start out of Zumbahua by arranging for one of the restaurants to open up early for breakfast. Take the main road out of town north to Quilotoa, first descending from the village to cross the river. After a few kilometres along a dusty road turn right, crossing over the bridge at the fork in the road. Have a local point it out if there is any confusion. As the landscape opens up at the top of the hill there will be a small road to the right leading up to the crater rim. There is a small settlement nearby and an overnight stay with a local family is possible, but you'll need a sleeping bag and extra food which the family can prepare for you.

From the lake you'll be able to see the road as it continues through the hills toward Sigchos. This smooth dirt track skirts the edge of a canyon and first passes through Chugchilán, a rustic village in one of the most scenic areas of Ecuador, some 20km from Quilotoa. Continue another 25km to Sigchos where a couple of basic hostels and a restaurant are available. Buses to Quito depart daily at 04.00 and 14.30.

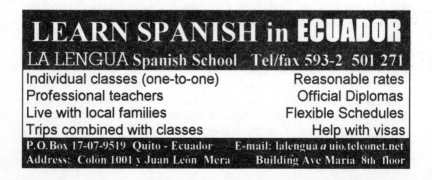

Chapter Four

The Central Valley

'I live not in myself, but I become
Portion of that around me; and to me
High mountains are a feeling, but the hum
of human cities torture.'

Byron

Lying in the middle of Ecuador, the 'Avenue of the Volcanoes' is not only the geographical heart of the country but also contains most of its major cities and almost half of the country's 12 million inhabitants.

QUITO

The most important city of the Central Valley is of course Ecuador's capital, Quito. Its high mountainous setting is marvellously invigorating and, with its well-preserved old town full of narrow cobbled streets and red-tiled colonial buildings, it is the most attractive capital in Latin America. Quito is proud of its 86 churches which, with their intricate wood carvings, superb colonial paintings and lavish use of gold leaf, are amongst the most splendid in the continent. The church of La Compañía and the monastery of San Francisco, both in the old town, are perhaps the most extravagantly gorgeous. There are also some fine museums. The Casa de Cultura at Av Patria and Av 12 de Octubre houses the collections of the Banco Central which chronicle the history of Ecuador through a well-conceived series of four galleries featuring pre-Columbian artefacts, colonial art, republican art and, finally, the modern paintings of Guayasamin and Kingman which explore the indigenous struggle for freedom. Information on tourist sights and a map of the city are available from the tourist office at Venezuela 976, tel: 514 044 in the old town, and Eloy Alfaro Av 1214 y Carlos Tobar in the new town by Parque Carolina.

You'll probably find yourself staying in Quito for some time as it is not only a charming city but is also well located as a departure point for other areas. Despite being only 25km from the Equator, Quito's altitude (about 2,850m) gives the city a pleasant climate. This is an excellent elevation to begin acclimatizing for high altitude and the following easy day hikes near

Quito are described with this in mind. These are followed by longer and more difficult hikes and climbs.

SHORT WALKS IN THE QUITO AREA

Cerro Panecillo (3,016m)
This walk, which has been featured in previous editions of the guide, has been omitted from this edition as it is now considered to be too dangerous.

Loma Lumbisi (3,045m)
Maps: IGM 1:25,000 Tumbaco or 1:50,000 Sangolquí
For those just arriving, this is a good way to test out your lungs at altitude on a 3- to 4-hour walk along a long flat hill lying just east of the capital.

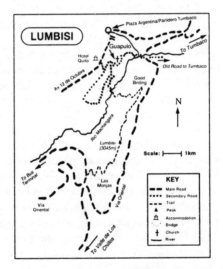

Below and to the west is the Río Machángara, once a pleasant river, but unfortunately now carrying most of Quito's sewage untreated out to sea. This hill is a protected area, preserving rural lifestyles a stone's throw from Quito. There are several very steep gullies on the west side of the hill that have escaped cultivation and are excellent birding spots.

You can catch a bus from Universidad Central going direct to Las Monjas, or any of the Chillos valley buses leaving from Plaza La Marin or Hotel Quito, and get off at the new Via Oriental interchange. From here head east up the hill. You will cross fields then connect with a dirt road which switchbacks up the hill, although it is also possible to take short cuts. The dirt road reaches the top of the hill and runs north-northeast along the summit ridge for over a kilometre before dropping down. Allow about an hour from the toll booth to the highest point.

Continue on this dirt road before it begins descending into thick eucalyptus forest and find the dirt road that turns back to the south. (If you go too far on the ridge you will eventually come to the new Vía Oriental – a six-lane highway!) Follow down about 0.5km and you will come to a new dirt road that switchbacks down to the Río Machángara. Cross the bridge to the other side and follow the cobbled road up past several small factories to the paved Av de Los Conquistadores. A right turn takes you to the famous Guapulo church and plaza, usually crowded with university students. From here you can walk up the steep old road to Hotel Quito through the historic neighbourhood of Guapulo. There is also a set of stairs a few metres to the left where you meet Av de Los Conquistadores. Frequent buses head uphill from the plaza to Quito. (See Lumbisi map.)

Ungüi (3,578m)

Map: IGM 1:50,000 Quito

This small rounded hill can clearly be seen in a west-southwest direction from the Panecillo. The beginning of the walk takes you through Marcopamba which is one of Quito's outlying suburbs and has a rural rather than an urban feel to it. You may even see a couple of llamas wandering by with loads of straw or firewood on their backs. The walk ends with some particularly fine views of the capital. It takes about 4 to 5 hours round-trip and there is some traffic on the road if you need a ride down.

Start by taking a No 8 Tola–Pintado bus to its western terminal at Cuartel Mariscal Sucre. Just before the end of the line there is a road at your right called Angamarca (maps show this as Chilibulo). Follow this road up the hill past a hospital on your left to the end where it makes a left turn to the southwest, and continue along its zigzagging route out of town. At any intersection take the major cobbled fork and follow the road through the countryside for about 1½ hours of steady walking which brings you to a pass. The road down from the pass will eventually bring you to Lloa which is a possible starting point for climbing Guagua Pichincha (see page 90). To climb Ungüi, however, you turn right at the pass. A dirt road heads right and goes around

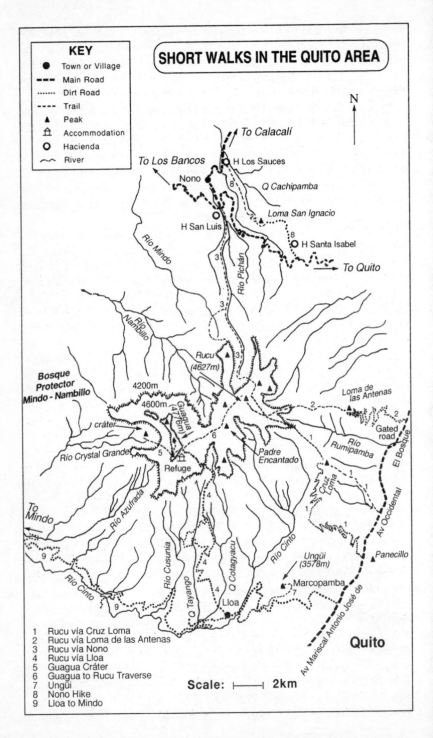

KEY

- ● Town or Village
- ▬▬▬ Main Road
- ∙∙∙∙∙∙ Dirt Road
- ▬ ▬ ▬ Trail
- ▲ Peak
- ⌂ Accommodation
- ○ Hacienda
- ∼ River

SHORT WALKS IN THE QUITO AREA

N

To Calacalí

To Los Bancos

H Los Sauces

Nono

Q Cachipamba

Loma San Ignacio

H San Luis

8

H Santa Isabel

To Quito

Río Mindo

Río Pichán

3

3

Río Nambillo

Rucu (4627m)

3

Loma de las Antenas

Bosque Protector Mindo - Nambillo

4200m

4600m

Guagua (4776m)

2

2

Gated road

cráter

Río Crystal Grande

5

Refuge

6

Padre Encantado

1

Río Rumipamba

El Bosque

Av Occidental

Cruz Loma

1

1

1

To Mindo

Río Azufrada

4

Panecillo

9

Río Cinto

Río Cusunia

Q Tayango

4

4

Q Cotagyacu

Río Cinto

Ungüi (3578m)

7

Marcopamba

9

Lloa

1 Rucu vía Cruz Loma
2 Rucu vía Loma de las Antenas
3 Rucu vía Nono
4 Rucu vía Lloa
5 Guagua Cráter
6 Guagua to Rucu Traverse
7 Ungüi
8 Nono Hike
9 Lloa to Mindo

Av Mariscal Antonio José de

Quito

Scale: ⊢——⊣ 2km

the back of the hill; in the crotch between this and the road you came up on there is a wide grassy lane on the east side of the hill which follows an aqueduct (marked *acequia* on the IGM map). This runs underground at the beginning but soon comes to the surface. Follow the aqueduct until you reach the point where there is a full view of Quito. Here you'll find rough tracks heading up and down the hill. At the top of the hill is a tiny stone building. Paths which appear to lead to the top before there is a full view of Quito are just water run-offs. If you continue following the aqueduct it will, after some 5km, join with a rough dirt road heading right and back down the hill towards Marcopamba, or you can make short cuts downhill through fields if you wish. Half a day is perfectly adequate but if you bring a picnic lunch you'll probably enjoy a full day gazing down on Quito. (See map opposite.)

Pululagua Crater
Map: IGM 1:50,000 Calicalí
The extinct volcanic crater of Pululagua is located about 20km north of Quito and is said to be the largest crater in South America. It is about 4km wide and 300m deep; its flat and fertile bottom is used for agriculture and in its centre there is a volcanic dome, Loma Pondoña (2,975m). The floor of the crater is at 2,500m elevation. The area is protected by INEFAN as a geobotanical reserve.

To get to the crater take any Mitad del Mundo bus which runs from Plaza La Marin, through the old town, and north on Av America. About an hour's ride will bring you to Mitad del Mundo where a huge monument marks the Equator – though it should be mentioned that the correct Equatorial line as determined by the most recent surveys lies several hundred metres away. Get off the bus at the monument and take the good tarmac road to Calacalí to the right of the monument. Walk, get a ride (expect to pay US50c or so), or catch a bus going to Calacalí to the marked turn-off for 'Reserva Geobotánica Pululagua', which is the first tarmac road to the right, some 4km beyond the monument. Less than 1km later this road ends at a parking area at the very edge of the crater. Usually there is a small kiosk to buy snacks and someone to guard your car.

From here you can walk down a very steep and winding footpath to the crater floor, then walk around on several field roads, or climb the Loma Pondoña in the centre. The descent into the crater takes about half an hour, and an hour to climb back out.

Nono hikes
Maps: IGM 1:50,000 Nono and Quito
Nono is a sleepy little village located about 15km as the crow flies northwest of Quito, but vehicles travelling on the beautiful winding mountain road from Quito to Nono cover twice that distance. The village is interestingly situated on the western flanks of the Western Cordillera and from Nono the road continues to the coast, dropping through lush tropical forests. This

road and the surrounding forest are particularly interesting for the number and variety of bird species. A new road serving this area has been completed through Calacalí to the coast. Since little transport uses the old winding road it makes an excellent mountain biking road for the so inclined. Nono itself is the centre of a fine network of jeep tracks and foot trails going into the surrounding hills, all making good day hikes or longer trips if desired. A possible one-day hike is described below, but armed with the IGM 1:50,000 topographical maps you will be able to find plenty of other possibilities, including a northern approach to Rucu Pichincha (see map, page 58.)

You can reach Nono in a couple of hours from Quito. First take the No 7 Marin–Cotocollao bus northbound. Get off at the end of the line, which is the Cotocollao Plaza. Wait at the corner of the plaza by the taxi stand for a ride to Nono. There are occasional buses, and often trucks will stop at this corner and pick up passengers for Nono and beyond. As mentioned, most vehicles will take the new northern route, though a few continue to go along the old road. This ride is very interesting because after you leave Quito you go past several kilometres of brickworks – but not brickworks in the sense of the smoke-belching stacks of Britain's industrial midlands; here you can see *campesinos* mixing, pouring, forming, drying, firing and stacking the mud bricks which are so commonly used in the construction of houses in Andean villages. The mountain road continues climbing through pine and eucalyptus plantations until it reaches a pass at nearly 3,400m, before dropping down through farmland to Nono at 2,700m.

If you are arriving via the new Calacalí road, the ride will be shorter but the scenery still beautiful. Very few vehicles actually go into Nono but it is only a few kilometres' walking from the junction to Nono. From here it's an easy walk into town.

From Nono there is a jeep track heading south to Hacienda San Luis and a footpath continuing south to Loma Yanayacu. You could continue south, walking cross-country to Pichincha. The route is shown on the Pichincha sketch map on page 58. There are trails east and west of this footpath, including an eastbound trail that goes to Quito. Trails also lead to the northwest of Nono to Cerro Chiquilpe and to the north to San Francisco and beyond. Finally, a mixture of tracks and trails climb southeast out of Nono over Loma San Ignacio and to the pass on the Quito–Nono road. This is the hike described below.

From where the bus or truck drops you off outside Nono walk northwest for about a kilometre into the village, then up the main road until you come to the church plaza at the north end of town. Turn east on a road which twists and hairpins for over a kilometre to the Hacienda Los Sauces, and here take the right-hand track (which is still wide enough for a jeep), skirting the *hacienda* and climbing steadily southeastwards for 2 to 3km to the Finca La Florida (which is wrongly marked on the IGM map). After the *finca* the track changes into a narrow grassy footpath climbing south and southeast almost to the top of the hill known as Loma San Ignacio. Go through two gates and near the top turn right through a third gate. The trail now widens out again and soon becomes a jeep track which continues for 3 to 4km past the Hacienda Santa Isabel and on to the main Quito–Nono road.

The whole hike will take about 3 hours of steady walking and is mostly uphill. It could be done in reverse which would be easier; the beginning of the jeep track is marked by a sign for Hacienda Santa Isabel on the right-hand side of the Quito–Nono road. The uphill route, however, climbs steadily but gently and is good exercise and acclimatization for those planning more strenuous trips into the mountains.

Tandayapa to Mindo Hike
Maps: IGM 1:50,000 Nono and Calicalí
This is an easy hike which takes you into a well-preserved cloudforest about 35km down the old road from Nono. The hike begins in Tandayapa on the Nono road, passes the Bellavista Lodge and finally exits on the new Mindo road. You mostly follow little-used dirt roads and footpaths, but there is almost no traffic.

The quickest way to get to the Tandayapa/Bellavista region is to take a bus (Cooperativas Amazonas, San Pedrito, Alóag or Kennedy) from the Terminal Terrestre in Quito. Get off the bus at the bridge just before the town of Nanegalito at Café Tiepolo of Fundacíon Tandayapa. The café may have information on short walks in the area. Turn left on to the dirt road to Bellavista, signed 'Pesca Deportiva'. You reach the trout farm after 4.5km (traffic at weekends goes this far), and from there it is about 1.5km to the small village of Tandayapa.

From Tandayapa, go straight through the village and uphill. The road that crosses the bridge to your left is the road coming down from Nono. The steep climb is rewarded by increasingly spectacular views. Follow the trail, marked with orange and white painted stones, which allows you to shorten the 6km road distance. The trail is known locally as the *chaquiñan* and goes through pastures and forest as it climbs to Bellavista Lodge. Here you can rent a room with good views of cloudforest. Bellavista is also a private reserve with other nature trails, waterfalls and over 150 species of birds.

You can continue from Bellavista by hiking along the dirt road 12km via Santa Rosa to the main road that continues to Mindo, San Miguel de Los Bancos and the coast. Equally, crossing old pastures at Bellavista, you come on to the dirt road down towards Nanegalito, 11km to the main road. Turn right when you hit the main road for Nanegalito and Quito, or left for the coast.

Cerro Ilaló (3,185m)
Map: IGM 1:50,000 Sincholagua
Ilaló is a long-extinct and deeply eroded volcano located next to the Quito suburb of Tumbaco. It is about a 45-minute bus ride from Quito to Tumbaco,

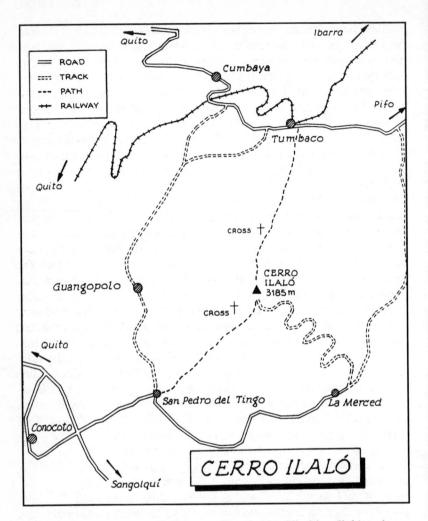

located 10km east and 400m lower than Quito. Climbing Ilaló makes a good half-day escape from Quito. Tumbaco is a delightful place and although essentially Ecuadorian in character it is home to many expatriates working in Quito. Its climate is rather like a warm summer's day in England and its gardens are full of bright tropical flowers, flashing hummingbirds and lazy butterflies.

To get there take any bus heading north on Av 6 de Diciembre and get off at the Plaza Argentina roundabout (also known as Partidero Tumbaco). You can take any bus heading to Tumbaco or beyond. Make sure that the bus goes as far as Tumbaco as some buses now wander around Cumbaya and never reach Tumbaco. There is a bypass of Cumbaya under construction. Get off at the traffic light in Tumbaco (you can't miss it, it's the only one in town) and walk east along the main road for a couple of hundred metres until the first right turn on pavement. Walk up this road for over a kilometre until the road forks. Here take a right fork on a paved road to Centro Comunal Tumbaco where there is a church with blue domes. A few hundred metres further you come to a major junction above several volleyball courts where you turn left on to a cobble road – this is a good place to park. Continue up this road staying on cobble until it turns to dirt and eventually deteriorates into a footpath on top of the ridge. This trail soon becomes a grassy track zigzagging up the hill and a few minutes later you reach a huge white stone cross which has been visible on and off from the beginning of the walk. You should allow almost 2 hours to reach this cross from Tumbaco.

This is a good place to stop and admire the view but you need another hour of hiking to reach the true summit. Continue past the cross on a narrow but well-defined trail which leads up a ridge, along a minor saddle, and up another ridge to a white triangulation marker at the summit. Occasionally the trail forks in which case you should always take the upper trail. The trail fades into grass at times but is generally easy to follow. From the top there is an interesting view of Quito to the northwest, nestled in the valley below Pichincha. To the southwest another white stone cross can be seen; a trail leads past this, complete with enchanting tunnels through scrub, and down to San Pedro del Tingo. To the southeast there is a dirt road which zigzags its way down to La Merced. Either of these can be used as an alternative descent route. Both places have hot springs and are rather crowded at weekends.

If you want to do this hike in reverse, buses ('La Merced', 'San Pedro', or 'Transportes San Rafael') leave frequently from Plaza La Marin in the old town for Tingo. (See Ilaló map.)

The three peaks of El Chaupi

John and Christine Myerscough
Map: IGM 1:50,000 Machachi
If you enjoy walking across rough open country and are not particularly interested in altitude records, this walk could be for you. It offers extensive views of snow-capped volcanoes and provides panoramic vistas of lush and fertile valleys without taking you over 4,000m. The three hills are usually free of cloud even when all the surrounding mountains are hidden, making this a useful walk during periods of unsettled weather. The walk can easily be completed from Quito within a day, being only 12km long with just under 1,000m of ascent. It is therefore possible to travel light with only a day pack. However, there is no water along the trail so it must be carried.

Take a Latacunga-bound bus from the Terminal Terrestre in Quito; they leave every 10 to 15 minutes. Ask to disembark at Minitrack Cotopaxi next to the El Boliche entrance to Parque Nacional Cotopaxi. The ride takes about an hour and on the way you will notice three rounded hills ahead and to the right of the road forming a horseshoe. These are the 'three peaks' of this walk.

On the opposite side of the road from the entrance to Cotopaxi Park there is a dirt road leading in the direction of the first hill, Loma Santa Cruz Chica, with the smaller mound of Loma Sal Grande in front of it. Walk down the dirt road passing under electricity cables and by a small conifer plantation. On your left, after about 15 minutes, you pass underneath another set of pylons and beyond them take the gravel road to the left. This road brings you to the foot of Loma Sal Grande.

Heading in a southwest direction you should be able to find small paths to take you towards the summit. Keep heading upwards, crossing occasional tracks which skirt around the hillside. Eventually the fields end and you have to continue up through *ichu* grass. Within about an hour of leaving the Pan-American Highway you should be on the top of Loma Sal Grande.

Even at this point, the view is incredible. Cotopaxi rises majestically to the east, along with the crags of Rumiñahui. If you have made an early start you may also see the morning train from Quito wind its way across the miniature landscape below.

From this crest you can view the rest of the walk. Follow the ridge to the south over a shallow col passing the edge of a young conifer plantation, then climb steeply up Loma Santa Cruz Chica, keeping to the left high above its craggy western side. It will take about another 45 minutes to reach the trig pillar on the top (3,890m) from where you may catch a glimpse of Tungurahua and El Altar away to the south if it is still clear.

From here descend a steep, grassy gully on the southwest side of the hill to the col between Loma Yuruquira and Loma Santa Cruz. Skirt below the southeast face of a small rocky knoll in your way and continue up to the summit of Laguna Yuruquira, then descend once more westwards crossing a col before beginning the ascent of Loma Santa Cruz, which at 3,945m is the highest of the three peaks.

Crossing the last col is a small but well-used path. If the weather is bad or if you wish to shorten the walk, turn right and follow this path which soon turns into a dirt road. It skirts around the north side of Loma Santa Cruz Chica and eventually brings you back to the Pan-American Highway near the Cotopaxi Park entrance. From here you can get a bus back to Quito.

Going up Loma Santa Cruz you may find a narrow path to take you part way. It fades out about halfway up and the remainder of the climb is over tussocky *ichu* grass. From the top of Loma Santa Cruz Chica to the top of Loma Santa Cruz takes about 1½ hours.

From the top of Loma Santa Cruz head northwards following the steep ridge downwards. There is no path but head for the dirt road that passes between this hill and your next peak, Loma Saquigua. On reaching this road turn right and follow it for approximately 400m before commencing your final ascent.

Loma Saquigua at 3,830m is the lowest of the three hills and has the gentlest slopes to climb. From the road to its grassy summit will take about an hour. The top gives a spectacular close-up view of the ice-capped volcano Iliniza Sur, and also enables you to look back with satisfaction along the whole length of the walk.

Finally descend to the northwest to join a clearly visible track which will take you to the small town of El Chaupi whose church can be seen some 3.5km away to the north. In El Chaupi there is a store which can provide a refreshing and welcome drink.

Small buses leave every 30 minutes to Machachi. The ride takes about half an hour. From Machachi buses leave frequently for Quito. The ride back along the Pan-Am also takes about half an hour.

ROCK CLIMBING AROUND QUITO

For the most part, the geology of Ecuador is not conducive to good rock nor has the sport of rock climbing taken hold with Ecuadorian climbers in general. We include rock routes up smaller peaks in various chapters of this guide.

In the Quito area there are a couple of interesting rock-climbing possibilities. Most noteworthy is the climbing practice-wall found near the Centro Deportivo in the *barrio* of La Vicentina. This is a small, castle-like structure on the south side of the roundabout at Toledo and Ladrón de Guevara, just a few blocks east of Av 6 de Diciembre and Patria in the new town. Short routes of varying difficulty are good for an afternoon of muscle-building.

On the Tumbaco road, about 1km down the hill from the Av 6 de Diciembre turn-off at the Plaza Argentina roundabout (Partidero Tumbaco), are some rock slabs on the left suitable for climbing but right next to a busy highway. You can't miss them because the obvious lines of ascent have been made more obvious with large painted arrows showing the route! Scrambling around in this area will turn up more slabs with more arrows and, hence, more climbs.

A better alternative is to continue on the road towards Papallacta and about 10km past Pifo are several outcrops which are suitable for rock climbing – though most have not been exploited. There is one small outcrop of competent andesite on the left side of the road directly behind a kiosk. Here there are several bolted routes that are rated at 5.9/5.10 and are about 30m long. A little further up the valley are some cliffs called 'El Castillo'. The rock is not great – it tends to exfoliate – but there are some climbable cracks.

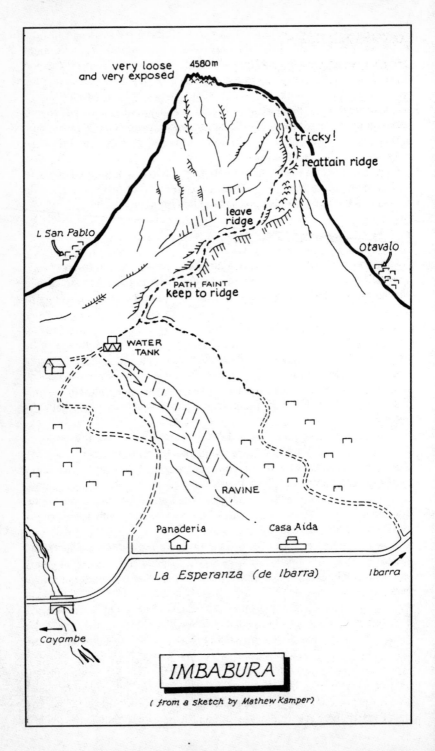

very loose and very exposed

4580m

tricky!

reattain ridge

leave ridge

L San Pablo

Otavalo

PATH FAINT
keep to ridge

WATER TANK

RAVINE

Panaderia

Casa Aida

La Esperanza (de Ibarra)

Ibarra

Cayambe

IMBABURA

(from a sketch by Mathew Kamper)

LONGER CLIMBS

Cerro Imbabura (4,580m)

Maps: IGM 1:50,000 San Pablo del Lago

This long-extinct volcano is located about 60km northeast of Quito near the town of Otavalo and the pretty lake of San Pablo. It can be climbed in one long day and although not technically difficult the extremely rotten rock at the top can make the last metres treacherous. Its first ascent is uncertain; it used to be climbed by local indigenous people who collected ice and delivered it to the town of Ibarra. There are no longer glaciers on Imbabura so this industry is now discontinued.

There are several routes approaching from different sides of the mountain. The most common and straightforward approach, however, is from the village of La Esperanza which lies about 8km northeast of the mountain. La Esperanza is easy to get to: buses leave frequently from Ibarra (20km north of Otavalo on the Pan-American Highway) or from Cayambe.

There are two very cheap and basic hostels in the rather strung-out village. The recommended Casa Aida, about US$2.50 per night with shared bath, is a friendly place with a restaurant serving mostly vegetarian food. They have great pancakes for breakfast.

Head south 100m from Casa Aida to a right turn on cobbled road just before the bridge over boulder-clogged Quebrada Rumipamba. The road passes a school and soon after becomes dirt. Stay on the track with a wide ravine (Quebrada San Clemente) on the right. It is best to ask for *el camino para la cumbre de Cerro Imbabura*. This way you'll get on the correct path without a lot of guesswork.

As the Quebrada San Clemente ends, switchback up through *páramo* grass and scrub to a cement water tank. This is where most climbers get lost. Do not descend into the valley to your left, but stay on the grassy ridge to your right. The trail is initially faint but soon becomes obvious. Follow the ridge until an elevation of 4,200m where you need to drop left below some rocks. After regaining the ridge, climb up a moderately exposed but easy rocky trail to the northeast edge of the U-shaped rim. From here you can see the summit pyramid about 1km away on the southwest side of the mountain. Continue around the rim and scramble on loose and exposed rock to the summit. The round trip from La Esperanza takes about 8 to 9 hours of steady climbing.

From the Otavalo side there are several ways to go, but the routes are difficult to follow and more technical. From the village of San Pablo del Lago (accessible by frequent buses from Otavalo), leave the town from the main square on the road to the right of the church. After about 2km the road turns right (east) and you continue up a track to the north with the mountain some 5km directly ahead of you. Where the road ends, head across fields for the highest point. Find a gully to take you up the craggy rim. The rock here is extremely loose and rotten. The summit is to your left on the southwest corner of the U-shaped rim. Most people that Mark talked to have got lost on this route.

You can also get to this route by starting from the village of Peguche (take a *ferrocarril* (train) or taxi from Otavalo). Ask for the trail to Agato in the Hostal Aya Huma which straddles the train tracks. From Escuela Agato head more or less straight up the slope to where it eventually meets up with the track out of San Pablo. For both routes it takes about 6 hours to reach the summit and 4 hours to return. (See Imbabura route diagram, page 66.)

Imbabura circuit
Map: IGM 1:50,000 San Pablo del Lago

If going around a volcano rather than up one sounds more appealing then try this circuit of Cerro Imbabura. Rather than cross-country *páramo* hiking, this route follows a cobbled path for much of the way and can be completed in one long day. It is an excellent introduction to life in small communities as it wanders through one village after another on its way around the volcano.

The hike starts in a counter-clockwise direction from the village of La Esperanza described in the Cerro Imbabura climb. For an early start you might decide to stay overnight here; Residencia Aida is basic yet comfortable, and popular with hikers. From La Esperanza the cobbled track heads north to Caranqui and then angles west past Chorlaví to Tahuarin. Here it begins to turn south, passing through the important weaving villages of Ilumán, Peguche and Agato. Beyond Agato you'll connect up with the paved road which circles Lake San Pablo and leads to the village of the same name.

In the plaza of San Pablo a road goes up left to Tañahualu Chico where it ends. Above Tañahualu a clear trail ascends toward the pass between Imbabura and Loma Cubiliche, offering splendid views of the San Pablo area. Beyond the pass the trail drops down to Las Abras where, just below the village, a left fork takes you down Quebrada Rumihuaycu to the cobbled road leading back (north) to La Esperanza.

This circuit has been a favourite of a group of dedicated Ecuadorian hikers who have turned it into an informal competition. The hike has taken as little as 7 hours and 20 minutes, though the most recent 'best time' can be ascertained at Café María in La Esperanza.

It is possible to hike up Loma Cubiliche from La Esperanza or from San Pablo in a day outing. The slopes are grassy so there are numerous routes to the top. One good walk begins in Zuleta. Take a bus from San Pablo or Esperanza to Zuleta and get off about 0.5km south of Aguas Guaraczapa. Here there is a good track which climbs southwest around the south flanks of Loma Cunrrú. It continues west along the ridge to Loma Cubiliche which has several small lakes in its crater. There are cows on the summit, but the views of Cerro Imbabura are great.

Laguna Mojanda

Maps: IGM 1:50,000 Otavalo, Mojanda, Cayambe and San Pablo del Lago

South of Otavalo is Cerro Fuya Fuya and the high *páramo* lakes of Mojanda. There are many hiking possibilities in this area. It is difficult to get tired of the ever-changing, yet always spectacular, views from the high wide-open *páramo* and the three lakes near the summit. A good road with occasional transportation goes all the way up to the lakes from Otavalo and footpaths can be followed across the pass and down several sides of the peak. You can easily pick your own route with the topographic map.

If you are planning a day hike it is good to leave Otavalo early, hiring a taxi (US$4) to go the 16km up to the lakes. You could walk but would have to plan to camp at the lake. The southern end of the main lake is suitable for camping.

One idea for a hike is the 5–6-hour walk from the main lake to Esperanza (*not* the town at the base of Imbabura) near Tabacundo. From the lake, climb south to the top of a low pass where there are three roads. Follow the middle road which ascends the western slope of a hill. At the top, as the road begins to drop steeply down the valley, take the vague trail which angles off to the left (east). It's easy to follow this trail east across the open *páramo*, first contouring under a ridge, then crossing shallow ravines. In the distance the twin towers of Esperanza's church will come into sight. The trail eventually begins to descend a forested ridge and continues through fields before reaching Esperanza. A good sidetrip is to head to Cochasqui, a tiny village above Esperanza which is known for the pre-Columbian pyramids of Tolas de Cochasqui. There are frequent buses back to Otavalo which is 1 hour away.

There is a popular annual hike from Quito to Otavalo, called Mojanda Arriba, which generally coincides with Otavalo's festival at the end of October. A considerable number of hikers gathers at Plaza Cotocollao in north Quito at 06.00 on the Saturday of the festival and they hike all day, camping that night in the village of Malchingui. The next day's hike continues over the pass and down into Otavalo where the town band plays a cacophonous welcome. This hike is not recommended for those solitary spirits wanting to get away from it all!

Cerro Pasochoa (4,199m)

Maps: IGM 1:50,000 Pasochoa, Píntag, Machachi and Amaguaña

This mountain is an ancient and heavily eroded volcano which has been inactive since the last ice age. It is located 30km south of Quito and is easily identified from the Pan-American Highway by its crater open to the west. It is an easy ascent and has been climbed many times from all directions except the west face where the crater walls are extremely steep and rotten.

If you have a car or do not mind a little road walking, the most direct and frequently done route is from the Tambillo-Sangolquí road. Along this road you need to find the turn-off to the 'Central Hidroeléctrica Pasochoa' – careful attention to the topographic map is essential. The turn-off is unsigned but there is a basic restaurant at this corner. Follow this cobbled road and make a left turn just past a soccer field. Climb steeply on good cobbled road to a fork down to the power station; stay left. Continue another 2km to where the road switches back on to a small ridge. A taxi can get you this far. Turn right on to the steep dirt track for another kilometre (possible with a 4WD) to a car park. The main road contours around Pasochoa following the Canal Pita Tambo.

From the car park, cross the stream to the east and head southeast across pastures to a dirt track. You can also find the turn-off to this track in the farming area of Runahuaycu on the Canal Pita Tambo road, but the gate is usually locked and it is a longer walk. Follow the dirt track as it contours up and to the east side of the mountain. There may be some bulls wandering around; give them plenty of room. At the end of the road, head up towards a rocky peak through *páramo* grass. Walk up the *left* side of the summit rock (be careful: the west side is a cliff). It takes approximately 2 to 3 hours to hike to the summit from the car park.

Another route is to take a bus to Machachi (frequent buses leave from Quito's Villa Flora bus terminal) and from the town square follow the east-northeast road heading towards Güitig (pronounced 'wee-tig') where the famous Ecuadorian mineral water comes from. After two hairpin bends and a bridge you reach Güitig some 3km from Machachi. Turn left at the main store, then right almost immediately (just before the church). If in doubt ask for Güitig Alto.

Continue on a cobbled road until just beyond Hacienda Mamijudy where you turn left. At the next major fork head right and keep going uphill until you come to a left turn for Hacienda San Miguel. Go through the cobbled and gated paddocks and continue on a dirt road down to a stream. Just before the stream there is a fork; take the left track which leads to a footbridge. Cross the stream and zigzag up the hill, then traverse northeast and head for a saddle south of the mountain. From here head north passing two smaller peaks to your left before reaching the main summit. You can descend the same way or continue due north, descending to the Tambillo–Sangolquí road by the first route.

On the northwest side of Cerro Pasochoa a forest preserve/environmental education centre has been established. It was declared a *bosque protector* in 1982 by the Ministry of Agriculture and turned over to Fundación Natura, a privately run conservation organization, for management. However, Fundación Natura may lose this reserve in 1997. This area is unique in that it preserves the last of the original forest and other vegetation that once covered the Quito basin area.

Several self-guided loop trails have been set up and the area claims almost a hundred species of birds. It is also possible to reach the summit from here but takes 5 to 7 hours round-trip. The last 100m of the climb involve some exposed scrambling on rock. The crater summit can be climbed from this approach in about 3 to 5 hours.

To get to Pasochoa Forest Preserve, take a bus to Amaguaña (buses leave frequently from Quito's La Marin bus area), about an hour away. Walk along the main road out of Amaguaña for about a kilometre until you get to the Pasochoa park entrance. From here it's about 6km or 1½–2 hours' walking to the information centre. If you feel competent with topographical maps you can cross fields and streams and make it in a shorter time. Alternatively, trucks can be hired in Amaguaña for about US$4 for the trip to the reserve.

There is a park entrance fee of US$7 for non-residents, and US$10 for a camping permit. There is also a very basic hostel by the information centre (take a sleeping bag).

THE INCA ROAD TO INGAPIRCA

Maps: IGM 1:50,000 Alausí, Juncal, and Cañar or you can get by with IGM 1:100,000 Cañar.

At the height of its power the Inca Empire extended from northern Ecuador to central Chile. This huge area was linked by a complex system of well made and maintained roads, the longest of which stretched over 5,000km from Quito to Talca, south of Santiago in Chile. This was the greatest communication system the world had known till that time; greater than the roads of the Roman Empire. Although today the road is in a state of disrepair and in many areas the route has been lost or forgotten it is still possible to find and walk along some remnants of this marvellous road system. There is a popular segment of this trail system at the southern end of the Central Valley which leads to Ingapirca, the most important Inca ruin in Ecuador. This 2- to 3-day hike is a fascinating glimpse of an Andean rural life which has changed little in hundreds of years.

Getting there The nearest major town to the beginning of the hike is Alausí where there are several cheap hotels. It is situated just off the Pan-American Highway, 290km south of the capital. Buses go there from Terminal Terrestre in Quito, but it may be easier first to go to Riobamba and then change to an Alausí bus at Riobamba's Terminal Terrestre. From Alausí you can get an early start, taking any southbound bus on the Pan-American Highway; ask to be let off at La Moya about 10km from Alausí. (You can camp in La Moya by the swimming pool with a nearby spring for clean water.) When you reach La Moya stand by the left fork of the road junction just past the bridge to hitch a ride up a steep and spectacular mountain road to the village of Achupallas some 12km away. There are also several trucks a day that leave directly from Alausí around noon for Achupallas. Either way you should be able to get from Alausí to Achupallas in a few hours. A more direct, but more expensive, alternative is to hire a

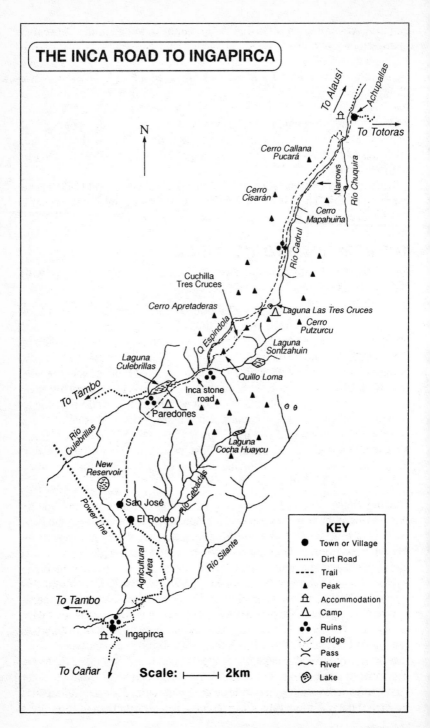

THE INCA ROAD TO INGAPIRCA

To Alausí

Achupallas

To Totoras

N

Cerro Callana
Pucará

Cerro
Cisarán

Narrows

Río Chuquira

Cerro
Mapahuiña

Río Cadrul

Cuchilla
Tres Cruces

Cerro Apretaderas

Laguna Las Tres Cruces

Q. Espíndola

Cerro
Putzurcu

Laguna
Sontzahuin

Laguna
Culebrillas

Quillo Loma

To Tambo

Inca stone
road

Paredones

Río
Culebrillas

Laguna
Cocha Huaycu

New
Reservoir

Río Cebadas

San José

El Rodeo

Power Line

Río Silante

Agricultural
Area

To Tambo

Ingapirca

To Cañar

Scale: ├─────┤ 2km

KEY

● Town or Village
········· Dirt Road
- - - - Trail
▲ Peak
⌂ Accommodation
△ Camp
∴ Ruins
)‿(Bridge
)(Pass
〜 River
◉ Lake

truck in Alausí (near the Hostal Tekendama) to Achupallas. This takes about 1 to 1½ hours and drivers charge between US$5 and US$7 per person for the trip.

Hiking directions In Achupallas head for the white arch below the plaza; take the track left (to the south) of the arch and soon pass the cemetery on your right. There are two options: follow the low road along the river or the high road below cliffs on the right side of the Río Cadrul valley. To take the high road after you cross the river on the bridge, switchback up the hillside on the road. Eventually the road/track heads up the valley. The other option is to follow footpaths on the other side of the bridge (there are several options – it's best to ask) along the west side of the Río Cadrul. Some 30 to 40 minutes out of town you recross the river on another footbridge and then follow the east bank of the Río Cadrul (marked as Quebrada Gadrui on some maps). You are headed for a rocky narrow in the stream between a pyramidal hill to your left (Cerro Mapahuiña, 4,365m) and a flat-topped hill to your right (Cerro Callana Pucará).

As you get closer to this narrow you will see a well-defined notch which you will have to climb. This is interesting as the trail goes up through a hole in the rock: a very tight squeeze and difficult to pass your pack through. Soon after the notch you should cross the river (it can be jumped in dry season) to climb to the upper trail on the other side. The Inca road contours along the west side of the Cadrul valley as it becomes more U-shaped and open. At 3,900m you reach the foundations of an Inca town. Within several kilometres you reach the Laguna Las Tres Cruces (by now you are on the Juncal 1:50,000 map). To this lake is about 6 hours of steady hiking from Achupallas but you can find flat spots near the stream to camp earlier if you wish. The area around the lake is boggy so it is best to camp on bluffs next to inlet or outlet streams.

The following day, follow the trail up beyond the lake and across a pass to the southwest. There is a shallow seasonal pond near the pass and a pile of stones marking the way (probably Incan). There are two paths beyond the pass – an upper road along the Cuchilla Tres Cruces or a boggier route in the valley of Quebrada Espíndola. For the upper Inca road contour up the ridge crossing some worn rocks. Much of the road is deeply eroded and seems like a stream-bed in places. Below you is the valley of the Quebrada Espíndola with the lower road plainly visible. Walk along the top of this ridge and admire the wonderful views as you follow it to its final peak, Quillo Loma. To your left is wild trackless countryside with many lakes, the largest of which is Laguna Sontzahuín. This area would doubtless provide several days of excellent off-the-beaten-track camping.

The trail becomes quite distinct again at the top of the ridge and then descends as a rocky path to the left of Quillo Loma to the lush and boggy valley bottom beyond where it meets the lower trail. You can quite clearly make out the remains of the old Inca road as a straight line in the grass at the bottom of the valley. At the point where the road crosses the stream you'll find the remains of the foundations of an Inca bridge. This stream has to be crossed; it is best to take off your boots and wade across. There is an obvious trail on the left-hand side of the Quebrada Espíndola which leads you past the southeastern shores of Laguna Culebrillas and to some Inca ruins known as Paredones (ruined walls) on a bluff above the lake.

Although it is only an easy half day from Laguna Las Tres Cruces to Paredones this is an excellent place to camp, relax and enjoy the countryside. To help preserve the area, set up camp near the ruins rather than in them and make an effort to carry out or burn trash you find around the ruins.

The ruin consists of a large main structure whose walls are still more or less standing; there are three main rooms and two smaller ones. The stonework is crude compared to Ingapirca and the famous Peruvian ruins and there is no evidence of typical Inca features such as trapezoidal niches. Around this main structure are the tumbled remains of several smaller buildings. Wildlife is rather limited; I saw caracara hawks and cinclodes. Flowers are prolific however, and you can expect to see gentians, lupins and daisies, among others.

The final day brings you to the ruins of Ingapirca. The walk will take you some 4 to 5 hours and thus leaves you with enough time to explore the ruins and then reach a town to spend the night.

From the Paredones head southwest on the Inca road which is here at its full width of about 7m. The trail soon swings south and continues straight across the countryside but is extremely boggy. The scenery is rather eerie with huge boulders strewn around like a giant's playthings. Frogs whistle repetitively and brooks bubble up from underground. You pass a new reservoir on your right that is not shown on any maps. After 2 or 3 hours the Inca road becomes difficult to follow. Head for the village of San José and take a right turn on dirt track to the village of El Rodeo. From here follow the road to Ingapirca, which is now in view. It seems closer than it is since you need to contour around several valleys. The terrain shows increasing signs of cultivation and habitation. You end up walking past fields and houses to a road which leads to the ruins themselves. (See Inca Road to Ingapirca map, page 72.)

Ingapirca

This area was occupied by the Cañaris for some 500 years before the construction of the Inca site. In the 1490s the Inca Huayna Capac conquered the area now known as Ecuador, and soon after this the construction of Ingapirca (which means 'Inca walls' in Quechua) began. It has long been known by academics and the plan drawn by La Condamine in 1739 was accurate enough to be used as a basis for the modern excavations of the ruins which began in the late 1960s.

Ingapirca, with its close-fitting, mortarless stonework and typical trapezoidal windows and niches, is the finest example of imperial Inca construction in the country, and was evidently built by stonemasons trained in Cuzco. The precise functions of the site can only be guessed at, but archaeologists think that the most evident and well-preserved structure, an elliptical building known as the Temple of the Sun, had religious or ceremonial purposes. The less well-preserved buildings were probably granaries or storehouses and part of the complex was used as a *tambo* or stopping place for runners taking messages along the Inca road from Quito to Tomebamba (present day Cuenca).

Ingapirca is 3,160m above sea level. An entrance fee of about US$4 is charged. There is a new visitors' hut and entrance station, along with an excellent site museum. It is funded by the Banco Central and is well laid out with many interesting maps and exhibits. A brochure in English with decent photos and text is also available for US$1. The nearby village of Ingapirca has several basic stores, restaurants and hostels. One recommendation is the *hostal* and restaurant 'Inti Huasi' owned by Julia Serrano whose father has been a guide at the ruins for more than 25 years. Buses leave every 3 hours for the Pan-American Highway during the day until 16.00. A truck costs about US$10 for the trip to El Tambo. There are also basic hotels in Cañar, about 17km from Ingapirca and on the Pan-American Highway.

Chapter Five

The Western Cordillera

'Never journey without something to eat in your pocket.
If only to throw to dogs when attacked by them.'

E S Bates

The Central Valley described in *Chapter Four* is flanked by the Western
and the Eastern Cordilleras. (These are often called the Cordillera Occidental
and the Cordillera Real.) The western is lower and less massive, although
it does contain Ecuador's highest mountain, the extinct volcano Chimborazo,
6,310m. This mountain range is about 360km long and 30–40km wide and
its average height is 3,000–3,500m above sea level. All the major mountains
and some hikes within the Cordillera will be described systematically,
beginning with the northernmost mountain.

VOLCÁN CHILES AND ECOLÓGICA EL ANGEL

Maps: IGM 1:100,000 Tulcán

Volcán Chiles (4,729m) is a single mountain located on the Colombian
border some 24km west of Tulcán and 130km northeast of Quito. Although
the volcano is extinct, steam vents and sulphur deposits are still found on
its slopes and studies of lava flows indicate relatively recent activity. There
is a crater which is about 2km wide and open to the Colombian side. It is
an easily and frequently climbed mountain and the ascent can be done in a
day. The weather tends to be cloudy and wet with occasional snow, so
dress accordingly.

Access Buses take 5 to 6 hours to reach Tulcán from Quito's northern bus
terminal, and there is plenty of accommodation in the town. From Tulcán,
Transportes Norte has a midday bus (leaving from Calle Sierra) to Chical
which runs along the Tufiño–Maldonado road and can let you off at the
trailhead for Volcán Chiles. Otherwise, you can get one of the occasional
buses and trucks to Tufiño, some 15km to the west, then hike west on the
road to Maldonado. You may want to hire a pick-up truck to take you about
15km along this road since there is little traffic. You'll see the mountain to
the north (to your right) and the Tufiño–Maldonado road passes within
3km of the peak. This should be the highest point on the road. You may see

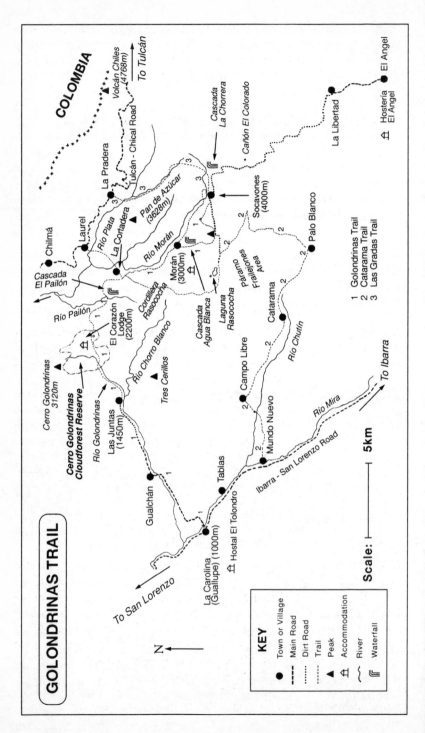

GOLONDRINAS TRAIL

COLOMBIA

To Tulcán

Volcán Chiles
(4768m)

El Angel

La Pradera

Cascada
La Chorrera

Cañón El Colorado

La Libertad

Hostería
El Angel

Chilmá

Laurel

La Cortadera

Río Plata

Pan de Azúcar
(3628m)

Río Morán

Socavones
(4000m)

Palo Blanco

Cascada
El Pailón

Cordillera
Rasococha

Moran
(3000m)

Páramo
Frailejones
Area

Catarama

1   Golondrinas Trail
2   Catarama Trail
3   Las Gradas Trail

Río Pailón

El Corazón
Lodge
(2200m)

Cascada
Agua Blanca

Laguna
Rasococha

Río Chutín

To Ibarra

Cerro Golondrinas
3120m

Río Chorro Blanco

Cerro Golondrinas
Cloudforest Reserve

Río Golondrinas

Tres Cerillos

Campo Libre

Río Mira

Las Juntas
(1450m)

Mundo Nuevo

Gualchán

Tablas

Ibarra - San Lorenzo Road

5km

To San Lorenzo

La Carolina (Gualupe) (1000m)

Hostal El Tolondro

Scale:

N

KEY

•   Town or Village
┆┆ Main Road
⋯   Dirt Road
⋯   Trail
▲   Peak
⌂   Accommodation
∿   River
≋   Waterfall

on the left side of the road a group of *frailejones* more or less in line with the Chiles summit. On the right side of the road is a visible trail heading towards the western ridge of the mountain. Follow this ridge for 30 minutes to a shallow lake, where there is a good camp spot. Follow the stream up the shallow ravine, then head left on a 35° sloped ridge. The route up this ridge and scree fields to the summit crater is cairned and takes another 2 hours. No rope is required.

The mountain is in the northern part of the 'Reserva Ecológica El Angel', an area declared a reserve in 1993. It is noteworthy as the only area in Ecuador aside from Parque Nacional Llanganates where the giant *frailejon* plant is common. (See Natural History in *Chapter One*.) A walk on the *páramo* here will soon enable you to see these strange plants. From Volcán Chiles you can link up with the Golondrinas Trail in the village of Laurel (see Golondrinas Trail).

GOLONDRINAS TRAIL

James Attwood and Piet Sabbe

Map: IGM 1:25,000 La Plata, Río Chutín, Estación Carchi, La Concepción

The high *páramo* above the township of El Angel in the Carchi Province is the starting point for a 3- to 4-day, 30km hike down the western slopes of the Andes; beginning at 4,000m, passing through three distinct ecosystems and finishing at the Ibarra–San Lorenzo train line in the subtropical Mira Valley 3,000m below. There are several trails which follow this route but the Golondrinas trail is the most accessible. Others like the Catarama and Las Gradas trails are equally interesting but can only be accessed with local guides since they are rarely walked and difficult to follow.

Access From the main plaza in El Angel (4-hour bus ride northwest of Quito) you can organize a ride in a pick-up truck to Socavones in the *páramo* (about 90 minutes), passing several smaller towns, *haciendas* and trout farms along the way. Sr Fernando Calderon (tel: 06 977 274) is recommended as a driver. With advance notice, he can also organize for your luggage to be taken by horses to an overnight stop in the village of Morán.

Hiking directions From the village of Socavones, walk down a dirt road on your left for about 300m, where a small walking track breaks off to the right. This leads to El Mirador, a lookout offering spectacular views of the lunar-like *páramo* with furry-leafed *frailejones* at 4,200m and pockets of cloudforest in the Morán Valley below. From El Mirador, backtrack to the dirt road and follow it southwest for half an hour or so. Here, the road veers sharply down to the left – a rocky hill on your right indicates the beginning of a walking path, which continues straight down into a grassy valley. This leads you to the edge of the *páramo*, past the Agua Blanca waterfall, before finally arriving at the ten-family village of Morán (about

5 hours' walking). Here, the Castro or Quintanchala families may be able to put you up. If not, a hostel – which in late 1996 was under construction – should be finished to offer more comfortable facilities. Villagers may ask you to register and pay a small entrance fee to their valley. They are seeking financial support to get their 3,000ha territory declared *bosque protector.*

In Morán you can also organize guides, horses and the following night's accommodation in the timber cabin and part-time research centre, El Corazón. Hiring guides in Morán (such as Hugo Quintanchala and Carlos Castro) is recommended both to make the 7-hour hike to El Corazón more interesting and to involve locals in tourism and environmental issues. This part of the trail is enjoyable on horseback from Morán to the El Pailón waterfall. On your way you may want to stop in La Cortadera for a bowl of soup with Gonzalo Meneces' family. From El Pailón to El Corazón the path may in parts be very muddy, especially in the rainy season. There are several sidetracks coming on to the main trail. As a rule stay on the widest trail and keep going downhill. The cabin in El Corazón is owned by Fundación Golondrinas and is uninhabited, but keys to the bunkbed room can be arranged with the residents of Morán.

The rich biodiversity of the wet evergreen forests surrounding El Corazón and covering the steep slopes of nearby Mount Golondrinas has been the topic of much interest within the international scientific community. The highest of the three Golondrinas peaks, at 3,120m, is three machete-swinging days away; out of most people's reach. However, several existing paths make memorable day excursions from the cabin.

Continuing on the trek to reach the village of Las Juntas, where the road to La Carolina and the Mira Valley begins, take the track leading from the cabin back towards Morán. Three hundred metres further on you reach a junction. This, and subsequent junctions, should be treated the same: always continue downstream. If you prefer more certainty follow the instructions of the Morán guides. The main track, well worn by horses, winds down through virgin rainforest, follows the Río Golondrinas (always on your left) past corn, *yuca* and *naranjilla* fields, and eventually arrives 5 hours later at Las Juntas (or Goatal). The Miers family offers hot meals. You can organize a lift here to La Carolina (1,000m), where the Hostal El Tolondro provides basic accommodation and meals. Buses and sometimes trains pass La Carolina to Ibarra and San Lorenzo on the coast.

Fundación Golondrinas – an organization geared to conserving existing highland rainforest and working with local people to introduce sustainable agro-forestry techniques in the area – offers a fully-guided 4-day version of the same route for US$200 (less for groups), or can help you get in touch with locals along the way. The foundation also organizes research and volunteer programmes. Tel: 593 2 226 602; fax: 502640.

It is possible to combine the Golondrinas trail with the excursion to Volcán Chiles, west of Tulcán. You can link up with the Tulcán–Chical road through the villages of La Cortadera and Laurel (see Volcán Chiles, page 77).

RESERVA ECOLÓGICA COTACACHI-CAYAPAS

The Reserva Ecológica Cotacachi-Cayapas was established in 1968 and preserves 204,420ha of Andean western-slope terrain ranging in elevation from the summit of Cotacachi (4,944m) to coastal rainforest (300m). Access to the reserve is difficult since most of the area is covered by thick cloudforest, montane or rainforest vegetation except the eastern edge which is in *páramo*. A walk from the *páramo* to the coast would be interesting but challenging. Most people visit the margins of the reserve from the Otavalo-Ibarra area. The Piñan Lakes trek, Laguna de Cuicocha and Cerro Cotacachi are located within the reserve.

It is also possible to access the park by travelling up the Río Cayapas from the coastal African-American community of Borbón, though few tourists do this. Remember if you travel to the northwest coast it is important to have malaria protection.

Piñan Lakes trek

Maps: IGM 1:50,000 Imantag covers the hike, but 1:25,000 Cerro Yanaurco provides a bit more detail of the lakes area, and 1:50,000 Ibarra shows the road to the trailhead at Irunguichu.

The Piñan lakes are northwest of Ibarra, a bit off the beaten track, yet worth a visit for the beautiful setting on the high *páramo* below the twin peaks of Yanaurco de Piñan (4,535m). The 3- to 4-day trek begins from the small settlement of Irunguichu, northwest of Ibarra. Transport direct to the village leaves Ibarra several times a day or you can take a bus to the larger village of Urcuquí and get a ride to Irunguichu from there. (See Piñan Lakes map.)

From Irunguichu a trail leads out of the village northwest toward a prominent hill called Cerro El Churo (marked Cerro Churoloma on the IGM 1:50,000 Imantag map). The steep ascent goes through small farming areas and *polylepis* forest and eventually skirts around the northeast side of El Churo. The trail then flattens for a short while as it picks up and runs west-northwest alongside a small stream for about 2km. This is likely to be the first water you'll encounter after leaving Irunguichu. There is good camping here or you can continue for another 2 to 3 hours to a small lake/stream junction. Beyond the flat area, the trail leaves the stream and angles north for another steep ascent toward a low pass between Cerro Hugo and Cerro Albugui. Past here the terrain flattens somewhat and you can find an area suitable for camping.

The next day head northwest up to Laguna Yanacocha or across to Laguna Burracocha to the west. Both of these lakes are good basecamps for short hikes in the area. It can be a little boggy around the lakes, but you can find a dry place to pitch a tent. The area has much to offer – herds of wild horses, lots of lakes, spectacular *páramo* vegetation, trout fishing in the

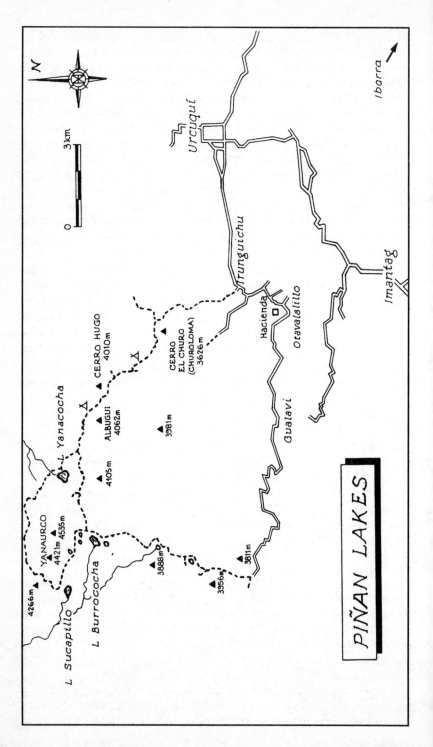

streams, etc. With an extra day, a circuit of the Yanaurco volcano can be hiked in about 6 to 7 hours. Traversing below the mountain in a clockwise direction will bring you to a low pass beneath the west peak. The trail begins as a wide cattle track and narrows to a footpath as it reaches the backside of the volcano. Several trails meander in and out but the route is straightforward. The circuit is a rolling affair – up and down the entire way around Yanaurco – littered with a variety of wild flowers and there's a good chance of seeing wildlife such as white-tailed deer and condors.

A climb to the summit will take about 5 to 6 hours depending on your starting point and the views from the top are some of the best in Ecuador. With clear weather the whole of the Ibarra/San Pablo valley is visible, along with more than 40 lakes scattered across the *páramo* below. There's not much of a trail but the route up to the summit is not difficult. Head northwest across a relatively flat area of *páramo,* keeping left (northeast) of a small hill. On the IGM 1:25,000 Cerro Yanaurco map this is left of the area marked Tatacho. Ascend the scree along the southeast ridge of the volcano. As usual, the rocks near the top are unstable, so watch your footing.

The route out goes south from Laguna Burrococha, descending along the ridge. Keep left (east) along the flanks of a *páramo* hill (marked Loma Chimborazo on the 1:25,000 map) angling southwest. You'll eventually come to a stream crossing and shortly afterwards pick up a clear trail heading south to the Hacienda El Hospital. This ought to take about 3 to 4 hours of steady hiking. From the *hacienda* there may be transportation all the way to Ibarra, or you can hike 3km uphill to Irunguichu.

Cerro Cotacachi and Laguna de Cuicocha

'In no other part of Ecuador is there anything equalling this extraordinary assemblage of fissures, intersecting one another irregularly and forming a perfect maze of impassable clefts. The general appearance of the country between the villages of Cotacachi and Otavalo is not very unlike that of a biscuit which has been smashed by a blow of the fist. The cracks are all V shaped, and though seldom of great breadth are often very profound, and by general consent they are all earthquake quebradas.'

Edward Whymper, 1892

Cerro Cotacachi (4,944m) and Laguna de Cuicocha are located 65km and 58km respectively north-northeast of Quito. A paved road leads to Laguna de Cuicocha. It is a collapsed volcanic crater now filled with a deep lake which averages 3km in diameter and is over 200m deep. The volcano erupted violently depositing angular blocks (which can be seen in the road cut at the crater rim) and a thick layer of volcanic ash into which streams have cut box canyons on the slope leading to Otavalo. During the eruption the volcano collapsed into the evacuated magma chamber creating a deep depression which is now filled with water. The islands in the middle of the lake are resurgent volcanic cones that began to refill the hole. The volcano is currently dormant.

To get there take any bus from Quito to Otavalo. In Otavalo, *busetas* (small buses) leave regularly for the 30-minute ride to Quiroga, where the Syndicate Cuicocha Camionetas (pick-up trucks) wait at the square to take passengers up to the Laguna. Cost is about US$5 for the vehicle. Walking to the lake from Otavalo along the road takes about 2½ to 3 hours and hitchhiking is also a possibility, but not dependable.

Once at the lake you'll find a restaurant and amenities such as boat rides around the islands. A path circles the rim, giving marvellous views of the deep blue lake with the snowy peaks of Cayambe and Cotopaxi in the distance. Among the many flowers growing by the path are several species of orchid and *puya* with bright green flowers. Giant hummingbirds visit the lupins and condors are sometimes seen.

Laguna de Cuicocha circuit
Map: IGM 1:50,000 Otavalo

The path begins at the reserve guard station and runs counter-clockwise around the lake; allow 4 to 5 hours. The trail is easy to follow since there are now signs at all the major intersections. Head for the highest point on the north side of the lake along a well-used trail on the crater rim – you will see the road to Cerro Cotacachi below and to your right. The trail veers to the backside of this hill and regains the rim on the other side. Here there are spectacular views of the two islands in the centre of the lake. These are the resurgent domes that began to fill in the crater after the catastrophic collapse of the mountain.

Continue to a point where the trail meets the road to Cerro Cotacachi. Keep on the trail to a covered veranda complete with trash bins! From here you descend to a bridge over a rocky stream bed which may be dry. After contouring in and out of several valleys that drain Cerro Cotacachi you eventually reach the rim again. Follow the trail to a fenceline and head right to a dirt road. Take a left on the road and descend to the entrance station. Just before you get to the entrance station there is a restaurant overlooking the lake directly above the visitors' centre. To the left of the restaurant are some *cabañas* that cost about US$10/day and sleep 2 to 4 people.

Recently this trail has been cleared and greatly improved. Steps have been added to the steeper parts, handrails provided on the precarious sections and a bridge now spans the river. Signs have been put up, information plaques added and picnic benches placed at two scenic lookouts. Camping is possible next to the bridge over the rocky stream bed, but water is not readily available during the dry season. Another established camp site is about 300m beyond the reserve guard station. It has picnic tables, grill and toilet facilities, but lacks water.

Climbing Cotacachi

Map: IGM 1:50,000 Imantag

Cerro Cotacachi rises impressively above the northern shore of Laguna de Cuicocha but the weather is often misty thus obscuring visibility. Whymper and the Carrels claimed the first ascent in 1880. This climb can be done in one long day if you have transport to the end of the road. A more pleasant climb would be with a camp at the base of the peak with the possibility of spotting a condor. The climb involves some exposed scrambling and may require the use of an ice axe if the slopes are covered with snow. (See Cotacachi route diagram.)

Approach Continue up the road to the Laguna de Cuicocha guard station where you need to take a sharp right (north) up the cobbled road which quickly deteriorates to loose gravel. The road ends 13km from the guard station at a military post with a radio tower. This post is staffed during the week and can help with emergencies – however it is not set up as a refuge. If walking you can take a short cut by following the power lines; it takes 2 hours. A hired vehicle from Otavalo takes about 1½ hours and costs US$15.

A couple of hundred metres before you reach the military post, the road crosses a ridge and turns sharply south. At this hairpin curve you'll find a trail that heads directly up the grassy *páramo* ridge to the base of Cotacachi. Camping is possible after about an hour's walk up this ridge with excellent views of Imbabura and Cayambe. Water can be found in a swampy area to the west of the ridge.

Normal route

From the base of the peak you need to corkscrew clockwise to the northwest side of the mountain. Stone cairns mark the way as you head west and up. This section of climbing up and across the slope is particularly dangerous because of rock and ice fall from above. A helmet would add safety. Look for a col on the southwest side of the peak. From the col drop down to the yellow scree (or snow) in the basin and scramble up to rock benches. To avoid loose scree it is possible to stay on rock to the right – a little exposed but not too technical. At the top of the benches climb up 10m of easy class 5 to the summit ridge. At the top of this, it's a 10-minute scramble to the summit along a knife-edged ridge of rotten rock with 200m drops on either side. There is a rock at the top of the 10m wall which can be used on descent as an abseil anchor. Allow about 3 to 5 hours from the military post to the summit.

Northeast ridge

A more technical alternative to the above route follows the northeast ridge to the summit. It consists of more rotten rock and for all this punishment you'll need a helmet, rope, climbing harness, carabiners and a few slings and a figure 8 or other device for abseiling. Follow the trail up the ridge to

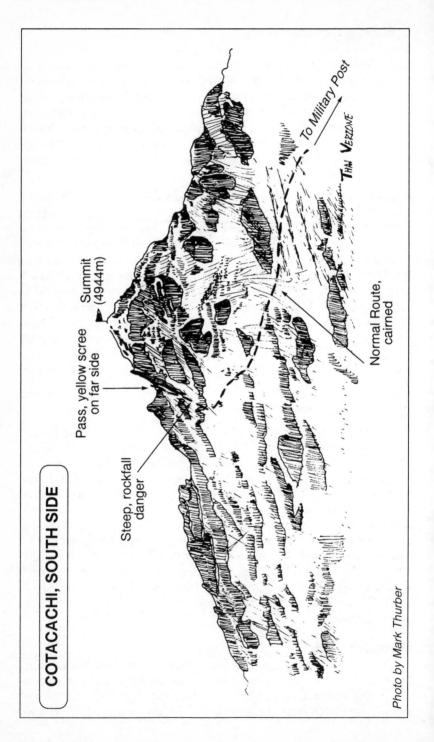

COTACACHI, SOUTH SIDE

Summit (4944m)

Pass, yellow scree on far side

Steep, rockfall danger

Normal Route, cairned

To Military Post

THAI VERZONE

Photo by Mark Thurber

the base as previously described. Rather than angle left, continue straight ahead, either up a river gully or along the grassy slope on the right of a bedrock layer. Aim for a small saddle and continue up the slope to the right. At this point look for the cairns which mark the route straight up the ridge. Follow a series of 'saddles' until you're confronted by an impossible-looking rotten rock wall. Take extreme caution as the handholds rarely stay put. Manoeuvre up a 15m chimney and follow up a short rock wall to the summit scree slope. Returning along the same route, it's a little easier briefly to follow the sandy ridge on the left to the point where you can cross over to the top of the rock wall for a short abseil to the saddle. From here it's a matter of retracing your steps (and continuing to avoid loose rotten rock!).

LAGUNA CUICOCHA TO LAGUNA MOJANDA

Maps: IGM 1:50,000 Otavalo and Mojanda

This 2-day hike will take you past several villages, through forested areas and across *páramo* from one crater lake to another. I've yet to do the hike myself, but it is quite straightforward and interesting for the changing vegetation zones which range from bromeliads to tree ferns to wild orchids. The trek more or less heads due south from Laguna Cuicocha through the village of Ugshapungu. Continue on a variety of footpaths toward Cerro El Quinde where the trail will cross a main road and angle southeast toward Cerro Blanco. Camping near the stream on the east side of the road would be a good stopping place. Heading southeast keeping Cerro Blanco on the left (east) there will be stunning views of the whole area. The route continues southeast until you finally reach Laguna Mojanda. Getting transport down the road to Otavalo should present no problem.

LA DELICIA TO APUELA

Maps: IGM 1:50,000 Imantag and Apuela

This day's outing northwest from Otavalo combines forested valleys with *páramo* ridges in an area superb for birdwatching. The trails can often be muddy and suitable waterproof boots may be desirable. (See La Delicia to Apuela map.)

The hike starts from the small village of La Delicia (also known as Las Delicias) which consists of a school, a tiny store and some four houses, about 2 hours from Otavalo. There is no direct transport but buses and trucks bound for the villages of Apuela and García Moreno pass through the settlement. Departing from Otavalo at the corner of 31 Octubre and Colón, the earliest truck leaves at 07.15 except Tuesdays, and several daily buses (Transportes Otavalo or Transportes Cotacachi) go until mid-afternoon.

From the store in La Delicia (where you'll be dropped) walk 200m back up the hill and around the bend to the last house. Here you'll find the beginning

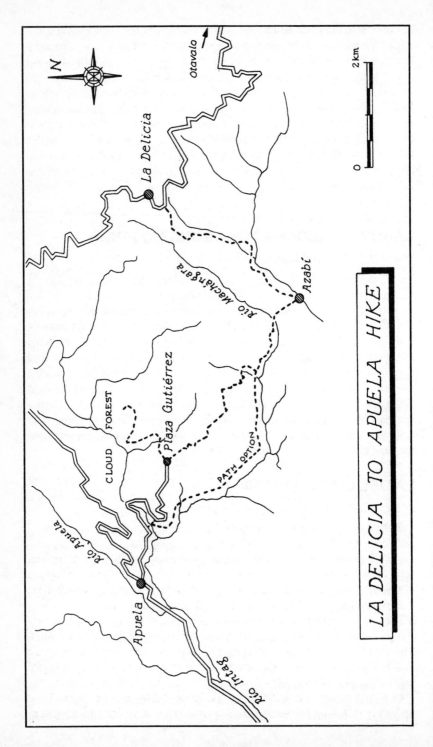

LA DELICIA TO APUELA HIKE

of the trail to the community of Azabí which is visible down the valley.

The descent begins through *polylepis* forest which is a good area for birdwatching. Once in the valley of Quebrada Agua Azul, the trail follows the river to Azabí. Here, just past the school, the track divides. Keep right for a short yet steep climb up the side of the valley where a good wide trail leads to Plaza Gutiérrez. As it descends the ridge to this hillside village there are some impressive views of the neighbouring valleys. In Plaza Gutiérrez there is a wonderful panorama of the entire area from the old church which is situated on a large (probably pre-Columbian) terrace.

Optional sidetrip An hour's walk upstream, north through Quebrada Flores, is a cloudforest area known as Intag Cloudforest Reserve. In addition to farming, American owners Carlos Zorilla and Sandy Statz have set aside much of the area as an ecological reserve with lovely guesthouses available for visitors. They charge US$25 per day with meals. Advance reservations are absolutely essential; they are frequently full. Write to Familia Zorilla, Casilla 18, Otavalo. Replies take at least a month to Europe or the US. There is a more direct route from Otavalo which is given with confirmed reservations.

Leaving Plaza Gutiérrez, a good jeep track winds west down into the valley and crosses the river. Halfway down to the valley there is a steep, narrow short cut which eliminates 0.5km and crosses a rustic suspension bridge. It then rejoins the main track following the Río Toabunchi into Apuela. From La Delicia this hike takes about 5 to 6 hours.

Occasional transport from Apuela makes the return trip to Otavalo in about 3 hours. There are two hostels in town if you decide to stay overnight. Hostal Veritas, rather basic, is on the plaza and Hostal Don Luis (probably better) is 200m up the hill. Don Luis faces one of the two eating places in town.

This area is full of lovely walks. To the southwest is the village of Vacas Galindo where several trails lead up into the hills. To the northeast a road winds up to Peñaherrera and on through Cuellaje to the Cordillera de Toisan.

THE PICHINCHAS

The Pichinchas, two volcanoes known as Guagua and Rucu, are located some 10km due west of Quito, so easily visible from the capital. They are normally snow free but an occasional high-altitude storm will cover them with a brilliant white layer – a pretty sight from the capital.

The two volcanoes are very distinct. Guagua Pichincha, which means 'baby Pichincha', is the highest and is presently active. Rucu ('old') Pichincha is lower, closer to Quito, and inactive. I have read half a dozen different versions of their elevations; the most recent IGM measurements put Guagua at 4,776m and Rucu at an unspecified but slightly lower elevation.

In 1983 a refuge was built on Guagua Pichincha by the Ministry of Civil Defence. Although the refuge is used mainly by scientists, the caretaker

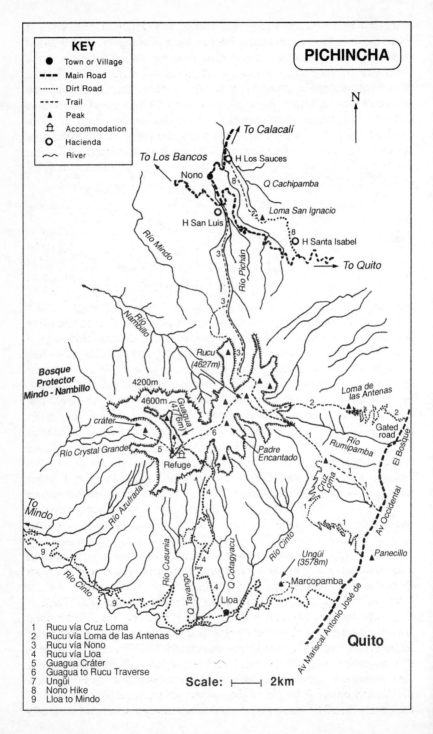

KEY

- ● Town or Village
- ▪▪▪ Main Road
- ⋯⋯ Dirt Road
- --- Trail
- ▲ Peak
- ☖ Accommodation
- ○ Hacienda
- ∿ River

PICHINCHA

N

To Calacalí

To Los Bancos

Nono

H Los Sauces

Q Cachipamba

Loma San Ignacio

H San Luis

H Santa Isabel

Río Mindo

Río Pichán

To Quito

Río Nambillo

Rucu (4627m)

Bosque
Protector
Mindo - Nambillo

4200m

4600m

Loma de
las Antenas

Guagua (4776m)

cráter

Río Crystal Grande

Refuge

Padre
Encantado

Río Rumipamba

Gated
road

El Bosque

To
Mindo

Río Azufrada

Cruz
Loma

Av Occidental

Río Cusunia

Río Cinto

Ungüi (3578m)

Panecillo

Q Tayango

Q Cotagyacu

Marcopamba

Lloa

Av Mariscal Antonio José de

Quito

1 Rucu vía Cruz Loma
2 Rucu vía Loma de las Antenas
3 Rucu vía Nono
4 Rucu vía Lloa
5 Guagua Cráter
6 Guagua to Rucu Traverse
7 Ungüi
8 Nono Hike
9 Lloa to Mindo

Scale: ⊢——⊣ 2km

will normally allow small groups of climbers to stay the night. A fee of about US$2 is charged and equipment lock-up is available. The refuge is extremely cold at night, so bring a warm sleeping bag.

Because of their close position to Quito and Guagua's activity, the Pichinchas have played a great part in both the factual and fictional history of Ecuador's mountains. They are mentioned by the first conquistadors and activity is recorded as far back as 1533. The greatest eruption was in 1660 when ash fell up to 500km from Quito and the capital itself was covered with 40cm of ash and pumice. The sky was filled with incandescent clouds and the sun was blotted out for 4 days – it must have been a terrifying time for the inhabitants of Quito and the surrounding highlands. Two centuries of inactivity followed. Minor eruptions occurred in 1868, 1869 and 1881. Recent activity in 1981 has precipitated a scientific interest and the area is now actively monitored. Vulcanologists claim that the volcano continues to be potentially dangerous although Quito is unlikely to be affected by anything more serious than an ash fall; the topography of the area would cause lava flows and lahars (avalanches of heated snow, earth and mud) to be diverted to the relatively uninhabited areas to the north, west and south of the volcano.

The climbing history of the volcano goes back further than that of other Ecuadorian mountains, with 1582 seeing the first recorded ascent by a group of locals led by José Ortiguera. All the famous scientific expeditions of the 17th and 18th centuries made successful ascents; first La Condamine and Bouguer of the French Geodesic Expedition in 1742, then Humboldt in 1802, and Ecuadorian President Gabriel García Moreno in 1844. The American photographer C Fardad spent a week taking photographs in the crater in 1867, Reiss and Stübel (the conquerors of Cotopaxi) spent several days there in 1870, and of course Whymper and the Carrels made an almost obligatory ascent in 1880. There were several other ascents during this period. Climbing in the 20th century has been dominated by Sr Pedro Esparza, who began climbing in 1926 and has made well over a hundred ascents of the mountain, often alone, thus earning for himself the nickname 'the solitary of Pichincha'. In 1959 Ecuador's first mountain refuge was built on Pichincha at 4,300m on the northeast side of the mountain by Fabian Zurita. Unfortunately vandals destroyed this soon afterwards and today the shelter is mainly for scientists, but the well-worn footpaths from Quito make this an easy and popular climb.

Various legends have been told about the mountain. One goes back to early colonial days when the inhabitants of Quito didn't dare to climb the volcano because of frequent explosions and eruptions. At last three adventurous Franciscan friars decided to explore but high on the volcano's slopes became lost in thick fog. Cold and frightened, the three found a cave to shelter in and the bravest went out to investigate the area and look for the way down. A long terrifying storm followed and the friar became hopelessly lost. The storm ended and his two companions left the cave in

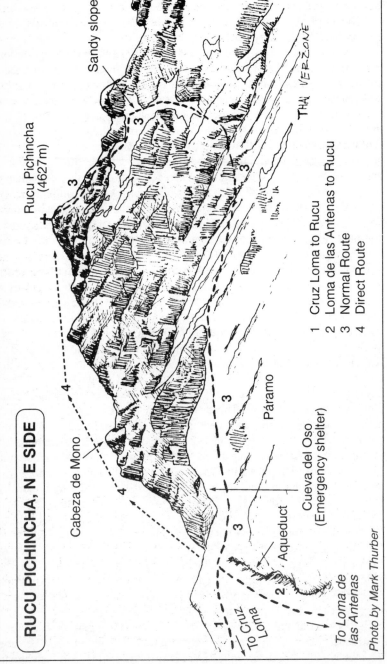

RUCU PICHINCHA, N E SIDE

Sandy slopes

Rucu Pichincha
(4627m)

THAW ZONE

Cabeza de Mono

Páramo

Cueva del Oso
(Emergency shelter)

Aqueduct

To Cruz
Loma

*To Loma de
las Antenas*

1   Cruz Loma to Rucu
2   Loma de las Antenas to Rucu
3   Normal Route
4   Direct Route

Photo by Mark Thurber

search of their lost brother, shouting and yelling but with no result. Despondently, they returned to the cave to spend the night. The next morning they went looking for him once again and were overjoyed to see him kneeling in prayer on a high summit. Happily they rushed up to embrace their friend, but their joy turned to terror when they discovered that he'd been turned to stone. They fled back down the mountain and reported to their superiors that the brother had become a rock pillar, praying eternally to God on a peak close to heaven. To this day, Pichincha's third highest peak, lying about halfway in between and a little north of Guagua and Rucu, is named El Padre Encantado ('the bewitched priest').

Climbing Rucu Pichincha
Maps: IGM 1:50,000 Quito and Nono
The approach to Rucu is becoming increasingly dangerous due to robberies in *barrios* on the west side of the city that you must cross in order to reach the peak. Aggressive dogs in the inhabited areas at the base of the mountain below Cruz Loma have been responsible for numerous bites. Armed assaults (including rape) along Av 24 de Mayo and in the area around Cruz Loma have happened all too frequently. Be wary of dogs, avoid altogether the walk up Av 24 de Mayo, and enquire as to the safety of climbing up to either set of antennae before you decide to go. Hike together in a group of five or more and carry no valuables. Contact the South American Explorers Club for the latest information.

Access There are numerous approaches from the city but the safest way to climb Rucu is by hiring transport or driving to Cruz Loma. It is also possible to climb to another set of antennae located to the north known as Loma de las Antenas (Antenna Hill). This hill can be reached from the neighbourhood of El Bosque but hikers and bikers have been robbed and you cannot drive to the top because there is a locked gate a third of the way up the road. Any route starting in the city will take about 10 hours round-trip. (See Rucu Pichincha route diagram.)

Cruz Loma
Take a bus from Quito's old town to San Roque market located directly west of the Panecillo, then hire a pick-up truck for about US$10 to take you past a military monument (Templete de Los Heróes) to Cruz Loma. If you arrive on a weekend day you will see other cars parked at Cruz Loma so you may be able to arrange a ride down. If you have access to a car, you can drive up to Cruz Loma by following the Occidental Highway through the tunnels to Av Libertadores. Turn right and continue up to Cima de La Libertad. About 100m before the military monument there is a dirt road turn-off to the left that switchbacks 45 minutes up to the antennae.

If you decide to walk up to Cruz Loma (it takes about 3 hours) head up Av La Gasca towards Via Occidental. At the on-ramp for Av Occidental turn left on a cross street, Enrique Ritter. Walk four blocks south to a dirtish road that passes under Av Occidental. Walk through the tunnel – the road swings right on the other side; you should climb out of the road-cut and cross a fence in front of you. Now you are on the edge of a eucalyptus grove; follow a road up through the grove to a clearing (0.5km). From here there are numerous routes: follow your nose or the description below. From the clearing find a path that turns left (south) back into the grove. This path leads unexpectedly away from Rucu but soon plants you on the shoulder of Cruz Loma. From here you can pick your way up the mountain to the antennae through pastures and small patches of brush.

From the antennae at Cruz Loma you head up an obvious northwest trail on a grassy ridge towards the base of the rock which is about 1½ hours away.

Loma de las Antenas

Take one of several buses northbound on Av América to Calle Mañosca. Walk up this street for about 15 minutes until it crosses the Via Occidental. Directly opposite Mañosca is a signed road leading to a fertilizer factory; ignore this and take the unsigned road some 50m to the right (north). Follow this road and take the first left up the hill, then continue taking the uphill fork whenever the road divides. 4WD vehicles and good pick-ups can negotiate this road as far as the locked gate of a *hacienda* about a third of the way up. The road continues up to the antennae, but the *hacienda* owner has closed the access road to private vehicles. Walkers will have no problem passing the gate.

To reach Rucu Pichincha from the Loma de las Antenas you take a path which goes over the hill behind the car park. This path follows a ridge which after 2 hours meets the trail from Cruz Loma.

Summit

Where the paths from either set of the antennae meet you have two options:

Either head right traversing the base of the cliffs to a sandy slope which leads to the summit (the easiest way);

or head straight up the rocks which are marked with paint splashes or white arrows in places. This second route is more direct although perhaps a little hair-raising for beginners. The route more or less follows the ridge, but you need to drop off the crest in places. The summit will take a further 1½ hours from the trail junction on both routes. There is also rock climbing to be had on Rucu's summit pyramid if you are so inclined.

Descent

You may be able to hitch a ride back to Quito from Cruz Loma or the Loma de las Antenas (a local para-penting group has keys to the gate at the *hacienda*). If you are walking, however, the quickest route is straight down from Cruz Loma to the city, following a faint path underneath the electric pylons from the TV and radio antenna. This will bring you out in the La Gasca area north of the route previously described. There are other paths as well if you feel in an exploratory mood but remember that descending on foot alone or in a small group puts you at risk of being robbed.

Climbing Guagua Pichincha

Guagua is accessed from the village of Lloa and is literally a walk-up. You can get there with a 4WD vehicle, arriving at the refuge just a 30-minute stroll from the crater rim. The walk up the road, however, is peaceful with great views and so far has none of the dangers of assault associated with climbing Rucu.

Approach Take a bus (No 8) or cab south on Av Mariscal Jose Antonio de Sucre to Calle Angamarca (shown as Chilibulo on maps), where transport departs west to the village of Lloa (this is also the beginning of the walk to Ungüi described in *Chapter Four*). From here you can walk to Lloa (2 to 3 hours) or buses depart several times a day (when full), more often at weekends. You may also be able to hitch a lift from a dump truck that is returning for a load of gravel at a mine several kilometres beyond Lloa. The road winds up through the growing *barrio* of Santa Barbara to a pass, then descends 4km to the agricultural village of Lloa. If you are walking it is quicker to take the old cobbled road just beyond the pass on the left down to Lloa.

Once you get to Lloa ask for directions to the refuge. Follow the track west out of town as it passes through some cultivation and eventually meanders up through *páramo*. Track junctions are signposted for the route to Guagua, but when in doubt, take right-hand forks. Allow about 5 to 6 hours of steady hiking to reach the refuge. The facilities are minimal but there are bunks and foam mattresses, and you can use the stove if the caretaker is there. If staying overnight, bring a sleeping bag and a stove, just in case.

By car, you can get up to just below the refuge, but there are many rough sections along the road, and a 4WD vehicle is essential in all but the driest of seasons. The dirt track turns into a mud wallow after a bit of rain. If you have any doubts about the strength of your car engine, burn super (octane 92) for the trip up to the refuge. It can really make a difference in the power output – and you'll need all you can get!

The easy route to the summit is to follow the obvious trail on the pumice slope to the crater rim. Head right along the rim for about 20 minutes to reach a metal cross which is slightly lower than the true summit further along the rim. There are more interesting routes to the summit up the rock to the right of the refuge as well, but they are exposed in places. For rock-starved climbers, this area is loaded with possibilities. A huge slab at the base of a rock face has several lines of solid climbing that can be top-roped, and the face itself may have potential though we haven't tried it out.

There is also an approach to the summit of Guagua from the north, although we haven't met anyone who has done it. Head to the village of Nono (see Nono Hikes in *Chapter Four*) and then head south on a jeep track to Hacienda San Luis. Continue south on paths and then cross-country to the Pichinchas.

Guagua Pichincha Crater

More interesting than climbing to the summit of Guagua is the descent to the crater floor. If you have your own transportation to the refuge, this trip can be done in one day. Otherwise, you'll need to bring camping gear for a stay at the refuge. It should be noted that in early 1993 two scientists were killed from volcanic gases in the crater following explosions from this active volcano. Therefore extreme caution should be exercised before entering the crater – find out if access is restricted. If in doubt do not enter the crater.

The trail to the crater floor is a steep path starting at the rim near a shrine. You'll want sturdy hiking boots for traction in the loose sand and for manoeuvring over the rough volcanic debris. The descent is often shrouded in mist, but rock cairns and wands mark the well-worn path. The smell of sulphur grows stronger as you descend. For both the descent and ascent, follow the path carefully. An occasional false trail could well end you up at one of the many precipitous cliff edges. At least one person has fallen and died in attempting to negotiate this track. As a safety precaution, parties should stay well within visual contact of each other at all times during the descent and ascent.

The trail winds down and angles to the right. After about 2 hours it flattens out as it reaches the crater floor and crosses a rock-strewn gully with a small freshwater stream running through it. This is the only freshwater source in this part of the crater but it often dries up in June through August.

The crater is an immense area, about 1.5km in diameter and 700m deep, resembling a strange looking valley. You can see and hear a huge geyser spouting steam halfway across the crater floor. Following the trail down toward the centre, you'll see on the right the huge central cone, 400m high, which produces the greatest amount of volcanic activity. Hills of lava scree and volcanic rock at its base are ripe for lots of exploring in what feels like the moon.

For the highlight of the entire excursion, head cross-country towards the prominent central cone and pick up the trail that follows around its base to the left. This trail descends out of the crater floor and winds through dense tropical vegetation caused by the heat of the thermal water stream running along on the left. At the bottom of the trail, about 45 minutes later, you'll discover natural thermal pools that provide a steaming hot bath for the weary hiker. A little exploring will reward you with several 'hot tub'-like pools, blocked off with rocks by former visitors. The return back up to the crater rim takes 3 hours.

Guagua to Rucu traverse

From the refuge you could return to Quito via Rucu Pichincha in one long day. It's a beautiful hike because the west side of Rucu has a large variety of flowering plants. From the refuge traverse north then east. Follow the ridge past Padre Encantado then climb up a basin that looks steep and long with a lot of loose rock. It's much easier than it looks and takes about a ½-hour to climb. Rucu is just beyond. If you look carefully you'll be able to follow a faint path for most of the way. The traverse takes approximately 4 to 5 hours. Carry water as it is usually not available unless the peaks are covered with snow or it is raining.

LLOA TO MINDO TRAIL

Maps: IGM 1:50,000 Quito, Alluriquín and Mindo

This is a 2–3-day trek for hikers and perhaps a 4-day trek for birders and botanists. The route takes you from the agricultural town of Lloa through cloudforest into western slope rainforest, skirting the southern edge of Bosque Protector Mindo-Nambillo. There has been some clearing in the river valleys for cattle, but a large amount of primary forest remains. It is amazing to think this area is so close to Quito! In the late 1980s a road was planned and partially constructed for this route but it was abandoned when it became clear that the construction and maintenance costs, due to unstable slopes and frequent landslides, were not worth the benefits the road would provide. Undoubtedly the area would have been deforested if the road was constructed; it is hoped that it will never be completed.

There is plenty of water but remember to treat it. You quickly drop to warmer elevations so one sweater is probably sufficient, but proper raingear is essential. The trail is very muddy; rubber boots are recommended. Though not essential, a machete may come in handy. There are places to camp along the river (Río Cinto) or it may be possible to arrange to spend a night in a wood shack at one of several *fincas*. Bring all food from Quito.

Hiking directions You begin by making your way to Lloa (see *Climbing Guagua Pichincha* page 95). The hike can begin here or you can arrange transport at least as far as Palmira. There should be some traffic as far as the second gravel mine (one hour walking from Lloa), but beyond here catching a ride could prove difficult. The walk along the road is quite pleasant. You will reach a turn-off to the left to the Hacienda La Palmira. Just beyond this turn-off is a dirt road up to some 'warm springs'. The springs are really only tepid and a bit grungy, but this makes a nice spot to camp. Landslides along the road make it difficult to drive more than a few more kilometres. The road eventually enters primary cloudforest with views of the box canyon of Río Azufrada – here you might smell sulphur from the vents upstream on Guagua Pichincha. This is probably the most dangerous place to be when Guagua Pichincha erupts again since lahars

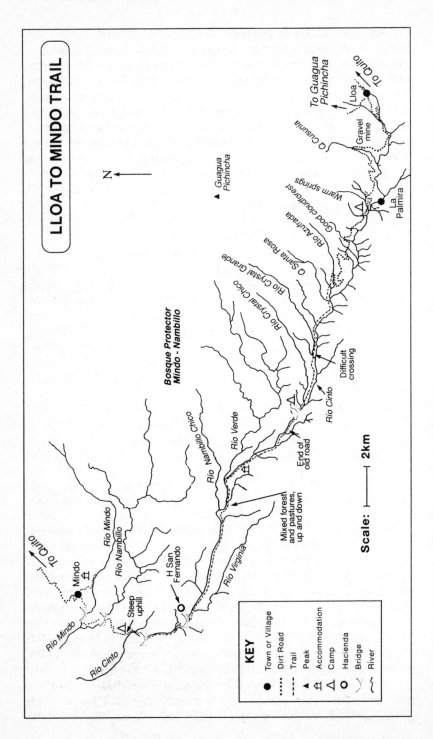

LLOA TO MINDO TRAIL

Scale: |———| 2km

KEY

● Town or Village
⋯ Dirt Road
⫶ Trail
▲ Peak
⚐ Accommodation
△ Camp
○ Hacienda
⤰ Bridge
〜 River

and toxic gases may pour down this drainage. Not to worry though, the chances of you being here when Guagua goes off are slim.

Wade across the thigh-deep river. Continue on the road across several small streams until you reach the Río Crystal Grande. During high water this stream is difficult to cross – narrow but waist deep. However, there is usually a log footbridge across the river since the route is used by locals. Find the streambed/road on the opposite side which eventually becomes road again. Follow it to a well-constructed bridge across the Río Cinto. There should be a sign that says 'Bosque Protector Mindo-Nambillo' on your right. Cross to the south side of the Río Cinto and follow the road past several *fincas*; you will cross into Hacienda Pacay which extends several kilometres downstream. Soon you reach the end of the road and follow the trail to the right into forest. The end of the road is about 6 to 7 hours from Lloa.

From here the trail stays on the left side of the river but is difficult to find at times because you will be alternating between muddy pastures and forest. When in the forest you should be on a more or less obvious track. About an hour past the road end you reach a large ranch house (also Hacienda Pacay). It may be possible to arrange a stay here if the caretaker is in. Here we saw about 30 red-billed parrots flying in a flock. The steep slopes on the opposite side of the Río Cinto are uncut since the river blocks access and consequently has abundant birdlife. Continue on a trail behind the large ranch house that leads past a corral and into the forest. Note the fragment of an aeroplane wing on the trail!

Again stay on the left side of the Río Cinto – you do not have much choice since the river is wide and rapid. Don't be discouraged if you lose the trail in the pastures – the key is to find the correct gate at the far end of each pasture where the forest begins. Birding is great in this section so take your time as you walk up and down the ravines feeding into the Río Cinto. About 2 hours from the ranch you pass over a waterfall in dense forest. Another hour brings you to a small ranch house on the left. Continue down to lower pasture on the right, enter the forest and you will soon cross landslide debris with a 50m-high cliff on the left. You are now entering *fincas* with tropical fruits such as bananas, guayabas and lemons – the lemons are quite sour but are a great addition to the water you are drinking.

You will soon arrive at an orange-roofed house on your left and slightly beyond a covered bridge across the Río Cinto to Hacienda San Fernando. A sign indicates it is 9km to Mindo and 22km to Lloa (probably as a toucan flies – it is certainly farther on foot). Do not cross this bridge, but continue downstream on the left side of the Río Cinto. About an hour later you will come to another bridge (logs with planks, but no railings) across a box gorge. Cross this and continue downstream on the right side of the Río Cinto for 30 minutes, cross an ankle-deep stream, then take a right-hand turn uphill. There should be a house in front of you with a concrete pad surrounding it. The trail to the right is an eroded road, the other end of the

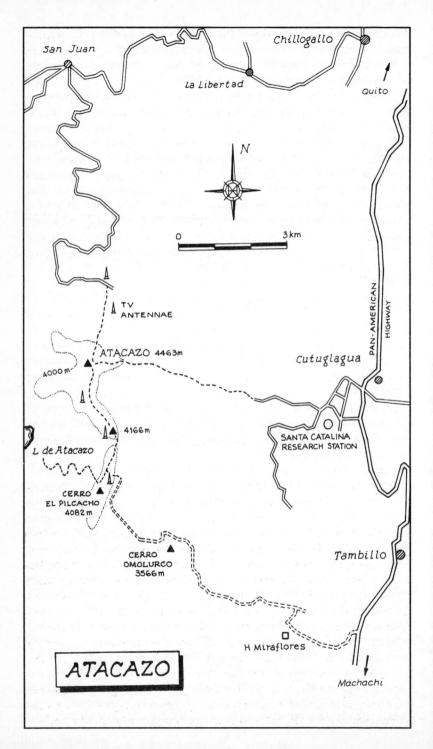

San Juan

Chillogallo

La Libertad

Quito

N

0   3 km

TV
ANTENNAE

ATACAZO 4463m

Cutuglagua

4000 m

4166 m

L de Atacazo

SANTA CATALINA
RESEARCH STATION

CERRO
EL PILCACHO
4082 m

CERRO
OMOLURCO
3566 m

Tambillo

H Miraflores

ATACAZO

Machachi

PAN-AMERICAN   HIGHWAY

Lloa–Mindo aborted road project. Continue up the steep hill – you have to cross the small ridge 200m above you. The views from the pass are incredible. From here it is about 2 hours to Mindo and the road is driveable so if you are lucky you might be able to hitch a ride.

In Mindo there are two hotels on the far side of town and both charge about US$5 per night. The one slightly out of town has a friendly owner and nice restaurant. There is also a more expensive lodge. Mindo is known for its guayaba orchards; the locals will complain that the numerous parrots wreak havoc on their crop. A jam is made from this fruit which is quite tasty. A bus leaves from Mindo at 06.30 every morning, arriving in Quito at 09.00 (US$3). You can hire a taxi to Quito for about US$30 or a taxi to the main road (7km), where there is traffic back to Quito, for US$5.

This trek can be arranged with an excellent bird guide out of Mindo: Vinicio Perez (tel: 02 612 955 in Mindo). He charges US$35 per day and speaks some English. He usually walks the trek in the opposite direction. (See Lloa to Mindo Trail map page 98.)

CERRO ATACAZO (4,463M)

Map: IGM 1:50,000 Amaguaña

Atacazo is an extinct and eroded volcano located about 20km southwest of Quito. With a 4WD vehicle you can get to within an hour of the summit. It is not a difficult climb and, unusual in Ecuador, the rocky summit is not composed of rotten and dangerous rocks but is quite solid. Because transport is somewhat of a hassle, this area is rarely visited, but it is worth the effort to get there. The spectacular summit views are of Quito and the Pichinchas to the northeast, and the countryside dropping down to the lowlands to the west. (See Atacazo map.)

There are numerous routes up Atacazo – it is just a matter of picking a line from the Pan-American Highway and heading for the summit. Perhaps the most straightforward is to take a bus south out of Quito on the Pan-American Highway to the turn-off just before the one to the Estación Experimental Santa Catalina and begin hiking towards the summit. This dirt road eventually peters out to trails and fields; follow your nose to the summit.

The way to drive to the summit is a jeep track from the tiny village of San Juan on the old Santo Domingo road, which also makes a pleasant walk. You can also get to San Juan by catching a bus at Plaza La Marin in Quito's old town to Chillogallo or La Libertad on the old Santo Domingo road. From here you will find occasional trucks (or you can walk or hitchhike) as far as San Juan 10km to the west. This beautiful mountain road climbs and hairpins steeply from La Libertad (3,000m) to San Juan (3,450m). Continuing westward from San Juan the old highway descends, offering fascinating opportunities to observe the ecological changes from *páramo* to coastal rainforest and with excellent birding. This route is great for mountain biking since all the traffic to Santo Domingo now goes through Machachi.

To climb or drive to Atacazo from San Juan take the southbound jeep road heading towards some TV and radio antennae. Anyone in the village will point out the road; it reaches the antennae in 10–12km, but there is almost no traffic. If you need drinking water you'll pass near the last streams about 2–3km before the end of the road.

From the antennae head south up gently sloping, grassy *páramo* to an obvious notch in the crater rim. It is an easy walk which will take a little over an hour. From here the highest point is to your left, a gentle scramble over grass and rocks. Below you is the delicately coloured crater, wide open to the west, and filled with pastel shades of sand and lava and brighter splashes of vegetation. It is not difficult to scramble down and explore 'These dwarf plant Japanese gardens' (Henri Michaux's *Ecuador: A Travel Journal*).

The descent can be made in different ways. The shortest is to head almost due east for 7km until you reach the Estación Experimental Santa Catalina. A more interesting descent is to head south on the crater rim for about 1km beyond the highest point, then head southeast along an obvious ridge to a small hill (4,166m) about 1km away; from here head south-southwest along another ridge to a long flattish hill (Cerro El Pilcacho, 4,082m) almost 2km away. A series of antennae dot these prominent points and can be used as landmarks for the descent. A short distance before you reach the top of El Pilcacho you'll find a trail crossing the ridge. Westward, it winds through interesting looking *páramo* to Laguna de Atacazo some 3km away; eastward it soon joins a trail heading southeast towards Cerro Omoturco, 3,566m, 2km away. From Omoturco a dirt road winds 7-8km to Hacienda Miraflores from which a road continues a further 2–3km to the Pan-American Highway. If you go north along the highway for about 3km to Tambillo, it will be easier to catch buses to Quito.

EL CORAZÓN (4,788m)

Map: IGM 1:50,000 Machachi

Corazón is yet another eroded and extinct volcano located about 40km southwest of Quito. Like Atacazo it is a good place to stretch your legs and lungs for a day if you have recently arrived in Quito. The route is straightforward and requires no rock-climbing equipment or experience. The first recorded ascent was in 1738 by La Condamine and Bouguer and this easy peak has been climbed many times since. Preconquest ruins have been reported on the northeast slopes, but they are very overgrown and have yet to be investigated. The name Corazón means 'heart' in Spanish and is said to refer to two gullies on the northwest slopes which, when seen from a distance, appear to join together roughly in the shape of a heart. (See Ilinizas and Corazón map page 104.)

To get to Corazón take a bus from the Terminal Terrestre heading south on the Pan-American Highway and ask the driver to drop you at the turn-off to Aloasí. Go through Aloasí on a good cobbled road for 3km as far as the railway station. About 100m past the station, take the dirt road going left. If travelling by car, this road will get you within 2 hours of the summit. The road winds its way through *páramo* – to get to the end you will need a 4WD vehicle. On foot, you'll have to keep pretty much to the road for the first few kilometres: fenced off, cultivated fields make heading cross-country fairly difficult lower down. Up higher look for trails leading west up across the *páramo*, otherwise it's probably easier to keep to the switchbacking road as tramping through the dense *ichu* grass is tiring and time-consuming. The road ends in the *páramo* on the northeast side of the summit rock in a valley. From here an irrigation canal leads towards a saddle between Corazón and a minor peak to the north. Follow alongside this canal until it runs out, then head up rocky scree slopes to the summit. There is no rock climbing except an easy 10m-high class 3 rockband just below the summit. Rock cairns and a few rocks painted with arrows mark the way. Allow about 5 to 7 hours of steady hiking to reach the summit from Aloasí.

There is another route from the north. Follow the main road from Machachi to Santo Domingo for 3km to Alóag and just outside of town near the railroad station take the left fork down a dirt road. About 12km down this road you'll find the Hacienda La Granja where it is possible to hire mules. From here head south across the *páramo* another 6km to the peak, reaching the saddle on the north side as described in the first route. On foot it will take about 5 hours to walk from the highway to the saddle.

THE ILINIZAS

Map: IGM 1:50,000 Machachi

These are two peaks located about 55km south-southwest of Quito. Iliniza Sur (5,248m) has the distinction of being the sixth highest mountain in the country whilst Iliniza Norte (5,126m) is the eighth highest. Prehistorically they were one volcano but today the two peaks are separated by a saddle and are about 1km away from one another. Jean and Louis Carrel of Whymper's expedition logged the first ascent of Iliniza Sur in May 1880, but Whymper himself never reached the summit despite two attempts in February and June of the same year. The first ascent of Iliniza Norte was interesting in that it was one of the few first ascents made by Ecuadorian climbers and the only Ecuadorian 'first' of one of the country's ten peaks over 5,000m. Ecuador's Nicolás Martinéz, accompanied by Alejandro Villavicencio, reached the summit in March 1912.

There is a simple refuge known as Refugio Nuevos Horizontes at 4,650m just east of and below the saddle linking the two mountains. The refuge is run by GeoEcuador (Calle Marchena #138 and Av 10 de Agosto, Second Floor, Quito, tel: 221 608) and usually has a hutkeeper in residence. To be sure check with the warden, Bladimir Gallo, in Machachi, tel: 314 927 or 314 258. His office is opposite where the buses leave for El Chaupi. The refuge has 15 bunk beds, fireplace, gas stove, and a few 'basics' like sodas

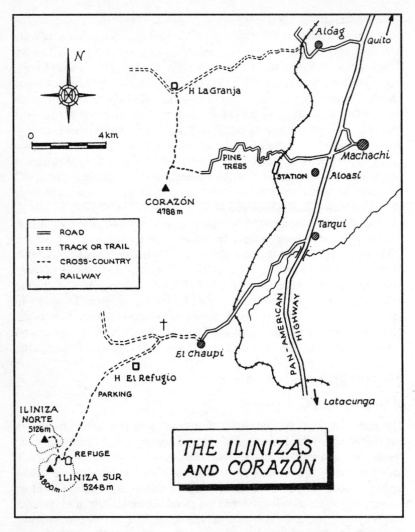

THE ILINIZAS
AND CORAZÓN

and cigarettes for sale. There is a small generator for electric lights. A nearby stream provides water that must be treated. Overnight stay for non-residents is US$10 per night. Free camping is possible but the area is exposed to weather.

The twin peaks of the Ilinizas offer some of the more enjoyable climbing in Ecuador. For the hiker, Norte is a challenging but fun scramble when free of snow. For the experienced climber, Sur provides several interesting and demanding technical steep snow and ice routes.

Access About 40km south of Quito and 8km south of Machachi on the Pan-American Highway there is a turn-off, located approximately 50m before a bridge and marked by a Vulcanizadora (tyre repair shop), to the small community of El Chaupi. Buses north and southbound on the Pan-American Highway pass this turn-off. From here it is 7km of cobbled road to El Chaupi; there is enough traffic to hitch-hike and buses pass here from the main square in Machachi every half hour on the way up to El Chaupi.

At El Chaupi turn right at the main plaza on to a road that passes to the right of the church. Walk or drive up this dirt road for 3km until you come to a left turn. If you come to a stream ford you have gone too far and need to backtrack 200m. This turn-off goes through fields, then crosses an avenue of pine trees where it forks (keep right) and eventually heads through a *hacienda*. About 3km from the turn off it switchbacks up a hill. Occasional grazing bulls in this area are territorial and require a degree of respect. If encountered, you should move slowly and quietly. The road above the *hacienda* is eroded and only passable with 4WD vehicles; hired pick-up trucks may have difficulty depending on when the road was last graded, or levelled to a suitable gradient. At 8.7km from El Chaupi you arrive at a flat grassy area (parking) and a shrine to the Virgin Mary with a blue cross. This is the normal drop-off point for hired transport. The track above the parking area could be navigated by a 4WD but is not worth the effort. Note that the parking area is not safe to leave unattended vehicles: break-ins are common.

Above the shrine the road switchbacks up to a broad rocky ridge eventually petering out into a footpath. The trail follows this flat crest to the base of a steep sandy ridge leading to the refuge which sits just below a saddle between the two peaks. The going is slow due to backsliding in the sand, but the way is marked by green paint dots on the rocks. At the top of the sandy ridge a well-established trail veers right to the orange refuge 'Nuevos Horizontes' (4,765m). From the parking area it is about 2 to 3 hours on foot to the refuge; if you are walking from El Chaupi to the refuge it takes 5 to 7 hours. There is no water between the shrine and the refuge.

Another option for those wishing to acclimatize a few days is to stay at Hacienda San Jose (3,400m). This 'bed and breakfast' is a farmhouse with several rooms and shared kitchen and bath. It costs US$10 and the friendly owner Rodrigo Peralvo can arrange horses up a trail to the refuge (4 hours). He can be contacted on tel: 891 547 or 09 737 985. If you are coming from El Chaupi, instead of turning right at the church head straight through town and follow the yellow and black arrows marked with 'Hacienda San Jose' for 3km.

Climbing Iliniza Norte (5,126m)

Despite the glacier marked on IGM maps, Iliniza Norte is a rocky mountain with no permanent snow. It can easily be climbed in 2–3 hours from the refuge. Technical equipment is unnecessary unless it has snow, in which case you will need at least an ice axe and perhaps crampons and rope.

From the refuge walk to the saddle between the two peaks. Most of the route to the summit is marked by cairns. Climb up the left flank of the southeast ridge, trying to stay high on solid rock. The trails below in the

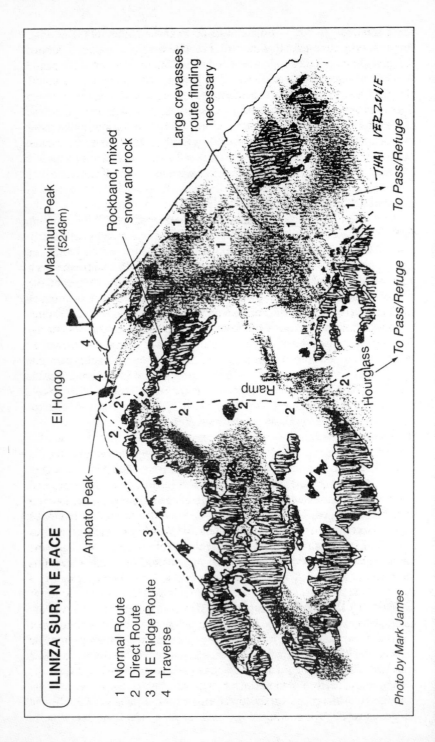

ILINIZA SUR, N E FACE

1 Normal Route
2 Direct Route
3 N E Ridge Route
4 Traverse

Maximum Peak
(5248m)

Rockband, mixed
snow and rock

Large crevasses, route finding
necessary

THAI VERZVUE

To Pass/Refuge

To Pass/Refuge

Hourglass

Ramp

El Hongo

Ambato Peak

Photo by Mark James

sandy scree are great for descent but hard work on the ascent. The ridge narrows; work your way up to the base of a false summit pyramid (5,060m). Traverse right on sandy ledges across the Paso de Muerte or 'death pass', which is far easier to cross than the name implies, to the base of the summit block. Follow the gullies with loose rocks to the summit. The true summit is marked by an iron cross. The climb is straightforward except for the danger of rockfall in the last few metres or when there is snow, making the Paso de Muerte more true to its name. When Mark climbed the peak the cross on the summit was buzzing and his hair was sticking up in punk-rock style from static electricity, so it's probably best not to climb during a thunderstorm!

Climbing Iliniza Sur (5,248m)

This relatively steep and crevassed mountain is one of the more difficult climbs in the country, and is not for beginners. There are two frequently climbed routes to the summit, the normal route and direct route. The direct route, which was for years considered the normal route, has become even more difficult, especially when there's a lack of snowfall. Some of the steeper sections can approach 80° in certain seasons so front pointing is necessary. This is a tiring technique, particularly at over 5,000m, and should be learned and practised at lower elevations if possible (in the Alps or the Rockies for example). It is best to bring an assortment of ice screws, flukes and snow stakes. Rockfall can be a hazard and a helmet is recommended. Avalanches occur often enough to pose a danger and a detailed route description is difficult due to constantly changing conditions. (See Iliniza Sur route diagram.)

Direct route (or ramp route)

The difficult direct route is via the north face. It begins from the Nuevos Horizontes hut then heads west into the saddle between Norte and Sur. From the saddle ascend the steep moraine then climb on to snow covered 'terrace' – a flat area where the northern glaciers terminate. After gaining the terrace, you will be almost exactly below the direct route which looks like the bottom of an hourglass between two large rock outcrops. Slopes steepen from 30° at the bottom of the route to between 50° and 55° inside the hourglass, with several 3m-long sections of 65° to 70°. You exit this ramp to the left and then negotiate a crevasse field. Finally there is a rockband that needs to be negotiated – difficult if covered by recent snow. Above the rockband, traverse or climb right to a ridge then left to the Ambato peak. To get to the Maximum Peak, follow the ridge by passing a rocky outcrop known as *el hongo* (the mushroom) and ascend Maximum. The descent is via the easier normal route described below, but it is easy to become confused if there are no tracks on the normal route. In good conditions the round trip can be done in less than 6 hours, but a full day is not uncommon. You should plan a pre-dawn departure to minimize rockfall and avalanche danger caused by the melting of the snow in the midday sun.

Normal route

This is an easier route to the summit, but still requires climbing experience and technical safety equipment. Follow the same route as the direct route up to the base of the steep north face. Traverse the glacier west (right) to the next snow ramp just beyond a low rockband. Take some caution here as rockfall is frequent. Ascend the slope as it winds right and to the northwest then more or less west, traversing the mountain. This area is quite heavily crevassed, requiring route finding depending on snow conditions. If there is deep snow, crevasses are not as much of a problem. After reaching a low angle bulge, continue corkscrewing right and up to the small rock outcrop, then head left and straight up the steeper snow slope (45° to 50°) to the Maximum Peak. From the hut, it is 3 to 4 hours to the summit.

Northeast Ridge

This is a challenging mixed snow and rock route with exposure along an interesting ridge crest. Bring a rack of three or four ice screws, three pickets, slings and a small rock rack. The rock is a poorly consolidated agglomerate so rockfall can be a problem in places. The rock is also difficult to protect, but with heavy snow cover you can place snow stakes. For the experienced mountaineer, this is a fun route.

From the refuge head up to the terrace, then traverse left to the northeast ridge. You can gain the ridge about a third of the way up by ascending to the right of the first knob on the skyline following up snowfields and rotten 5th-class rock to the ridge crest. Alternatively continue around to the base of the ridge and climb the ridge from the bottom. Just past the first knob follow easier class 3 rock and snowfields along the crest to Ambato summit.

Celso Zuquillo

A more difficult route is known as the Celso Zuquillo (after one of its first climbers) or East Ridge route.

South Ridge

The most difficult route of all was done by the French and Ecuadorian climbers, Joseph Bergé and Marco Cruz, in October 1973 and goes up the south ridge. A bivouac and highly technical ice climbing are required. The route was repeated by Martin Slater, Travis White and Peter Hall in March 1974 and again by George Gibson and Allan Miller in June 1977.

Southwest face

The southwest face was climbed by Tom Hunt and Jorge and Delia Montpoli in September 1982. This route is approached from the 3,600m Loma de Huinza pass on the Sigchos road, south of the mountain. Head for the base of the westernmost glacier located just north of the prominent, crumbling rock towers that divide the south and west sides of the mountain (8 hours). Camp here. Climb the left side of the heavily crevassed glacier to a 40° snow ramp which bears further left and above the first rock walls. Ascend a steep couloir to the right (75°, 50m) and at the top angle right along a mild ridge to a 5m ice wall. Ascend the final 100m to the summit via the southwest knife ridge. Total climbing time from camp was 5 hours for 900m of ascent.

HIKING IN THE ZUMBAHUA AREA

The high *páramo* and rocky peaks around Zumbahua are an undiscovered treasure that have maintained a character which is distinctly Andean and indigenous. There are remnant cloudforest patches, interesting *páramo* vegetation and walks into the coastal rainforest or back into the central valley. The people are mostly warm hearted but sometimes distrustful of outsiders. A recent earthquake in 1996 which killed several dozen people and destroyed thousands of houses has instilled fear among the indigenous people. It is important to be respectful and sensitive when visiting this region. When choosing places to camp put your tent away from villages unless invited to stay near or inside a *choza* (grass hut). We have described several routes but cross-country travel is possible with the appropriate maps. (See Zumbahua to Tambo Loma, Chugchilán Area and Sigchos to La Unión maps.)

Zumbahua to Angamarca hike
Maps: IGM 1:50,000 Pilaló and Angamarca
This 2-day trek takes you from Zumbahua over rarely visited *páramo* to the isolated town of Angamarca. The area is mostly above 4,000m and is sparsely populated with Quechua-speaking *campesinos* who raise llamas and mostly still live in *chozas*. The broad green valleys surrounded by rocky peaks and the cold weather make you feel like you are in the more expansive *cordilleras* of Peru. Most llama populations in Ecuador were eradicated by the Spanish but we were told that the llamas in this region are original pre-colonial stock. They have been purchased by US llama breeders because of their high quality. The highlights of the hike are views of the peaks of Ilinizas, Cotopaxi, Laguna Quilotoa and Chimborazo. There is also an interesting canyon with remnant cloudforest vegetation. On this hike the people are incredibly friendly and do not beg; please do not give them money or candy unless you are paying for a service.

Access Take a bus from Quito to Latacunga and get off at the traffic light. Buses leave from here to Zumbahua every couple of hours. It is also possible to catch the more frequent buses to Pujilí and hitch the rest of the way to Zumbahua. Get off in Misaruni (small store and bridge over Río Huaniupulog), approximately 2km before Zumbahua.

Equipment The weather is cold and snow is possible so bring sweaters and a Gore-Tex jacket. You could arrange to stay in a *choza* or camp, but in either case bring a sleeping bag. There is plenty of water on the route but it must be treated.

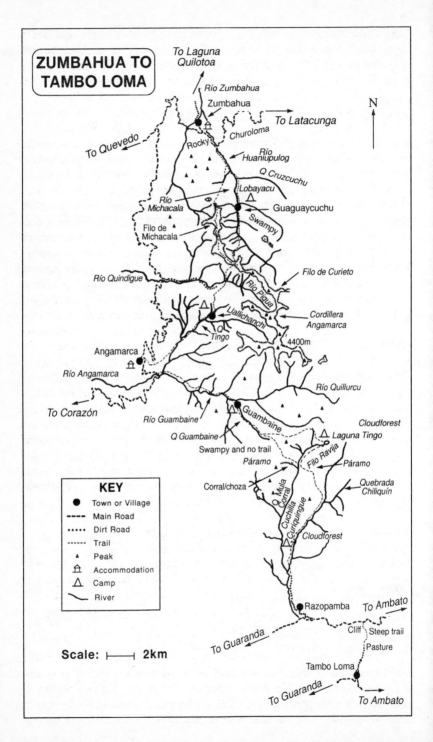

ZUMBAHUA TO TAMBO LOMA

To Laguna Quilotoa
Río Zumbahua
Zumbahua
To Latacunga
Churoloma
Rocky
Río Huaniupulog
Q Cruzcuchu
To Quevedo
Lobayacu
Río Michacala
Guaguaycuchu
Swampy
Filo de Michacala
Filo de Curieto
Río Quindigue
Río Piqua
Llalichanchi
Cordillera Angamarca
Q Tingo
4400m
Angamarca
Río Angamarca
Río Quillurcu
To Corazón
Río Guambaine
Guambaine
Cloudforest
Q Guambaine
Laguna Tingo
Swampy and no trail
Páramo
Filo Ravjia
Páramo
Corral/choza
Quebrada Chiliquín
Q Mula
Corral
Cuchilla Curiquingue
Cloudforest

N

KEY
● Town or Village
---- Main Road
••••• Dirt Road
- - - Trail
▲ Peak
⌂ Accommodation
△ Camp
∿ River

Razopamba
To Ambato
To Guaranda
Cliff
Steep trail
Pasture
Tambo Loma
To Guaranda
To Ambato

Scale: ⊢——⊣ 2km

Hiking directions Begin at the small store in Misarumi and walk south along a dirt path on the right side of the river. This is a beautiful canyon that narrows just before you arrive at the community of Michaca (1 hour). Continue right and south past the villages of Loayacu and Guaguaycuchu in a broad green valley. Just after the valley narrows again and turns southeast leave the valley and head southwest up the prominent draw (natural gully) of Quebrada Saniahuaycu. There are only game trails but the walking is easy. Reach the pass to the west of Cerro Tixan; the views from this rocky ridge are incredible. Below you is the broad valley of the Río Pigua and the orange roof of Hacienda Chinipamba. Drop down to the river. This is a nice place to camp, about 5 to 7 hours from Misarumi.

If you would rather walk on the ridge you can head up Quebrada Satram just before Michachi to the pass between Cerro Sachacocha and Sachapata and continue south. We came up the valley but this looks like an easy ridge walk in stable weather.

The following day, climb over a small pass and descend to the isolated community of Llallichanchi, which consists mostly of *chozas*. Arrive at the concrete school and contour over to the other side of the valley. Follow the well-defined trail down to the canyon, eventually getting to a narrows with good cloudforest and abundant birds. Follow this valley as it becomes wider and more agricultural eventually crossing to the right side of the river. As you approach Angamarca it is best to stay high on the right side of the valley. From Río Pigua to Angamarca it is about 5 to 6 hours of hiking.

There are no hostels in Angamarca but a bed can be arranged at one of the shops in the village square. Note the ornate carvings on the church doors, the work of artisans trained in a school set up by a respected Italian catholic missionary living in the town. Buses come from the semi-tropical village of Corazón and continue back to Zumbahua, usually leaving in the morning. However there is usually some form of transport in the afternoons or evenings. It is 3 hours by bus back to Zumbahua; look out for some incredible views as you climb up from Angamarca.

Angamarca to Tambo Loma hike
Maps: IGM 1:50,000 Angamarca, Simiatug
You can continue the above hike from Angamarca to Tambo Loma, a small community located on the new Ambato–Guaranda road near the peak of Chimborazo. It is possible to resupply food in Angamarca. Alternately you can get a bus from Zumbahua to Angamarca – there are several a day – to begin this hike. The hike takes about 3 days and you will see very few people, so come prepared.

From the town of Angamarca walk or get a ride down the road to Barrio San Pablo (3km). Just past a school before you cross the river follow a narrow dirt road up a hill to the community of Shuyo Grande. From here find the main trail on the north side of the Río Guambaine – ask for the trail to the community of Guambaine. The trail is wide and obvious with great views of the Guambaine valley and surrounding peaks. About 3 hours upstream you cross to the south side of the Río Guambaine and climb another ½-hour to the community of Guambaine which consists of a concrete school and several dozen *chozas* scattered on the hillside. The people of this village are friendly and may let you camp on the volleyball court.

The trail climbs along the south side of Quebrada Guambaine with some interesting hoodoos (rock towers) on the north side of the valley. The valley opens to a broad swampy basin called Hondonada de Yuracucha. Here you can continue on the north side of Cerro Chaso Carapungu, eventually dropping down to Laguna Tingo, or take the more direct route to the pass on the west side of Loma Negro Huanuna. Taking the Loma Negro Huanuna route, drop to Quebrada Mula Corral past a circular corral and *choza* on your right. The route to Laguna Tingo is longer but there it is possible to camp below a large *polylepis* forest. It takes about 4 to 6 hours to reach Laguna Tingo or Quebrada Mula Corral from the village of Guambaine.

From Laguna Tingo it is easiest to cross around the north side of Filo Ravija and descend Quebrada Chiliquin. If you are camped in the Quebrada Mula Corral you can descend the valley through *páramo* grass to the confluence with the Río Calamaca or cross on the north side of Cerro Yanantzay and descend on a good trail to the Río Calamaca. This trail descends on the west side of the Río Calamaca valley and crosses the river just above the confluence with the Río Sigsiyacu – about 4 to 5 hours from the lake. A new dirt track has been constructed to this point and it is an easy 2-hour walk from here to the Río Ambato and the old road between Ambato and Guaranda. Buses pass along this road four times a day and there is moderate traffic for hitchhiking.

You can complete the hike by walking downstream on the road about 4km to a trail that heads south steeply up Cerro de Pailo Loma. The trail begins about 5 minutes beyond the bridge over Quebrada Paila Huaycu and immediately beyond the overhanging cliff next to the road. The trail climbs to a dirt track which brings you to Comuna Tambo Loma on the new Guaranda–Ambato road with much more traffic. It is about 3 hours from Río Ambato to Tambo Loma. From here you continue cross-country to the refuge at Chimborazo or catch a bus to Ambato (it is difficult to get a ride after dark).

Zumbahua to La Unión de Toachi hike

Maps: IGM 1:50,000 Pilaló, Sigchos, San Roque, Manuel Cornejo Astorga and Alluriquín

This 6–7-day hike from *páramo* to the lowlands traverses a number of vegetation zones. It begins in the colourful indigenous town of Zumbahua, ascends to the crater rim of Quilotoa then passes the villages of Chugchilán and Sigchos, eventually descending the Río Toachi valley. A highlight of the hike is a 2km-wide lake in the centre of the collapsed caldera of Quilotoa.

Along the Río Toachi valley small pools and streams offer numerous opportunities for swimming and an incredible variety of orchids and birdlife is present. The trail is often muddy in parts.

Hiking directions There are numerous trails so it is important to have topo maps or enough Spanish to ask directions from the *campesinos* you meet. The trip can also be shortened to 4 to 5 days by starting from Sigchos instead of Zumbahua.

From the village plaza in Zumbahua descend the hill to the bridge and continue on the dirt road north to Laguna Quilotoa. After a few kilometres along a dusty road turn right at the fork and cross the bridge. Walk past Quilopungo, a small school and playground, continue past the Ponce turn-off, and finally up to a colourful painted tombstone-shaped sign for Quilotoa. The road to the right takes you to the cluster of houses near the crater rim. The walk is 12km and takes approximately 3 to 4 hours. There is usually some traffic so you can hitch if you do not want to walk this stretch.

The views of the barley fields and pumice plain along the way are spectacular. You can camp at the rim or stay in some basic huts including Cabañas Quilotoa, Posada Quilotoa and Refugio Quilotoa. There is a small community here that sells *cuadros* (small colourful symbolic landscape paintings) and they have been known to wake campers early in the morning to peddle their wares. A more secluded option is to hike down to the lake at the bottom of the crater, which takes approximately 1 hour. The trail down starts in a notch in the rim to the left of the parking area and descends steeply on a dusty path. The lake water is alkaline so it is not recommended for drinking – bring enough water for your needs.

From the rim of Quilotoa you can walk or hitch a ride down the dirt road to Chugchilán. It is 22km and 6 hours of walking. The other option is to head around to the northwest side of the crater to Loma Quilotoa. Look for the third low sandy spot about 45 minutes along the west side of the rim. The most common mistake is to leave the rim too early. Follow a row of eucalyptus trees down to Huayama. In Huayama walk through the town past the cemetery, take the second right down to the canyon of Río Sihui (cement bridge) and up to Chugchilán. This route to Chugchilán is 11km and takes 5 hours.

Just 1km beyond Chugchilán there is a pleasant and inexpensive hostel, the Black Sheep Inn, run by an American couple. This is a good place to check up on current trail conditions and other day hikes in the area such as to the pre-Columbian ruins of Atalaya and a cooperative cheese factory.

There are several ways to get from Chugchilán to Sigchos – the Black Sheep Inn has good information. One route is to head up to the Cordillera Chugchilán and back down to Sigchos. Follow the main road out of town for about 20 minutes then take a left turn up a dirt road leading towards the cheese factory. The road switchbacks and you can find short cuts. Continue to Gusumbinialto village church (3 to 4 hours) with views of the coast,

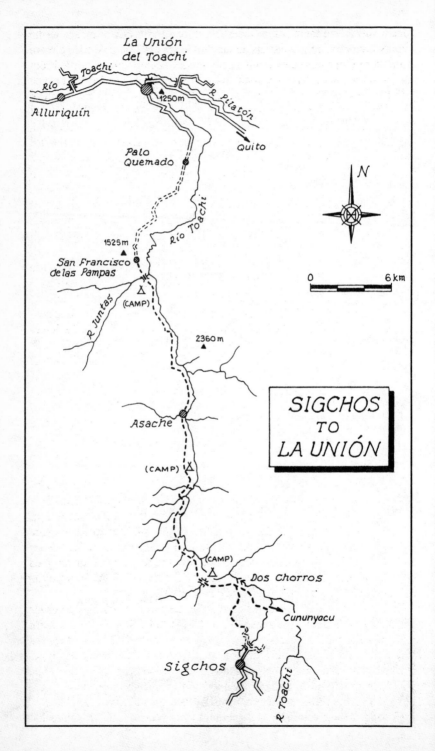

La Unión
del Toachi

Río Toachi

Alluriquín

1250m

R. Pilatón

Quito

Palo
Quemado

Río Toachi

1525m

San Francisco
de las Pampas

R. Juntas

(CAMP)

2360 m

Asache

(CAMP)

(CAMP)

Dos Chorros

Cununyacu

Sigchos

R. Toachi

N

0   6 km

SIGCHOS
TO
LA UNIÓN

Toachi valley and the Ilinizas. Take a right turn and follow the track to the Ruinas Pucurá. Continue to Hacienda San Gabriel (3 hours), where there is another set of ruins nearby and a good place to camp with a spring. From here find the path or take the road down to Sigchos (about 1 to 2 hours).

In Sigchos, there are a couple of small *residencias*. From the north of town, follow the dirt road that runs along the east side of the church. Ask for the track to Sibicusi. As the last of the straggling village is left behind, the road turns left (west) alongside a deep wooded valley. Stay on the dirt road as it crosses the river valley and climbs out to the northwest. At the pass where the track levels, a wide open pasture lies ahead and the road bears off to the left. Take the foot trail which angles left through the pasture and continues straight down the ridge. The trail is clear for a couple of hours until it comes down into a flat area where you'll see a farmhouse. Just before the house a small trail leads off to the right, marked by a small gate before the newly built local school. Follow this down as it crosses several pastures. Along the way you'll pass a small deserted wooden house which could be used for shelter. The trail weaves back and forth as it continues down the slope, passing a few small farms and several pleasant springs. The final part of the descent, as the track passes two thatched adobe houses, requires a bit of route finding to connect with the lower path. The trail heads to the right and leaves you with an extremely steep (100m) descent through a pasture, ending up at a junction with another trail coming from Cunuyacu to the east.

At the trail junction are two waterfalls known as Dos Chorros and from here it's a ½-hour walk to the valley floor. After the first of many log bridges, the trail follows the west bank of the Río Toachi. Shortly you'll come to a field on the right which is good for camping; a house nearby has a water source. From Sigchos to the campsite it can take 6 to 7 hours if you don't spend too much time marvelling at the fantastic views.

The next day's walk is along a scenic trail following the Río Toachi. You'll cross several small tributaries excellent for bathing. The birdlife is abundant. The village of Asache, 5 to 6 hours down the trail, is a delightful place to stop for the night. The people are friendly and the place has a nice feel to it. It may be possible to sleep in the community house or with Rosa and Marío Ortun. Across the river are the Montes de Santo Cristo, an area of steep forested mountains. A new logging road is being put in from the east and the villagers expect to have electricity soon.

The following day continues alongside the river, crossing numerous tributaries with many small cascades and waterfalls. Stopping for a swim may be hard to resist. Occasionally you'll see a single wire cable stretched above the wide Toachi. Believe it or not, this is what the locals use to get across to the other side. Tying a simple sling around the cable, they then slip their upper bodies through the loop and cross hand over hand to the other side. This technique is not recommended for the uninitiated!

Finding decent camping spots through this section can be somewhat

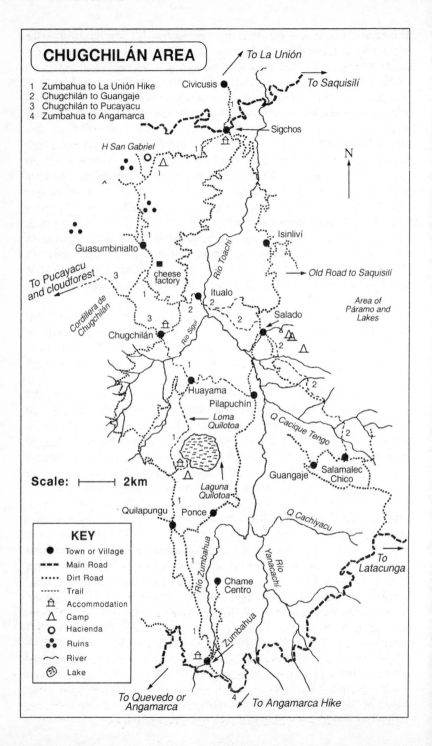

CHUGCHILÁN AREA

1 Zumbahua to La Unión Hike
2 Chugchilán to Guangaje
3 Chugchilán to Pucayacu
4 Zumbahua to Angamarca

To La Unión

Civicusis

To Saquisilí

Sigchos

N

H San Gabriel

Isinliví

Old Road to Saquisilí

Guasumbinialto

Río Toachi

cheese factory

Itualo

Area of Páramo and Lakes

To Pucayacu and cloudforest

Salado

Cordillera de Chugchilán

Río Sigui

Chugchilán

Huayama

Pilapuchín

Loma Quilotoa

Q Cacique Tengo

Salamalec Chico

Guangaje

Laguna Quilotoa

Scale: ⊢——⊣ **2km**

Quilapungu   Ponce

Q Cachiyacu

To Latacunga

KEY

● Town or Village
━ ━ ━ Main Road
••••• Dirt Road
- - - - Trail
⛩ Accommodation
△ Camp
○ Hacienda
⁙ Ruins
〜 River
🔄 Lake

Río Zumbahua

Chame Centro

Río Yanacachi

Zumbahua

To Quevedo or Angamarca

To Angamarca Hike

problematic, but, unless you're really moving fast, it's not feasible to hike all the way to Las Pampas in one day. You'll occasionally pass deserted buildings that can be used instead of struggling to set up a tent.

About 1 to 2 hours before reaching the village of Las Pampas the trail crosses the river junction of the Toachi and the Juntas. Nearby an old stone bridge spans the river. You'll probably want to set up camp before crossing the junction.

On the other side of the stone bridge the trail makes a steep, short climb and then drops down into a small valley before beginning the real (and steep) ascent up to Las Pampas. It's a tough trail especially in the rainy season when it becomes pure mud.

Las Pampas has one basic *residencia* on the plaza and several places to eat. There is a road head, but the only regular transport is a 07.00 milk truck to La Unión de Toachi, which takes about 2 hours, and a daily bus to Latacunga which departs at 09.00. You can also visit uncut cloudforest 2½ hours up a trail, staying at a basic refuge called Ortin (owned by Cesar Ortin, the brother of the family in Asache). Biology students use this refuge to explore the surrounding forest.

On foot, it's about 6 hours of easy walking along a dirt road to La Unión. The road leaves the north side of town, passes through the ridgetop village of Galápagos and continues on to Palo Quemado, an old mining town. Though the goldmine is now shut down, the village maintains its huge church and the look of prosperity.

From Palo Quemado the road continues north past several tiny settlements and eventually drops back down into the Toachi valley. It's unlikely that you'll see any vehicles until the last few kilometres before La Unión. In the town of La Unión de Toachi, frequent eastbound buses are easily flagged down for the return to Quito. If you'd like to soothe away the weariness you can take a bus to the town of Alluriquín, about 5km west, and stay overnight at Hotel Florida which has a sauna and Turkish bath.

Chugchilán to Guangaje hike
Maps: IGM 1:50,000 Pilaló, Sigchos

Another option from Chugchilán is to head east across the *páramo* to Guangaje – a 2-day hike with views of the crater of Quilotoa. From Chugchilán walk down the road towards Sigchos and at the first road junction on the left take a path right into the canyon towards the villages of Chinalo and Itualo. Take the path through Itualo to the Río Toachi. Follow the riverbed upstream to a bridge, cross the river and head up the steep hill in front of you. Follow the path to Punteo where you take the left fork to the pleasant village of Guantualo (market Monday mornings). Go straight on here, passing through fields and between houses. On the canyon rim go straight down into the valley crossing a small stream, then head up to the church of Salado. It is 3 hours to this point. You can hike up from the church to a small lake where there is a good camping spot.

The next day follow the road for a about 100m until a track veers up the ridge to the left. You will meet the road again on a hairpin bend; cross it there and the trail brings you up to the Loma Malingua with great views of Laguna Quilotoa. Continue gently uphill. At Quebrada Malingua you join the road again. From there a path goes level to your right and later down to the Quebrada Chinchil. In front of you are the villages of Guangaje and Salamalec Chico.

From Quebrada Chinchil head up the canyon until you reach a road at Salamalec Chico. From here you can follow the road to your right towards Guangaje where there are buses to Latacunga. It is approximately 5 hours from Salado to Guangaje.

Chugchilán to Pucayacu hike

Maps: IGM 1:50,000 Sigchos and Pucayacu

It is also possible to hike from Chugchilán to the subtropical village of Pucayacu. Climb out of Chugchilán to the Cordillera de Chugchilán then follow a track which turns to a better trail. The hike takes 2 days and passes through some great cloudforest. We have not done the hike but the trail is not difficult to follow. Enquire at the Black Sheep Inn for details.

HIKING AND CLIMBING IN THE CHIMBORAZO-CARIHUAIRAZO AREA

Maps: IGM 1:50,000 Quero and Chimborazo.

The glaciers on the mountains are inaccurately represented; they have greatly receded in recent years and on Carihuairazo occupy barely half of the area assigned to them on the maps. Thus part of the hike appears to cross glaciers but this is not so. Most of the other topographical features are accurate.

> 'Señor, we understand perfectly, that in an affair like yours, it is necessary to dissemble – a little; and you, doubtless, do quite right to say you intend to ascend Chimborazo – a thing that everyone knows is perfectly impossible. We know very well what is your object! You wish to discover the TREASURES which are buried in Chimborazo...'
>
> Edward Whymper, 1892

Chimborazo and Carihuairazo are two extinct glaciated volcanoes located about 150km south-southwest of Quito. Chimborazo is the tallest mountain in Ecuador at 6,310m and for many years it was thought to be the highest mountain in the world. It still retains the distinction of being the point on the earth's surface which is farthest from its centre; this is due to the earth's Equatorial bulge. It is higher than any mountain in the Americas north of it: McKinley is about 75m lower. Chimborazo's reputation as such a high mountain led to many attempts on the summit during the 17th and 18th centuries before it was climbed by Whymper and the Carrels in 1880. Carihuairazo is also an impressively high peak; at 5,020m it ranks tenth in height in Ecuador and was conquered, also in 1880, by the Whymper expedition with the Ecuadorians David Beltrán and Francisco Campaña.

The more deeply eroded peak of Carihuairazo is located 10km northeast. Despite its 5,020m and glaciers it appears diminutive alongside Chimborazo.

Both mountains are heavily glaciated and snow- and ice-climbing equipment and technique are required for their ascents. The normal routes are relatively straightforward but have claimed lives. For the non-climber, an excellent hike is from the Pan-American Highway to the Ambato–Guaranda road. This crosses the pass between the two mountains with beautiful views of these and other major peaks. For the mountaineer, combining the hike with ascents of both peaks provides an exceptional experience. (See Chimborazo/Carihuairazo map.)

Access From Quito's Terminal Terrestre take a Riobamba bus along the Pan-American Highway. About halfway between Ambato and Riobamba you will see a sign on your right for Mocha. Stay on the bus for a further 5–6km as the road climbs steeply until a turn-off to Mochapata. There is no sign; the right-hand turn-off is a steeply descending cobbled road, which crosses the Quebrada Yanayacu via a stone bridge which is plainly visible from the highway. Allow about 3 hours on the bus from Quito.

Hiking directions Walk down the cobbled road, cross the stone bridge, and look for trails climbing the small hill in front of you. Take one of these over the hill (avoiding a detour through Mochapata), cross a railway track, and you will soon come to a rough road where you turn left. In clear weather Chimborazo's steep and rugged southeastern flanks are visible to the west; this side provides the most difficult ascent routes and the view is splendid. Carihuairazo is seen to the northwest but from this angle the major glaciers are not properly appreciated.

Walk about 3km along the road until you come to a right-hand turn on to a dirt road passing the swampy Laguna Patococha and continuing about 1km to the unsigned settlement of Doce de Octubre at about 3,560m, and not marked on the IGM map. You may be allowed to sleep in the village hall (four bare walls, no facilities). Alternatively continue about 1km along the steeply descending dirt road to the banks of the Río Mocha where you can camp. If you have a heavy load of gear, you can rent mules in Doce de Octubre (though this may take 2 or 3 days to arrange) to take you to the hut at the base of Carihuairazo. A 4WD vehicle will reach the settlement, after which you must rely on mules or backpacking.

From Doce de Octubre to the dilapidated hut at the base of Cerro Piedra Negra takes about 8 hours of hiking. After crossing the Río Moche below the village, climb out of the river canyon and take the second left fork passing a house and climbing north-northwest. Take the mud road that climbs the side of a hill above the area known as Mauca Corral. The road switchbacks up Loma Tulutuz and ends at two grass huts behind the hill. Follow this for another kilometre until you can see two sharp ridges heading

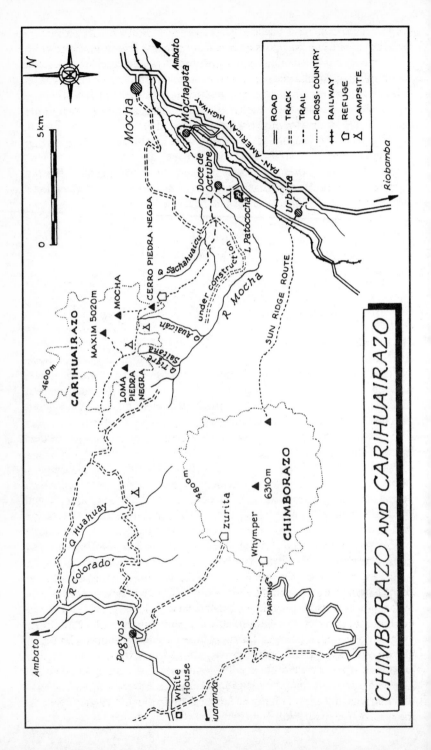

CHIMBORAZO AND CARIHUAIRAZO

northwest towards Carihuairazo. They are separated by a small river, the Quebrada Sachahuaicu. Cross a stream and climb the left-hand ridge (Filo de Sachahuaicu) and follow cowpaths along the gently rising ridge top which heads west and then curves northwest toward Cerro Piedra Negra (c4,480m) which is a southern spur of Carihuairazo and about 4km away. Keep your eyes peeled for the small, dilapidated hut about 0.5km to the east of Cerro Piedra Negra and by the right flank of a small conical hill. When you seem to be heading away from the hut, leave the ridge and go north cross-country towards it.

The hut is now in total collapse and may be difficult to see, but the surrounding area is suitable for camping and still used as a base to climb the Moche peak of Carihuairazo (see *Climbing Carihuairazo,* page 122). From the hut it is an easy scramble to the top of Cerro Piedra Negra from which there are views of Ambato as well as four major peaks: Carihuairazo to the north, Chimborazo to the southwest, Tungurahua to the east, and El Altar to the southeast.

From the hut area the hiker continues roughly westwards along the south flanks of Carihuairazo. First climb on to the ridge joining Cerro Piedra Negra with Carihuairazo and continue north along it for about a kilometre until you are near the head of the Aucacán river valley on your left. This ridge is narrow and exposed in places. Then drop down from the ridge, cross the Quebrada Aucacán high up by the central glacier of Carihuairazo, and scramble up the opposite side of the Aucacán valley to the top of the ridge. It's easier than it looks, especially if you follow the diagonal slash of vegetation which is clearly visible on the far side. At the top are flat camping areas with meltwater running off nearby. Other good campsites are found near lakes at the head of the Quebrada Tigre Saltana valley, about half an hour roughly west from the ridge. Both sites are often used as base camps for the ascent of Carihuairazo's main (Maxim) peak (see *Climbing Carihuairazo*, page 122). Allow a full day to reach this area from the hut. This is such a pretty area that it is worth camping early and exploring. A good sidetrip is to the western flanks of Carihuairazo where many interesting high Andean lakes, streams and bogs can be investigated.

The hike continues roughly north over a pass between Carihuairazo and Loma Piedra Negra (not to be confused with Cerro Piedra Negra), a pyramidal peak west of Carihuairazo. There is a trail around the eastern and northern flanks of Loma Piedra Negra. It is rather indistinct in places but frequent cairns are an aid. Once you have rounded Loma Piedra Negra the trail fades and you strike west down a gently sloping plain for about 3km until you come to a road. Follow this road to a hairpin turn with a sign to Vicuna Reserve, and take the hard right fork (not shown on the map) to get to the Ambato–Guaranda road in 1½ hours. Here you can flag down a bus to take you into Ambato (turn right) or Guaranda (turn left). For ascents of Chimborazo it is about 6km to the turn-off for the Whymper refuge in the direction of Guaranda.

Climbing Carihuairazo

There are two main peaks, Maxim in the centre and Mocha to the southeast. Maxim is the highest at 5,020m according to IGM figures, although some authorities put Maxim at 5,116m and Mocha at 5,030m. Whatever the correct altitude, both peaks are glaciated and require ice axe, crampons and rope. The rotten rock at the top of both peaks is a little exposed.

Maxim Peak

Access The most direct approach to Maxim peak is from the Ambato–Guaranda road. About an hour out of Ambato you'll see a large sign on the left side of the road which says Río Blanco. A short way down the road there are a group of buildings and a school, Colegio Manuela Cañzares, on the right. Have the driver let you off here. Follow the road going left from the community and this will take you up toward Laguna Negra (about 3 to 4 hours' walking) and beyond to Quebrada Tigre Saltana. You can drive this section of road with a 4WD vehicle but it can be tricky since it is sloped in places. A drawback is that this route passes through a *vicuña* reserve and technically you should have permission from the MAG office in Cuenca. Some groups get stopped, others go through without seeing anyone. What seems to be the easiest solution is to 'pay' on the spot for permission to enter if you're stopped.

You can camp at a pleasant lake called Laguna Negra (not to be confused with Laguna Cocha Negra) about 45 minutes' walk up the *páramo* from the road. It is best to hide your things or hire someone from the MAG office to watch them while you are climbing. Another hour higher up there is a camp just below the glacier, west-northwest of peak 4698. To get to this camp head to the left of peak 4698 and eventually up to the ridge behind this peak, then follow the cairned trail to a flat rocky field usually with water or possibly covered by snow. By camping here you reduce the climbing time by about 2 hours, yet it's risky leaving anything out and unattended anywhere in the area. It is also possible to camp at the head of Quebrada Loma Saltana where there is usually a lake.

Climbing by the direct route Maxim Peak is most easily climbed by the direct route but there are numerous variations. From the flat area west-northwest of peak 4698 head up the moraine slope to the glacier. Once on the snow an obvious line leads to the right for the summit ridge. There may be a few crevasses depending on conditions. The last 100m may be a moderately steep mixed snow and rock scramble. Once on the ridge, traverse left along a rotten exposed knife-edged crest. The top few metres are loose and there is some danger from rockfall. Allow 2 to 3 hours for the ascent.

Mocha

The route up Mocha is steep and provides an interesting route-finding problem. It can be climbed directly from the Carihuairazo hut (described earlier) in 4 to 6 hours. A pleasant alternative is to place a high camp on the upper slopes below the Mocha glacier.

Climbing Mocha by the glacier route From the hut climb up on to the ridge joining Cerro Piedra Negra with Carihuairazo and follow the ridge towards Carihuairazo for about 1km. At one point, this section becomes rather narrow and steep with large drop-offs. A rope may provide more security, or you can drop off down and traverse below the ridge crest. Flat spaces are found at the end of the ridge for a high camp. From here there is no standard route because the glacier is constantly changing. You can try climbing up the scree along the left-hand side of the lower slope, then climb on to the glacier above the serac field at its tongue and skirt the large ice fall in the centre of the glacier (but beware of rockfall from the cliffs bordering the ice). Route finding through crevasse fields may be necessary. The summit is to the right and is composed of rather rotten rock.

CLIMBING CHIMBORAZO

There are five summits: the Whymper (or Ecuador) summit at 6,310m, the Veintimilla summit at 6,267m, the North summit at about 6,200m, the Central (or Polytechnic) summit around 6,000m, and the Eastern (or Nicolás Martinéz) summit of approximately 5,500m. The last, although the lowest, is the most difficult. The routes to the highest summit will be discussed more thoroughly. (See Chimborazo route diagram.)

Chimborazo can be and is climbed year round but June and July are considered the best months. August tends to be windy and September is not too bad, but October and November have long spells of bad weather. Late December and early January are good, but the rest of the year has predominantly bad weather, with April the worst month. A tent is only needed by hikers doing the full hiking route described.

Access The best way to reach the mountain is by bus from Ambato to Guaranda. Sit on the left-hand side of the bus for the best views. About 56km from Ambato you will come to a dirt road on your left leading to the Whymper refuge. This road is marked by a deserted white house of cement blocks (often painted with colourful political slogans) on the left-hand side, immediately beyond the junction. It is the only house on the left-hand side for many kilometres. From the junction walk southeast on the dirt road for 3 to 4km until you come to a hairpin bend. Here you can turn left up a small gully and climb due east for a further 3 to 4km until you see the parking area and lower refuge below the larger Whymper refuge. (The lower refuge has some facilities, but most parties stay at the Whymper refuge some 200m above and a ½-hour away.) Allow 3 to 6 hours from the junction to the car park at the lower refuge (the high altitude slows you down). If you don't want to go cross-country you can follow the road around to the parking area but this is 10–12km. If you'd rather hire transport, a

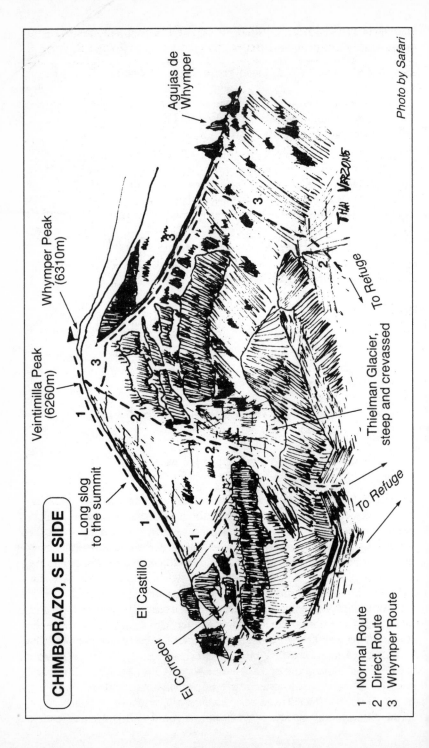

CHIMBORAZO, S E SIDE

Veintimilla Peak (6260m)

Whymper Peak (6310m)

Aguijas de Whymper

Long slog to the summit

El Castillo

El Corredor

Thielman Glacier, steep and crevassed

To Refuge

To Refuge

Thin Varzons

1 Normal Route
2 Direct Route
3 Whymper Route

Photo by Safari

taxi can be hired in Ambato at the Terminal Terrestre for about US$15–20 or the equivalent in sucres. Better still is to go by taxi from Riobamba, especially if you plan to stay overnight before going to the refuge the following day. You ought to be able to get a taxi for US$15 or less, and the road up to the refuge via the village of San Juan is straightforward. Riobamba has a better variety of accommodation and restaurants, and a lovely market on Saturdays. At the parking area and lower refuge, a narrow trail takes off from the left of the refuge for the ½-hour climb up to the Whymper hut. There have been recent break-ins in the parking lot but the military is now patrolling the area. The Whymper hut is well appointed with bunk beds and foam mattresses for about four dozen mountaineers (use your own sleeping bag), toilets, cold water, a kitchen with utensils and a propane gas stove (though this has been known to run out of gas during and after a busy weekend), a small supply of basic foods for sale, a fireplace, and a huge visitor's book with which to while away high-altitude storms. There is a hut guardian who will keep an eye on your belongings when you climb; he will also charge you a fee of US$10 per day to use the hut.

Normal route

This route has become the normal approach to the Chimborazo summit over the past few years, replacing the Whymper Route. Its steepness is more continuous but offers a direct line to the summit. The route will vary slightly from year to year, so it's best to check with the refuge guardian for the latest information. From the hut, follow the path which leads to the prominent scree slope to the left of the Thielman glacier. Climb up the scree to the huge horizontal snow ramp (El Corredor) just below a prominent rock outcrop (on the descent, this section ought to be negotiated quickly as danger from rockfall increases as the snow softens). Traverse El Corredor right up to the main glacier then angle left up a steep snowfield to a pass above a rock outcrop called El Castillo. The area below El Castillo can be crevassed. As you ascend from El Castillo you will eventually begin to head northwest (right) toward the Veintimilla summit. The snowfield is usually marked with flags and footsteps. There may be a large crevasse just below the Veintimilla summit which can be passed on the right. From here it is nearly a kilometre east over a gentle snow basin to the main summit, a slog that can take anywhere from 20 minutes to an hour, depending on the snow conditions. Late in the day this snow basin is filled with notoriously soft snow and at this altitude it takes great energy to wade through thigh-deep snow. Therefore it is advisable to start as early as possible (midnight) so that the final slog to the summit is easier. Some climbers have spent the night near Veintimilla summit and finished the climb the next day – this is an adventure for experienced, acclimatized and well-equipped climbers. The ascent normally takes 8 to 10 hours (although one party took 20 hours!); allow 2 to 4 hours for the descent.

The route should be marked with wands during the ascent, and it's not a bad idea to mark the path up the scree to the snow ramp in advance during daylight hours. It's surprisingly difficult to find the track up through the scree in the middle of the night.

Direct route
A variation on the normal route is to head straight up Thielman glacier and meet the normal route where it leaves El Corredor. This route is not recommended since it is subject to avalanches and could be heavily crevassed.

Whymper route
Having long been the most popular route on Chimborazo with historical connections to boot, this line of ascent is no longer considered practical or safe. The icy traverse under the seracs has been the site of several deaths over the past few years and conditions have continued to deteriorate.

The route begins by following a trail to the right of the refuge to Agujas Whymper (Whymper Needles). Continue on the ridge crest and aim directly towards the Veintimilla summit. Pass between some rock outcrops where the snow begins to steepen. Depending on conditions, crevasses may be present. Continue directly up the steep snow slope to the left of the large rockface. From here two routes are possible to the Veintimilla summit. Either follow the original Whymper route by traversing left and joining the normal route, or a more direct variation may be followed only if snow is stable by continuing up the steep snow slope straight to the Veintimilla summit.

Old route
This is no longer a popular route, but we have retained the description in case conditions change.

The old route begins at the village of Pogyos (also spelt Poggios or Pogyo) which is a tiny group of buildings on a bend of the road about 50km south of Ambato on the old road to Guaranda. About 1 and 4km before Pogyos are two roads to the left, which may help you to locate the village; the bus driver sometimes knows it.

Pogyos is the last place on the route where you can find water, but you'll probably want to sterilize it. Mules can be hired inexpensively to carry water and your gear up to the remains of the Fabián Zurita refuge at 4,900m, about 900m above Pogyos. To get to the refuge cross the Ambato–Guaranda road and follow a dirt track that leaves the road a few hundred metres west of Pogyos and heads southeast across the sandy *páramo* to the hut, which is 3 to 4 hours' walk away.

The hut was built in 1964 and is the oldest still in use in Ecuador. The orange octagonal shelter is now in a very dilapidated condition with a door that doesn't close properly, a leaky roof, and plenty of trash scattered around. Nevertheless it provides basic shelter for about ten people.

The climb from the hut to the summit is becoming more demanding as the glacier recedes. The route goes up the loose scree above the hut to the snowline and then continues on the snow to the base of a large red rockband known as the *murallas rojas* ('red walls'). At the base of the red walls traverse to your right and continue upwards on snow along or a little beyond the right edge of the walls. Once beyond them, head towards the peak above you, watching for crevasses which will be predominantly to your right. As you get high on the peak start heading left and to the side of it – this peak is the second or Veintimilla peak. The rounded summit is about 1km east of Veintimilla. The climb takes 8 to 12 hours. A midnight departure is recommended as the summit snow plateau becomes very soft and slushy and avalanche danger on the slopes increases after midday.

When Rob tried this route in 1982 he found that the glacier had receded so much that the scree slog up from the hut took several hours. A huge bergschrund had formed between the scree and the glacier and it was difficult to find an easy way on to the snow.

Piedra Negra and Sun Ridge routes

These two routes on the eastern side of Chimborazo involve rock climbing and mixed rock/ice climbing respectively. The area is rarely visited but is located in a spectacular setting formed by a natural amphitheatre of rock and snow. Even if the climbing proves to be too challenging, the area is excellent for exploring and hiking.

Access Transport along the Ambato–Riobamba road will pass the turn-off for the old URBINA train station about halfway between the two cities. From the main highway get off at the 'entrada a Urbina' (possibly there's a sign, they seem to come and go) and walk 3km up the dirt road to a refuge which has been set up in the old train station. It has bunks and foam mattresses, a gas stove and a small store. A fee of US$6 per night is charged, but several local climbing clubs are trying to get the price lowered.

From the refuge, a trail leads directly up the *páramo* and begins a steep ascent to the terminal moraine at the foot of Chimborazo. At the top of the moraine, there is a small lake with a flat area for camping, about 4 to 5 hours from the refuge. This is a good base for climbing both Piedra Negra and/or the Sun Ridge route. Another option for camping, particularly if you're not planning to climb, is to continue along the moraine to the right for another 1½ hours where there are magnificent views of Carihuairazo and the surrounding area and plenty of water from streams.

Climbing Piedra Negra

This enjoyable climb is not to be confused with either Cerro Piedra Negra or Loma Piedra Negra, both of which are located across the valley on Carihuairazo. This route was first climbed in 1984 by the Polytechnic Climbing Club but has not been repeated with much frequency. An assortment of technical rock gear is necessary. From the moraine camp you will see the entire east side of Chimborazo clearly – an impressive view. To the northeast (right) is a large rock formation, Piedra Negra, with a long moraine leading directly up to its base, about 1 to 2 hours from camp. At the base, traverse right (northeast) to the obvious ridge and climb to the summit. The difficulty is rated about 5.5 based on the Yosemite decimal system and takes a maximum of 2 hours from the start of the traverse.

A more difficult option, again requiring technical rock gear and experience, is the route up the east wall of Piedra Negra.

This climb, first ascended by Hugo Torres and Francisco Espinosa, begins on the east face just past the obvious overhanging junction of the east and southeast faces. A few metres to the right is a smaller overhang (good to belay below this) with the climb starting in a crack next to it. The crack runs out quickly, and you'll continue up, face climbing between two large rocks to a small belay ledge. Because of the rarely climbed condition of the route, pitons may be more useful for securing belay stances than chocks or nuts, but several well-placed small nuts may do.

The second pitch continues up the face to another, larger ledge. Just below this belay the rock turns a little ugly with downward-sloping holds. From this belay, the third pitch climbs a chimney to the ridge, about one rope length. At the ridge, the route goes left, in 4th class scrambling up and across some big loose rocks. The top is about ½–1 hour away. There is no easy downclimb; you'll have to descend to the ridge and then rappel/abseil the rest of the way.

Above the second pitch, at the wide ledge, there are several alternatives for reaching the top. One is to go left at the chimney rather than climbing in it, and you'll find easy rock leading to the ridge.

Sun Ridge route

This climb ascends to the Nicolás Martínez summit of Chimborazo and is considered by many climbers to be one of the most beautiful mixed rock/ ice routes in all of Ecuador. It requires both rock and snow experience and equipment, along with regular camping gear. Carry an assortment of ice screws, stakes and various sizes of rock protection. A bivouac will more than likely be necessary below the summit, so you'll need to come prepared for that as well. From the moraine camp, follow the same route up to Piedra Negra. Traverse left under the rock and head for the main snow ridge. Once on the glacier, traverse across the snowfield toward the immense rockface of the Chimborazo summits. Camp is set up on the glacier well below and in line with the start of the rockface. Allow about 3 to 5 hours of hiking from the moraine camp.

From the glacier camp, you will see a wide snow ramp to the left on the rockface which leads up into a couloir. Ascend about halfway to a logical point where you can begin a traverse left across the rocks. Be careful of loose rock in this section. The traverse continues across to an area of huge rock slabs/boulders stacked on top of each other. In spite of appearing ready to give way at any minute, this area is quite stable. Climb these slabs up and left to just below a ridgeline. Here the route begins another traverse across a mixture of steep snow and rock up and down across small ridges. (The feasibility of crossing this section depends on the season. If there has been little snow, you'll have to continue up to the main ridge to make the traverse, but this is more difficult.) The traverse continues left and flattens out at the top of a wide snow ramp. It should take about 5 to 7 hours from the camp to reach this point. Here you can make a choice. If the going has been difficult, or the group is moving too slowly, this ramp is an excellent escape route and easy descent back to the lower glacier and camp.

If continuing, traverse for a bit further to a snowfield which is the beginning of the upper glacier. Head left up the snowfield to a section of huge snow 'mushrooms' which begin the final approach to the summit. A bivouac is normally made just after gaining this part of the glacier. The snow and ice are steep, of poor quality, and some route finding is necessary to make your way up towards the summit. From the top of this snowfield you can look up left to pinpoint the final approach to the summit. It should take about 3 to 5 hours of climbing from the bivouac to reach the summit. The descent backtracks to the easy-exit snow ramp for the fastest return to the lower glacier.

An easier alternative to this mixed route is to traverse from the snow camp below the rockface to the snow gully used for the descent in the above climb. Climb this to meet up with the other route, and continue up to the summit following the above description. From camp, this could take about 7 hours to the summit and another 3 for the descent.

Other routes

Many new routes remain to be climbed on a mountain of this size. There are also routes which have had only one or two ascents. Among these are the following: the eastern summit via the Moreno glacier in the southeast, the main summit from the north, and the central peak via the Humboldt glacier in the south. These routes are suggestions for highly advanced climbers only. Otherwise stay on the standard routes; if you need a guide see the appropriate section in *Chapter Three*.

PARQUE NACIONAL CAJAS

Maps: At the entrance station they have a free planometric map of the area with trails and routes indicated. This is useful in conjunction with the following topograpic maps: IGM 1:50,000 Chaucha, Cuenca, San Felipe de Molleturo and Chiquintad.

At the southern end of the Western Cordillera is found an enchantingly beautiful area of *páramo* and cloudforest. For the naturalist the principal attraction is the variety of plants, and a careful ornithologist will see a good number of bird species. The hiker is faced with a profusion of lakes of all shapes, sizes and colours; the area boasts 275 named lakes and countless minor ponds and tarns. This is the Parque Nacional Cajas, a reserve of almost 29,000ha set aside for preservation in 1977 and named a national park in December 1996.

The Parque Nacional Cajas is one of the best-managed conservation units in Ecuador, which is probably due to local Cuencano pride in the area. On any weekend, hundreds of local anglers and recreationalists drive from nearby Cuenca into the park. Most visitors do not travel far from the road, so you can find solitude on an overnight backpacking trip into the centre of the park.

The preserve lies about 29km west of Cuenca. This charming city, the nation's third largest, is worth a few days' exploration. Getting a bus for the 9-hour trip to Cuenca from Quito's Terminal Terrestre is straightforward or you can take one of the several daily flights. Once in Cuenca you should visit the tourist information office which is on Hermano Miguel between Jaramillo and Cordova. Here you can obtain city maps and brochures about the area. (See Cajas map.)

Access There is at least one bus a day which leaves at 06.30 from the San Francisco market on Pres Cordova between Torres and Aguirre. This bus has also left from Plaza San Sebastián at the corners of Bolívar and Talbot, so check locally. The bus (marked Sayausi-Miguir) takes about 2 hours to reach the park information centre and ranger station by Laguna Toreadora in the northern part of the park. Here you need to pay a US$10 park entrance fee. It makes the return trip to Cuenca at 15.00. You can hire a taxi in Cuenca to Miguir for about US$12. There is a refuge with a few bunks and a kitchen (a small fee is charged) but it's better to bring your own tent as the guardian is not always there. Camping is permitted throughout the park and is free. Another route into the park is on the bus to Angas, on the southwestern border of Cajas. Buses leave from Av Loja by the river on Tuesday, Wednesday, Friday and Saturday at 06.30.

Once you get away from the immediate environs of the park station you will find that an effort has been made to mark some of the frequently used trails. Still, those which wander some distance from the main area usually peter out fairly quickly so hiking here is largely a cross-country affair. A strong hiker with a good sense of direction can cross the park in 2 days. The vegetation is primarily *páramo* grasses and way trails exist up most valleys and to most lakes so the walking is straightforward. Nevertheless, several people have died from exposure so it is important to have warm clothes and raingear. We describe several recommended routes although perhaps your best bet is to bring enough food for a week and just amble around gently; you'll see very few people and the scenery is really marvellous.

The major part of the land area is *páramo* and many typical *páramo* species may be seen. Most exciting of all is perhaps the condor which is still occasionally sighted. You will hear as well as see the Andean snipe. Highland thickets of the dwarf quinua tree dot the landscape and are filled with a fascinating variety of primitive plant and fungal life: the trees and ground are covered with mosses, lichens, liverworts, mushrooms, toadstools and other fungi. One of the most colourful and common flowers is a small, bulbous, yellow and red flower known locally as *sarazhima*. You'll see rabbits and, with luck, a white-tailed deer or fox. The lakes are filled with trout and sport fishing is permitted. Towards and beyond the park's western boundaries are almost impenetrable cloudforests. There is one area of the park, however, which is known for its accessible cloudforest: the eastern part near Laguna Llaviuco. This is one of the very few areas of cloudforest on the eastern slopes of the Western Cordillera. It is reached by a short signposted dirt track leading from the main park entrance road about a third of the way between the village of Sayausi and the park station. Many more bird species are found here, including the grey-breasted mountain toucan (*Andigena hypoglauca*), the multi-coloured masked trogon (*Trogon personatus*), and various tropical woodpeckers. Another park station is being planned for this vicinity.

The altitude of the park averages around 4,000m with no areas rising above 4,500m; hence there is no snow yet it can get rather chilly at night and in the early morning. The weather varies so much that it's best to be prepared for all temperatures. Mornings are usually clear with lots of sun, good T-shirt hiking, but by late afternoon clouds often roll in and rain is always a possibility. Visits can be made year round although April to June are said to be the wettest months and August and September the driest.

Miguir to Río Soldados hike

Begin on an established trail that leaves Miguir to the Laguna Sunincocha. You pass through second-growth cloudforest to *páramo* vegetation. In this zone there are marvellous hummingbirds such as the shining sunbeam, viridian metal-tail, sparkling violet-ear, and the spectacular sword-billed hummingbird whose bill is three times the length of its body. The lakes also harbour Andean gulls, speckled teal and yellow-billed pintails. As the trail becomes less distinct stay on the south side of Laguna Sunincocha and follow the draw (gully) south past Laguna Valeriana Yacu to a pass. From here you look down to Laguna Inga Casa and the Río Soldados drainage. It is about 4 to 5 hours to this pass from Miguir and there are good camping spots next to the lakes on the opposite side of the drainage. The walk out to Soldados the next day takes 3 to 4 hours. There are only four buses a week to Cuenca via Soldados, so don't rely too heavily on transport out.

Ingañan trail

There is a portion of an Inca trail that crosses the park from Laguna Llaviuco to Laguna Luspa known as the Ingañan – probably a trading road from Cuenca to the coast. It is in ill-repair or lost in places but there are some interesting ruins above Laguna Mamamag that are presently being excavated. You can access the trail from several drainages near the park headquarters or from Miguir. Beginning in Miguir, follow an established path to Laguna Luspa. At Laguna Luspa take a path on the left (north) side of the lake; this will bring you to a stream that flows into Laguna Luspa. From here head east on a trail eventually ascending to a divide, from which point you will be able to see Laguna Osohuaycu. Continue down to Laguna Osohuaycu. The trail then passes north of Laguna Osohuaycu, a large basin surrounded by rocky peaks in the centre of the park that makes a good base for day hikes. The trail then descends to Laguna Mamamag where you

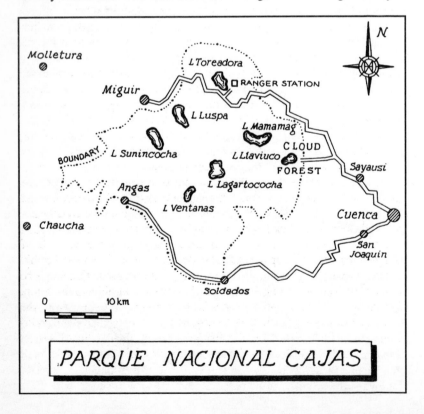

PARQUE NACIONAL CAJAS

should stay on the south side of the lake, cross over the small ridge near the mouth of the lake, and then descend through cloudforest on an established trail. Soon you reach a flat, U-shaped, grassy valley bottom and follow the wide Inca road to Laguna Llaviuco and a gate where you should be able to get a ride with fishers back to Cuenca. This trip takes 2 to 3 days. The area near Laguna Llaviuco has recently been purchased by ETAPA (Empresa de Telefonos Agua Potable y Alcantarillado, tel: 831 900) and access may be restricted in 1997.

Río Mazán to Laguna Toreadora hike

Although this area is presently closed to tourists and reserved for scientific studies, it is likely to be open for hikers in the near future so we include a description of the route. Enquire at local travel agencies or ETAPA for information on access.

This 4-day hike is said to be especially stunning for its changing scenery and vegetation, and the many bird species found in the area. It's a great opportunity to see mountain toucans, highland parrots, masked trogons, woodpeckers and the great Andean condor. Not having had the opportunity to get out and do it myself, I can only offer the following route description. However, in conjunction with the IGM maps of the area (mentioned earlier) there should be no problem in getting from one end to the other.

The hike begins near the park boundary of Cajas in an ecological area called Mazán Forest Reserve. This cloudforest reserve is protected by a local conservation group, Amigos de Mazán.

From Cuenca take the Cajas road to the Mazán reserve entrance. Get off the bus at Hacienda Gulag which is about 8km out of Cuenca and 5 minutes past the village of Sayausi. Follow the *hacienda* road left into the valley and then turn right at the gated bridge. An hour's walk will bring you to the Mazán reserve. A trail heads southwest through the reserve following the Río Mazán in beautiful cloudforest. Continue southwest to Laguna Totoracocha where you'll find good camping beside the lake.

The next day, follow the route as it angles northwest, passing to the east side of Laguna Tintacocha. Trails throughout the area will often come and go, but finding your way with map and compass should be easy enough. Past Tintacocha the track heads in a northerly direction, passing Laguna Lagartococha and on to Laguna Osohuaycu (staying on the east side of both) where camp is set up the second night. From here you should be able to pick up a clear trail heading north directly to the ranger station and park entrance of Cajas at Laguna Toreadora. This should take about 5 to 6 hours of *páramo* hiking. An option would be to continue northwest from the north point of Laguna Osohuaycu to Laguna Luspa along an old Inca trail. From here you can hike out to the village of Miguir, but finding transport from this little village back to Cuenca may be problematic.

ROCK CLIMBING
Cajas
From the refuge at Laguna Toreadora, you can look across the road and see a prominent rock block some 300m away. About 20 minutes of uphill walking will get you to its base. In the centre of the face is a large (35m) flake with three established routes and several other possibilities. The overhanging face on the main block can also be climbed but bolting is necessary. A top rope can be set up on the flake.

Godzilla is a 5.10b climb first achieved by Juan Rodriguez and Juan Carrasco. It begins near the centre of the flake at the base of a tree. Look for a finger crack leading up to a roof. Past this roof the thin crack continues up to a second and runs out to the right while the route angles left, up the face to a ledge. The descent is a matter of downclimbing a chimney (5.6) on the right side of the flake. Another chimney (5.7) on the left side can also be climbed, but both are somewhat dirty.

200m east (left) of Godzilla is another rock formation (25m) with an off-width crack starting in its centre which gradually narrows to a fist, then finger crack, called **Salsipuedes**; 5.9.

In addition, there are many huge rocks scattered in this general area which would serve well for an afternoon of bouldering.

Cuenca area
In search of good rock, a few stalwart Ecuadorian climbers have pioneered many routes and opened up several areas suitable for climbing. Of these climbers, Juan Carrasco and Juan Rodriguez seem to have been the most active, claiming many first ascents. While the majority of rock routes described here are not particularly noteworthy by American or European standards, at least for now they offer a sampling of the best available in the country. As mentioned previously, Ecuador is not a rock-climbing destination but if you're already here and longing for the feel of rock, the following suggestions and descriptions may be useful.

If you happen to be staying in Cuenca for a few days, you can get in a little climbing practice by 'buildering' – sport climbing on buildings – or, in this case, 'bridgering' (?) near the Tomebamba river. Follow Av 3 de Noviembre southeast as it runs parallel to the river and crosses under a broken bridge (*puente roto*) just past Vargas Machuca. The three centre pillars on the west face of the bridge range from 5.7 to 5.8 and a top rope can be set up on the bridge railings.

About 6-8km outside Cuenca, just before the village of Sayausi (buses leave from Plaza San Francisco), is a popular restaurant called Las Cabañas that serves the best trout (*trucha*) around.

After lunching here, continue along the road toward Sayausi until you come to a dirt road heading left. Follow this road down to a covered wooden bridge about 100m away, cross over and backtrack along the river on the other side to just opposite the restaurant. Here you'll come to an 8m-high boulder called **Piedra de las Truchas** (trout rock) with two climbable faces and lots of routes.

The east face has several established climbs. **Vía Murcielago**, 5.8, starts as an off-width crack leading off of a flake near the centre of the face. It narrows to a finger crack near the top.

To the left of this climb is **Cebiche de Trucha**, a 5.11 face climb which starts from a low rock ramp; it's overhanging and fun. **Encebollado** follows up the northeast arête, not difficult at 5.8. Top roping is possible on the south side and there are other climbs and more possibilities on both the south and north faces.

Another nearby area is located outside the village of Cojitambo. Here you'll find a dome-shaped rock formation, spanning 800m with a 200m rock wall, overlooking the village. To get there, take a bus from Cuenca to Azogues (40 minutes) and get off at the end of the line. The bus for Cojitambo (25 minutes) passes nearby, at the hospital road junction. You'll have to ask where to wait. Once in the village you'll see the huge east face – about a 20-minute walk from town.

Dead centre in the wall is **Ruta de la Gruta**, a 5.7 crack, dirty with vegetation; the second pitch is better. On the far left is **Viuda Alegre**, a nicer, wide, 5.10 hand crack leading up to a roof. At the roof you can go left (dirty) or traverse right (nice) to a walk-off. Above this area, closer to the ridge and higher up, is a rose-coloured wall with two good cracks of about 30m running up to the south ridge. From here you can hike to the top and walk off via the easy west slope.

More climbing can be found to the south of Cuenca in a beautiful area near the village of San Fernando. To get there you first have to take a bus from Cuenca to the town of Girón on the road to Machala. Here take another bus to San Fernando which is situated at the foot of massive **Mount Pablo**. The area is loaded with climbing possibilities and is good for camping, hiking and birdwatching. Sometimes groups come up here for hang-gliding practice. From the village hike up to Laguna Buza, 15 minutes away, where you'll find good camping. The approach to the base of San Pablo is somewhat difficult, requiring a steep bushwhack through dense vegetation and forest to reach the rock walls towering as high as 300m. This could take as long as 3 to 4 hours but the area is worth exploring.

Another suggestion that may not offer world-class climbing but promises to get you off the beaten path is the gorge of **Río Ridcay**, about an hour down the Cuenca-Machala road near the village of Lentag. In Cuenca hop on a bus from the main bus terminal going to Santa Isabel and ask to be let off at Lentag. From here find the dirt road that takes off left down to the river. After about a ½-hour's walk you'll come to a bridge. The rock walls of the gorge will be visible to the right. Cross the bridge and head down into the gorge. Climb on.

136

Chapter Six

The Eastern Cordillera

'The journey not the arrival matters.'
T S Eliot

This is perhaps the most interesting region for the adventurous outdoor traveller. The Eastern Cordillera is, on average, higher and more massive than its western counterpart and counts amongst its mountains the famous volcanoes of Cotopaxi, Cayambe, Antisana, El Altar and Sangay, which rank respectively second, third, fourth, fifth and seventh highest in the country. The last named is considered to be the most continuously active volcano in South America, if not the world.

The high eastern slopes of these mountains are bordered by a relatively thin strip of *páramo* which changes abruptly to almost impenetrable high mountain cloudforest on the lower slopes before merging into what is commonly called 'jungle' but is in fact the tropical rainforest of the lowlands. Hot air masses rise up the eastern flanks of the mountains depositing enough rainfall to make the high mountain cloudforest the wettest part of Ecuador; indeed, with some areas averaging over 5,000mm of rain per year, it is one of the wettest regions on earth. It is also extremely thickly vegetated so the middle and lower slopes have been little disturbed by people. The story is often told of the *hacienda* owner who, upon being asked how extensive his land was, replied, 'I don't really know – as far as you can go to the east'. Even today the eastern slopes are so little explored that *haciendas* with ill-defined limits to the east still exist. These are the haunts of the rarely seen mountain tapir and the Andean spectacled bear, the two largest wild land mammals in Ecuador, both considered endangered species. Their rarity is due not only to hunting and land encroachment but also to the almost impenetrable nature of their environment – no-one really knows how many of these elusive animals are left.

The mountains themselves tend to be covered with more snow than those of the Western Cordillera because of the higher precipitation on the eastern slopes. The peaks are normally climbed from the western side, partly because the heavily populated Central Valley lies on this side and partly because the eastern side is difficult to get to, often clouded in, and the summits are more heavily corniced. Adventurous climbers seeking new routes could look for eastern approaches to these mountains.

As with the Western Cordillera, the mountains of this range will be dealt with systematically from north to south; descriptions of both climbing and hiking routes will be given and walks into the rarely visited eastern slopes are also described.

RESERVA ECOLÓGICA CAYAMBE-COCA

The Reserva Ecológica Cayambe-Coca was established in 1970 and protects an area of over 400,000ha of diverse and largely unexplored forested and *páramo* wilderness. It occupies an area between Ibarra and Papallacta, straddling the Eastern Cordillera and extending down to the Oriente. Although some colonists and indigenous tribes live within the reserve, the inaccessibility of the eastern Andean slope has protected the unexplored centre from intrusion and development. On flights to the Oriente you pass over this maze of knife-edged ridges, frothing rivers, dense cloudforest and rainforest and understand why not many people wander into this country. You do not have the wide navigable rivers of the lowland rainforest or the open *páramo* slopes of the Andes that make travel in these areas relatively easy. A wild adventure would be a traverse from the Eastern Cordillera down the eastern Andean slope to the Oriente using the good IGM 1:50,000 topographical maps that might prevent you from getting hopelessly lost. For the sane hiker and climber there are numerous established routes that are accessible from the edges of the reserve.

The peaks of Nevado Cayambe, Cerro Sara Urco and Volcán Reventador (described in the *Oriente* chapter) all lie within the boundaries of the reserve. There are many lakes in the *páramo* around the towns of Papallacta, Oyacachi, Olmedo and Sigsipamba which can be walked to on trails used by *campesinos* and fishermen. There are also several short lowland rainforest walks.

The administration of the reserve is divided between Andean and lowland rainforest regions. The INEFAN office in Cayambe (located at km1.5 on Pan-Americana Norte) is managed by Luis Martinez and can provide information on road and trail conditions, guides and weather conditions for the western side of the reserve. The two INEFAN offices in the Oriente, in El Chaco (located 2km along the Via San Juan) and in the small town of Lumbaqui, can provide information on the eastern side of the reserve. Jorge Aguirre splits his time between these two offices and the staff for the reserve is small but friendly and helpful.

Laguna Puruhanta

Maps: IGM 1:50,000 Cayambe, Nevado Cayambe, San Pablo de Laguna, Mariano Agosto

On the northern end of the reserve is Laguna Puruhanta, a large lake (3km long and 1km wide) which is popular with trout fishers. The area is partly grazed but still features a large amount of native cloudforest and *páramo* vegetation. There are several access points. The most common and shortest is to hike from Shanshipamba near the gorge of the Río Pisque. You can also walk from the village of Pesillo to the west or from Laguna San Marcos to the south.

Hiking directions

From Shanshipamba Take a bus from Ibarra to Pimampiro (45 minutes). Reach Shanshipamba by hiring a taxi or catch an occasional bus from Pimampiro (1½ hours). It is a full day's (7 hours') walking from Shanshipamba to the lake with camping possibilities along the way.

You have two options to get to the lake. The first is to climb up through the cloudforest to the ridge south of Shanshipamba. Not many people go this way unless they are hunting and we could not obtain specific information on the route, though a trail is indicated on the IGM map.

The more straightforward route is along the Río Pisque gorge. Take the track out of Shanshipamba up to a flat pasture area with a dilapidated *hacienda*. Just before reaching the white house, follow the main track to the right towards the Río Pisque. Follow a well-defined and sometimes muddy trail for approximately 3 hours to where you can see pastures on the opposite (west) side of the river. You can cross over to the furthest upstream pasture near the confluence of the Río Palaucu to avoid a nasty stretch of trail on the east side of the river. The trail on the west side enters forest near a tin-roofed shack. You cross the Río Molinyacu and after an hour of hiking come to a log over the Río Pisque where you join the trail on the east side of the river. From here it is about 2 to 3 hours of muddy hiking through alternately swampy and cloudforest vegetation to the mouth of the lake, where there is a stream-gauging station and a campsite.

This hike has some of the best cloudforest vegetation of any intra-Andean trek and spectacular views of the Río Pisque gorge and surrounding mountains. A good local guide is Juan Pupiales, who lives near the main square in Shanshipamba and charges about US$7 per day. He also has a boat hidden somewhere on the shore of the lake that he will rent to his clients for about US$8 per day. Rubber boots are highly recommended.

From Pesillo Take a bus to Pesillo from the town of Cayambe (see *Laguna San Marcos* 'Access'). From the central *hacienda* of Pesillo, which is now a school and cheese factory, take the dirt road that heads up Quebrada Queseras Cuchu. After 5 minutes follow the trail on the left along powerlines which soon joins a dirt track. You can see pine-covered Loma El Panecillo to the south and eventually will get spectacular views of Nevado Cayambe. Continue on the track (contouring on the south side of the hill). When the track turns south, head left up to the pass following a trail up the ridge towards Loma Turupamba and follow the contours of the land on the west side of Loma Chafina to a pass east of Loma Ventana. On the other side of

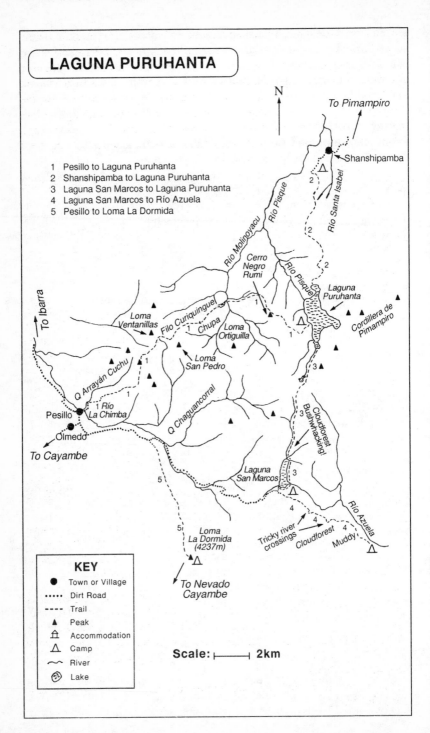

LAGUNA PURUHANTA

N

To Pimampiro

Shanshipamba

1 Pesillo to Laguna Puruhanta
2 Shanshipamba to Laguna Puruhanta
3 Laguna San Marcos to Laguna Puruhanta
4 Laguna San Marcos to Río Azuela
5 Pesillo to Loma La Dormida

Río Molinoyacu

Río Pisque

Río Santa Isabel

Cerro Negro Rumi

Río Pisque

Laguna Puruhanta

Río Pisque

To Ibarra

Loma Ventanillas

Filo Curiquinguel

Chupa

Loma Ortiguilla

Cordillera de Pimampiro

Q. Arrayán Cuchu

Loma San Pedro

Pesillo

Río La Chimba

Q. Chaguancorral

Cloudforest Bushwhacking!

Olmedo

To Cayambe

Laguna San Marcos

5

5

Río Azuela

4

4

Tricky river crossings

Cloudforest

Muddy

5

Loma La Dormida (4237m)

To Nevado Cayambe

KEY

● Town or Village
•••• Dirt Road
---- Trail
▲ Peak
⌂ Accommodation
△ Camp
∼ River
◉ Lake

Scale: ├———┤ 2km

the pass you should see the Ventana ('window'), a natural rock arch, below you. Cross over to the east side of Loma Ventanas and follow around to Filo Curiquingue Chupa. Pass a *choza* and ascend to peak 3953. From here you need to cross through cloudforest and a stream which lies between you and Cerro Negro Rumi. From peak 3953 it may be easier to head for the grassy slopes of Loma Ortiguilla to the south instead of crossing through the cloudforest. Once on the slopes of Cerro Negro Rumi it is *páramo* and easier walking. From the top of the ridge descend the steep trail to the west side of Laguna Puruhanta. It is 8 hours to the lake.

From Laguna San Marcos (see *Laguna San Marcos* 'Access') It is 1 long day or 2 short days of cross-country hiking to Laguna Puruhanta. Once on the north side of the lake stay to the right of the river bushwhacking sometimes through thick forest, but mostly walking in the *páramo*. Bring a machete.

Laguna San Marcos
Map: IGM 1:50,000 Nevado Cayambe
Laguna San Marcos is located on the north side of Nevado Cayambe and is also a popular destination for trout fishers who drive to the lake. The lake is just across the continental divide and is strongly influenced by weather from the Oriente. Hence when it is wet in the Sierra it is often dry in this area and vice-versa. The road into San Marcos was constructed for a hydrologic study for a potential hydroelectric project which has subsequently been abandoned. This is the gateway to the seldom visited cloudforests east of Cayambe. Luis Martinez, the highland director of the Cayambe-Coca Reserve, says it is beautiful but wild country with potentially dangerous river crossings and thigh-deep mud. There are also mountain tapir, Andean spectacled bear and deer. A series of glacial outwash plains extend up to 15km east of the summit of Cayambe. These plains are covered with low heath vegetation and are swampy in places but offer much easier walking than the surrounding cloudforest-covered ridges. You can get to the edge of lowland rainforest where the rivers drop off these plains and descend on steep gradients (probably waterfalls) to unknown forests. For a well-prepared expedition this would be the jumping-off point for a traverse to the Río Aguarico in the Oriente.

Access Take a bus to Cayambe (1½ hours), then take a bus to Olmedo (1 hour). Hire a vehicle to take you to the pass above Laguna San Marcos or walk from town (3 to 4 hours). If you are driving you need a 4WD vehicle to reach the lake, but you can park your car at the pass if in a normal vehicle. Do not leave valuables in your car – there was a problem with break-ins several years ago.

The weather is unstable and often rainy, but January through March is said to be drier.

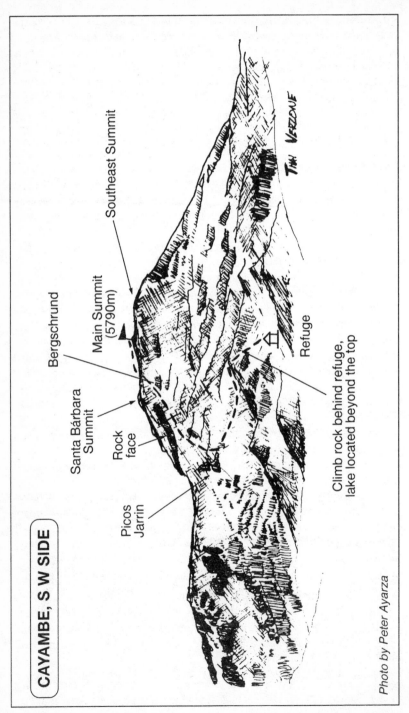

CAYAMBE, S W SIDE

Bergschrund

Main Summit (5790m)

Southeast Summit

Santa Bárbara Summit

Rock face

Picos Jarrin

Refuge

Climb rock behind refuge, lake located beyond the top

TINA VERZOLUE

Photo by Peter Ayarza

Equipment Rubber boots, a machete and lots of plastic bags. You may have some tricky river crossings so bring extra food and a length of rope.

Hiking directions Laguna de San Marcos is a pleasant spot to camp, fish and enjoy the forest. It is easy to see mountain tapir tracks near the lake. The guard (Marco) is friendly and can give advice on day hikes or longer treks.

If you are just camping at the lake you can hike around the lake (1 to 2 hours) or continue down the Río Azuela on a washed-out road, crossing several deep river canyons cut into the flat glacial outwash plains.

For overnight and longer treks continue down the old road south of Río Azuela which eventually turns into a muddy track. You can make an overnight camp in Toldadas (you will need rubber boots but should not have to cut a trail) or continue on longer treks to the lakes east of Nevado Cayambe.

From the guard station and turn-off to Laguna San Marcos, walk on the road east to Quebrada San Pedro. This is the first of three river crossings on your way to Toldadas. If dry the water is ankle deep; if it has been raining heavily then water may be waist deep and dangerous. You follow the old road and ford across the Quebrada San Pedro past the broken-down buildings of an aborted hydro project. Continue on the road to the deep canyon of Río Boqueron; the road has been washed away so look for a trail on the left as the road begins to descend the canyon wall. Cross the river at a destroyed water-gauging station and ascend to the opposite side. About 20 minutes later you need to descend to the Río Arturo canyon and climb to the other side. Soon you lose the wide road and the trail becomes a muddy path. It is frustrating but easy to follow. About 4 hours from San Marcos you arrive at Toldados, a beautiful plain with fern plants, a few palm trees and great views of waterfalls and surrounding hillside cloudforest. The area is soggy but it is possible to find relatively dry spots to camp.

You can continue downstream to lower elevation forest along the Río Azuela where the trail is said to peter out in La Chorra. Perhaps the most adventurous hike is south along the Río Jeronimo to Lagunas Patacocha, Yanococha, and the Planada de La Virgen. There is supposed to be a hot spring on this plain with several lakes. Plan on at least 3 days to reach the Planada de La Virgen and 2 days for your return. The reserve office in Cayambe can help arrange a guide. There is no record of anyone dropping down to Río Salado and exiting at Río Aguarico in the Oriente. This looks like the best route on maps but is probably well-nigh impassable.

Nevado Cayambe (5,790m)

Maps: IGM 1:50,000 Cayambe and Nevado Cayambe

Nevado Cayambe, a massive glaciated extinct volcano, is located about 65km northeast of Quito and is both Ecuador's third highest peak and the third highest peak in the Americas north of the Equator. At about 4,600m on the south side, it also enjoys the distinction of being the highest point on the earth's surface through which the Equator directly passes. It was first climbed in 1880 by, you guessed it, Whymper and the Carrel cousins. Although technically not very difficult it is rather dangerous due to crevasses and avalanches. In 1974 such an avalanche killed three well-known Ecuadorian and French climbers: Joseph Bergé, Carlos Oleas and César Ruales. A refuge, which has been recently refurbished, is located on the southwest flanks of the mountain at 4,600m and named after the three climbers. It has a permanent guardian, running water, gas stove and cooking facilities, and toilets. It is now under the administration of the San Gabriel Climbing Club and the overnight charge is US$10. (See Cayambe map and route diagram.)

Snowstorms and high winds are more frequent on Cayambe than on many other peaks. It can be climbed year round although October through January is said to be the best period.

Access Catch one of the many buses leaving Quito's Terminal Terrestre that go to the town of Cayambe. It is 25km from the town of Cayambe to the refuge, which can be driven most of the way with a normal vehicle and all the way with a 4WD, or at least a vehicle with a strong engine and clearance. There are no buses and hitchhiking is difficult except at weekends when there are some daytrippers from Quito. A truck can be hired in the central square in Cayambe for a lift to the refuge (US$20–25); all the drivers know the route. They will drop you off 2km below the refuge, where the road steepens and becomes quite rocky.

If you are driving your own vehicle look for a sign on the southern edge of town which indicates a turn-off to the east towards Nevado Cayambe. Continue down this road about 30m then turn right. Now heading south, in approximately 200m you will cross an indistinct bridge; turn left just beyond it. There should be a rock painted with 'Cayambe' at this junction. The road from here is cobbled most of the way to the refuge. There are several turn-offs but the locals know the way. You will pass through a short tunnel at Hacienda Piedmonte Bajo (6km) and continue up to Hacienda Piemonte Alto (14km). There is a guard station for the Cayambe-Coca Reserve which is presently unstaffed and does not charge an entrance fee, but this may change. The road flattens before reaching steep switchbacks. Usually this is where hired transport will leave you and it is about 1 hour's walk to the refuge (4,700m).

There is so little traffic midweek that if hitchhiking you'll have to walk most of the way which makes a good hiking trip even if you don't intend to climb the mountain. There are broad views of the ancient lava flows of this now extinct volcano as well as of the Glaciar Hermoso ('beautiful glacier') near to the refuge.

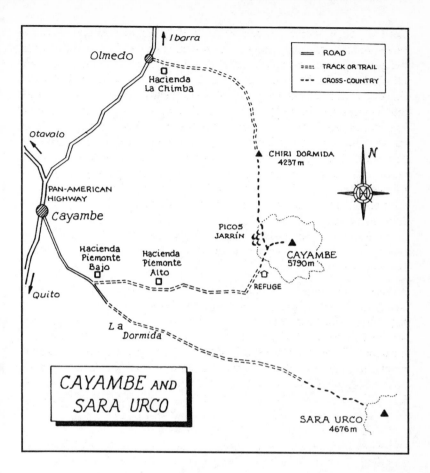

Climbing Cayambe

To climb Cayambe, get as early a start as possible to take advantage of the frozen snow: departure at 23.00 is not unreasonable. It is essential to be down on the lower glacier by 10.00 since later in the day the snow softens and there is a risk of avalanches. There are numerous crevasses which, if hidden by fresh snow, are extremely dangerous. It is important to carry wands for your descent.

Normal route From the refuge scramble up the rocky hill. There are numerous trails, but it is easiest to stay to the right where there are cairns. After reaching the top of the hill (4,830m) in 45 minutes, drop slightly and continue to the right of a green tarn. If you want to avoid hut fees you can camp next to this tarn. Traverse around the right side of the rock outcrop to the base of the glacier. There are numerous small crevasses at the toe of the glacier, but not too much of a problem. From here head approximately northeast towards Picos Jarrin, an emergent rock outcrop on the ridge. A

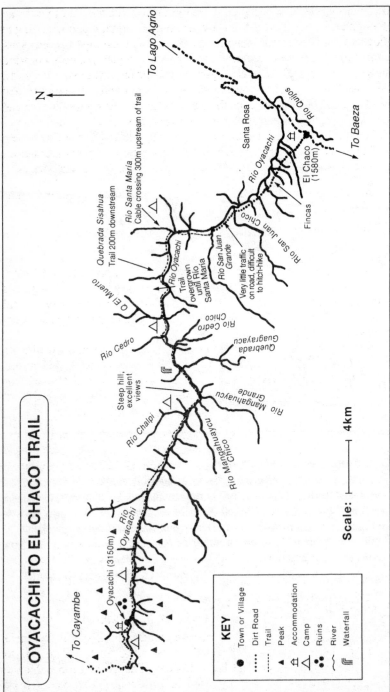

OYACACHI TO EL CHACO TRAIL

Scale: |————| 4km

KEY
● Town or Village
⋯ Dirt Road
⋯ Trail
▲ Peak
⌂ Accommodation
△ Camp
•• Ruins
River
〽 Waterfall

common mistake is to be too far to the right where you must pick your way through a crevasse field. After about an hour of climbing before getting to the Picos, turn east towards another small emergent outcrop (5,200m). Pass either side of the rock and head east-northeast to gain possibly corniced snow on a flat ridge. There is a massive rock and ice cliff to your left and a crevasse field in front of you. Conditions are constantly changing so you need to pick your way through the crevasse field to the right of the ice and rock cliff. The crevasses are large and deep, but obvious.

Reach a bowl with a large crevasse or bergschrund at 5,600m. Route finding around the gaping bergschrund will be necessary. This is a dangerous spot and is where Berge, Ruales and Oleas died. There are two options:

(1) descend into the bergschrund crossing a snow bridge and climb steep snow to the ridge

(2) traverse across the very steep snow slope to the far right of the bergschrund and up the steep slope.

Option 1 is preferable when possible, since there is high avalanche danger and exposure on the steep slope to the right. Once you reach the ridge it is a short hike to the summit (5,790m) with fantastic views. The bergschrund in recent years has presented difficulties and ice climbing may be necessary to pass – bring some ice screws.

During good weather, Cayambe is frequently climbed despite its dangerous reputation so you can sometimes follow footprints and wands from previous parties. Follow the same descent route and watch for avalanche danger and softening snow bridges. Expect to take about 8 to 10 hours to the summit and another 2 to 3 hours back to the refuge.

Old route The old route avoids the refuge completely. You head for the village of Olmedo about 10km northeast of Cayambe town. Mules and guides may be hired from Hacienda La Chimba, in Olmedo's western outskirts. It takes 5 to 8 hours to reach Chiri Dormida where water is available. Camp here. From Chiri Dormida a further 2 to 3 hours are needed to reach Picos Jarrín from where the route continues as on the new normal route. Since the construction of the refuge this route is rarely used.

Cayambe is one of the less explored of Ecuador's major peaks and new routes could be attempted by highly experienced climbers. The mountain has rarely been climbed other than by the Picos Jarrín route described.

Oyacachi to El Chaco hike

Maps: IGM 1:50,000 Oyacachi and Santa Rosa de Quijos

This 3-day hike takes you from the small mountain village of Oyacachi (3,200m), located south of Nevado Cayambe, along the Río Oyacachi, to the frontier jungle town of El Chaco (1,600m). The local legend is that the Oyacachis fled the Incas in the 15th or 16th century, retreating from Cayambe to the Oyacachi valley on the eastern side of the Sierra. From here they persisted relatively unmolested, trading with people in the highlands and the jungle. The Oyacachis never came under the *hacienda* system but the Jesuits had a mission in Cangahua (until they were expelled by the king of Spain in the 18th century) and used this route to supply their missions on the Aguarico and Napo rivers in the Oriente.

This route to the jungle, therefore, is believed to be quite old – it is paved with cobblestones similar to the Inca Trail to Machu Picchu in Peru – but the exact age is not known. There are some interesting stone ruins called Huasipamba near the present town of Oyacachi that are at least a few centuries old. There are also several *fincas* below these ruins that are terraced and probably pre-Columbian.

The cobblestoned trail takes you through the heart of the Cayambe-Coca Ecological Reserve and this is truly wilderness hiking. The trail has fallen into disrepair in the middle section between two big river crossings (Río Cedro and Río Santa María) where bridges were destroyed by an earthquake in 1987. Now only cables precariously stretch across the channels and it is necessary to have a pulley and harness to span the rapids below. The locals slide across on barbed-wire loops attached to their belts or makeshift rope harnesses, but they cannot get their cattle across so the area between these rivers is not deforested and there are good opportunities for birding and animal spotting.

A road was built to Oyacachi in 1995 and access is now much easier for hikers. The government should restore the route down to El Chaco as a national archaeological and natural history trail. It is one of the most interesting walks in Ecuador and would attract people from around the world, as does the Inca Trail in Peru. As it is, the hike is for the prepared and intrepid. (See Oyacachi to El Chaco map, page 146.)

Access Take a 1½-hour bus ride from Calle Manuel Larrea and Portoviejo in Quito to the town of Cayambe. These buses run every 30 minutes until about 19.30. In Cayambe hire a taxi for approximately US$20 to take you 1½ hours on a dirt road to Oyacachi. You can get a bus as far as Cangahua and perhaps can find a pick-up truck to take you the distance to Oyacachi. Walking from Cangahua would take a full day. The village of Oyacachi has no hotels, but you can arrange to stay with a family or camp next to the hot springs on the far side of the river. There is great fresh bread in the carpentry shop on the main street near the church and basic supplies in several small shops. You can pay a visit to the cheese factory up the hill and there is a restaurant under construction near the hot springs. Oyacachi is known for woodworking, and spoons, bowls and sculptures can be purchased. Trout fishing is possible in the streams.

You may want to hire a guide and mules to carry your gear as far as Río Cedro. Mules cost about US$7 per day and a guide charges US$10 per day plus his food. David and José Parión have experience guiding and are the people to contact – they live near the carpentry shop.

Equipment We recommend rubber boots for the mud but, since it is quite rocky, hiking boots would be a good idea for those with weaker ankles. A tent and stove are not absolutely necessary if you plan to stay in one of the wood shacks along the trail. Definitely bring good raingear, one sweater, gloves for vegetation, a machete and insect repellent. For cable crossings you need a strong iron pulley that can pass a 4/5 inch steel cable and that can be disassembled (a normal climbers' pulley would be chewed up by the steel cable). You can purchase a pulley at Kywi on Av 10 de Agosto in Quito for about US$15. Also bring 45m of cord and a climbing harness.

Hiking directions The trail is always on the left side of the Río Oyacachi. Do not try to cross to the other side; the map incorrectly shows a trail on that side of the river.

Find the cobbled trail that leaves the east side of the village of Oyacachi. The first day you will walk along a well-defined muddy trail alternating between pasture and forest. About 30 minutes out of Oyacachi you will encounter an abandoned group of three-sided stone structures with window frames. The Río Cariaco (not named on map) is crossed on a suspension bridge 1½ hours from Oyacachi. The Oyacachi valley soon narrows from a broad U-shaped glacial valley to a steep-sided V-shaped valley. The Río Chalpi is reached after another 2½ hours and can be waded during moderate flow – it is only ankle deep. A cable exists downstream that can be used during high water. From here the trail narrows, becomes more rocky and involves more up and down hiking. About 8 to 9 hours from Oyacachi you arrive at the Río Cedro which is as far as mules normally can go. There are two streams to cross. The first you need to cross on a log; the second involves a cable crossing. You can stay in wood shacks on either side of rivers. It is customary to leave some food or money for the owner. Camping is best on the far side of Río Cedro.

If you have not tried the technique of cable crossing, an explanation is in order. Depending on the type of pulley you are using it must be disassembled and reattached to the cable so you may need pliers to unscrew some bolts. Tie a cord to the pulley so that it can be retrieved from the opposite side of the river after each person has safely crossed. Put on a climbing harness and loop it over the hook on the pulley – do not tie it to the pulley! If for some (very unlikely) reason you are swept into the water you do not want to be attached to the cable because you would not be able to swim to shore. For the same reason do not clip the hip belt on to your pack. Once safely on the other side the next person can retrieve the pulley and climbing harness with the cord. We found that with a pack it was easier to maintain a sitting position with one hand on each side of the cable. If you fall in, get yourself free of the cable and pack and swim to shore. I do not recommend using the barbed-wire loops that the *campesinos* attach to their belts.

The trail from the Río Cedro has numerous hills and is overgrown and difficult to find in places. It is also the most beautiful section of the hike

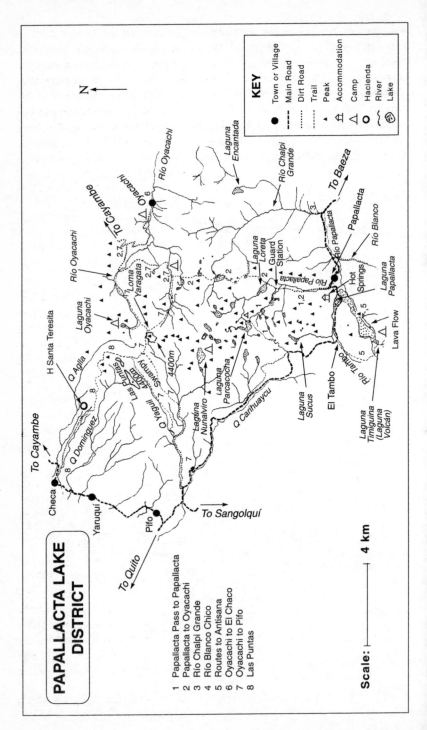

PAPALLACTA LAKE DISTRICT

1 Papallacta Pass to Papallacta
2 Papallacta to Oyacachi
3 Rio Chalpi Grande
4 Rio Blanco Chico
5 Routes to Antisana
6 Oyacachi to El Chaco
7 Oyacachi to Pifo
8 Las Puntas

KEY
Town or Village
Main Road
Dirt Road
Trail
Peak
Accommodation
Camp
Hacienda
River
Lake

Scale: —— 4 km

with great views of primary forest on the opposite bank of the Oyacachi. In two spots you are walking along the bouldery bank of the Río Oyacachi. You are confined to a narrow valley so if you lose the trail it must be somewhere on the slope above or below you. The trail is never more than 100m in elevation above the Río Oyacachi. About an hour from Río Cedro you reach Quebrada El Muerto. The next landmark is Quebrada Sisahua (4 hours from Río Cedro), a gravel-clogged channel where you need to walk downstream to about 200m from the confluence with the Oyacachi and find the faint trail up the bank. About 6 hours from the Río Cedro there is a wooden shack with a view of Río Santa María just beyond. You will reach the banks of this river an hour later to see the ruined foundations of a suspension bridge and a 15m-wide river with Class 5 rapids. Do not try to wade across this river unless it is low water; there is a cable 300m upstream. The landing on the far side is a little awkward on a large boulder. Camping is best on the opposite side of this river.

The trail leaves the gravel banks below the old bridge foundations and from here is well travelled. In about 30 minutes you will see a suspension bridge across the Río Oyacachi which has collapsed into the river. Look for a cable crossing which may be tricky since the river is quite wide here. Note: ask in Oyacachi about this crossing as there are plans to repair the bridge. Once across to the right side of the river it is about 1½ hours to the end of the road. The walk on the road to the town of El Chaco takes about 3 hours depending on the soreness of your feet. Frequent buses pass through the town of El Chaco on their way back to Quito (4 hours).

Papallacta Lake District

The Papallacta Lake District contains hundreds of rocky peaks and glacially carved lakes. It is mostly *páramo* at high elevation and lower down is a mixture of grassy areas with remnants of cloudforest. The area is regularly burned by *campesinos* who have used it for hundreds of years for grazing their cattle. Still the area supports white-tailed deer, Andean fox and Andean spectacled bear populations. The lakes were stocked by the military in the 1940s with rainbow trout, making it a fishers' paradise. We saw a local *campesino* packing over 50 trout back to his home in Papallacta.

Although it is only about 2 hours' drive from Quito, rainy weather and lack of infrastructure have limited recreational use of the area. This is changing as new roads are being built by EMAAP, the municipal water authority of Quito. An access road was bulldozed from Papallacta to Laguna Parcacocha and a road linking Oyacachi to Papallacta is currently under construction. The park service (INEFAN), with the aid of the Nature Conservancy and US AID, have been working to provide long-term protection to the area, but this may prove a difficult task with easier vehicle access.

Trails exist but cross-country travel is relatively straightforward with a compass, map and proper gear. The area is wet and driving hail in a white-out is not uncommon. There are few forested areas so getting shelter from one of the storms is difficult. Occasionally you will run into a log-framed structure built by the *campesinos*. A piece of plastic could come in handy to drape over the beams of the logs to sit out a storm.

Papallacta Pass to Papallacta hike

Maps: IGM 1:50,000 Papallacta and Oyacachi

This is a great 1-day outing from Quito with an optional overnight stay at the hot springs of Papallacta. Take any bus heading to Baeza or beyond. Get off at the pass or at La Virgen, which is a shrine located precisely on the continental divide. Locate the antennae to the north, and follow the unpaved side road to this summit (called Poterillos), passing several *páramo* lakes. The views from Poterillos are some of the best of the Lake District. Follow the ridge trail northwest, then drop down steep grassy slopes on a trail to the east side of Laguna Parcacocha. This is a nice spot to stop and perhaps swim if it is sunny. Follow this track past several lakes and eventually though remnant cloudforest. Connect with the Rio Papallacta road where there is an INEFAN guard station. Turn right and head down to the hot springs. The hike takes 5 to 7 hours. There are numerous buses back to Quito from the town of Papallacta.

The hot springs have been remodelled recently with several pools, changing rooms, a hostel and *cabañas*, and a restaurant. This somewhat upmarket hostel has an indoor thermal pool (US$13 a night). Alternatively there are several more basic hostels in town (US$3 a night). The hot springs only see crowds at weekends so you may well have them to yourselves midweek. They are the best hot springs we have found in Ecuador. The views of Antisana can be superb on a clear day.

Oyacachi to Pifo hike

Maps: IGM 1:50,000 Cayambe, San Pablo del Lago, Mariano Acosta

This is a 2-day hike from the village of Oyacachi to the town of Pifo. For access see *Oyacachi to El Chaco hike,* page 147. Follow the new road out of Oyacachi (not shown on IGM maps) to the 'Y'-junction just below the pass. Turn left on the road that contours up the broad Oyacachi valley. Pass a water diversion tunnel through a ridge to bring Oyacachi water to the thirsty mouths of Quito. About an hour's walking from the intersection you reach the Río Oyacachi. From here there is no established trail, only thick brush and boggy ground, but the way is clear and the views are worth the work. It takes 2 to 3 hours to reach the head of the valley below Loma Yaragata. Climb west for 30 minutes to a grassy bench below steep slopes. One option from here is to hike to the north to Laguna Oyacachi for a secluded camp spot.

Head south-southwest towards the slopes of Yaragata. You should encounter a trail that skirts the north side of this peak and the south side of a flat area known as El Tambo (shown only on 1:25,000 scale map). Along this horse trail are obsidian outcrops and interesting *páramo* plants. Eventually follow the trail to the saddle below Loma Yunguillas. Climb to the top of Yunguillas and follow the rocky ridge (no cliffs) southwest. Drop down to Quebrada Mullumica where a house is located. From here follow the road back to Pifo. From the Laguna Oyacachi to Quebrada Mullumica it is approximately 4 to 6 hours of steady walking.

Alternatively from Yunguillas you can cross Loma Ingaraya and drop into the Quebrada Yanquil. There is no obvious trail, but you can follow cowpaths down this broad U-shaped valley which is a bit boggy. Where the stream valley becomes steep and the valley V-shaped, follow a disused irrigation ditch on the left-hand side of the valley. Eventually crest on to the pastures of Loma Cole Pugra, and follow the ridge down to the road. Walk down the cobbled road to the Quito–Papallacta road, arriving near the town of Pifo.

Papallacta to Oyacachi hike

Maps: IGM 1:50,000 Papallacta and Oyacachi
The hike from Papallacta to Oyacachi takes 2 days and requires route-finding skills through hilly terrain of *páramo* and grasses. It has the advantage of starting and ending in towns with thermal springs. There are excellent views of rocky peaks to the east and large trout-stocked lakes. A road (closed to public traffic) is planned for this route which will make the walk easier.

Access Take a bus to Papallacta (see *Reventador* description, page 229). You can arrange for truck transport to Termas Papallacta (hot springs) where you can spend the night. If you decide to begin your hike from the town, head up the hill to a sign that marks the turn-off to the springs. Follow the dirt road, switchbacking up pasture which eventually levels out in a broad glacial valley. You will pass a large trout farm just before reaching the parking lot of the thermal springs. This is a good base for exploring surrounding cloudforest flora and fauna.

Continue following the road up the valley. You can arrange for transport to the end of the road, but the walk is pleasant and car traffic is limited. There are many interesting orchids, trees and birds. Evidence of the last glaciation is present in the glacially polished and striated andesitic bedrock outcropping along the road. After about 5km you reach a 'Y' in the road where the INEFAN guard station is in a small concrete house. This is where the hike from Papallacta pass connects to the road.

Follow the right branch of the road to Laguna Loreto where a small dam is located at the mouth of the lake. This is where the road is being constructed to Oyacachi so either walk on the dirt track or follow the directions below.

Cross the dam and head north-northeast up the grassy hill following an unmarked trail. Stay right of the rocky hill to the left and you will soon reach a small flat area. Contour up the slope in a northerly direction until reaching a larger flat area. Cross the small stream on a log bridge – this is also a good place to camp. Follow the trail that skirts the edge of this flat area in a counter-clockwise direction. You will pass a turn-off to the east; keep heading north uphill. The trail passes a log frame shelter and hugs the northeast side of the valley above an unnamed lake. In the distance is a pass which must be crossed. The descent from the pass goes to the left of two small lakes in somewhat swampy terrain. The large Laguna Mangashina (unnamed on IGM map) can be seen below. This lake would be a nice place to camp and I saw several Papallacteños with a catch of over a hundred trout. It is approximately 3 to 4 hours from the end of the road at Laguna Loreto to Laguna Mangashina.

Follow the trail on the east side of the lake to the outlet stream, then cross and climb up the steep hill on the opposite side to a bench with a flat, rather swampy area to the northeast. Loma Yaragata is a prominent, pyramid-shaped peak to the west. Head north, avoiding the swamp, soon arriving at a lake hidden from view. Look for a low pass to the west of a loaf-shaped hill in front of you. From this pass descend the slopes on the left side of the stream drainage to a beautiful valley containing Laguna Picocha (unnamed on map). There is another log-framed structure above the lake which is an excellent camping spot.

Cross the outlet stream and head north over a low ridge, skirting to the west of the flat swampy area until gaining a 2m-wide stream. Wade across knee-deep water and follow the northern bank downstream. There should be 20–30m cliffs on the opposite bank. After about 30 minutes you reach a bluff with a trail; ascend to the top of the bluff. Head north-northeast and soon you will get a view of the Oyacachi valley. Descend through the cloudforest or find the landslide scar scrambling down a slippery trail. Reach some grassy slopes and follow them to the flat valley floor. The trail ends on a very steep grassy nose just in front of a small hill that is oddly detached from the main slope. The notch at the bottom divides two stream drainages. If you are coming from the other direction it is important to find this low divide. From the notch follow the east on mushy flat ground, crossing Río Oyacachi and soon arriving at the road. From Laguna Mangashina it is approximately 4 to 6 hours. An hour of walking on the road brings you to Oyacachi. Here you can buy basic supplies and soak in a large concrete pool which is warm but not as nice as the thermal waters in Papallacta. There are no hotels in Oyacachi but you may be able to arrange to rent a room in a house. At the time of writing there was no bus service to Oyacachi, but pick-up trucks do travel back to Cayambe several times a day.

Las Puntas

Maps: IGM 1:50,000 El Quinche, Oyacachi and Sangolqui
The name of this serrated ridge of peaks means 'the points'. This area can be seen on a clear day from the Hotel Quito, located only 28km east of the

city, but oddly it is rarely visited. If you want to avoid the weekend crowds on Rucu Pichincha, Las Puntas will probably offer solitude. There are dozens of separate small peaks that offer good rock climbing and many opportunities for first ascents.

The rock consists of a layer of andesite covered by an agglomerate (mixture of lava cobbles and ash that were deposited and welded together while the material was still partially molten). The surrounding hillsides are covered by the ash deposits that fill the central valley. The upper agglomerate unit is knobby with many handholds and footholds, but they are not secure and placing protection is difficult.

Access To get to Las Puntas from Quito take a bus going north from 6 de Diciembre to the Plaza Argentina roundabout (Partidero Tumbaco). Catch an El Quinche bus at the eastern exit on the road which heads into the Oriente. The bus goes through the villages of Cumbaya, Tumbaco, Puembo, Yaruqui, Checa and El Quinche. Get off at Checa 1½ hours from Quito.

Hiking directions Walk out of town uphill, cross a railway line just beyond the village and take the obvious cobbled road to the right. There are several turn-offs but stay on this main cobbled road up Loma Achachi to Hacienda Santa Teresita (3,250m). It is possible to drive with a 4WD vehicle as far as Hacienda Santa Teresita and, for the adventurous, to the top of Loma Grande in front of you. There is water at the *hacienda*, the last good water before reaching the east side of Las Puntas. Stay on the cobbled road that continues to the right above the *hacienda*. Pass another small house, then the road becomes black dirt. The road forks above this house; take the right fork that switchbacks up Loma Grande passing through many barbed-wire gates (do not forget to close them after you pass). The left fork takes you to Quebrada Aglla which is the valley to the north of Loma Grande with what looks like good multiple-pitch crack climbing on the far side of the valley. The road reaches the top of the hill with views of Las Puntas. Continue on the road until it arrives at a gentle pass (4,115m). You can camp here, but there's no water. It is approximately 6 to 8 hours of walking to reach this point from Checa, perhaps 2 hours by car if the road and weather conditions are good. A track through the grass heads up towards the crags of Las Puntas Chiquito, but deteriorates to a cowpath that contours around the base of the rocks. You will reach a grassy ridge and have to drop down below some rocky gullies, then climb to regain a saddle between Loma Puntas Chiquito and Loma Contrayerba. Crossing these gullies is a little tricky. The cliffs of Quebrada Aglla can be seen across the valley to the north, and an irrigation channel is below you. From the saddle, traverse on a cowpath to the east side of Las Puntas. The trail is difficult to follow on this side and requires some bushwhacking through colourful *páramo* vegetation. There are many seeps on the east side for water.

From here you have many opportunities for hiking. You can return to Checa the way you came or down the Quebrada Aglla valley. A pleasant-looking lake for camping is located at the headwaters of the Quebrada Aglla at the base of some cliffs and can be seen from Las Puntas.

Las Puntas to Oyacachi hike
Traverse the east side of Las Puntas to Loma Ingaraya and crest to the top of this exposed ridge to find the trail. Head south to Loma Yanguil which looks like a large rock on the ridge. Just past this hill look for a trail heading east towards a flat swampy area known as El Tambo and continue to the Oyacachi Valley.

Other hikes in Reserva Ecológica Cayambe-Coca
Río Salado hike It is possible to ascend the Río Salado starting from the Baeza to Lago Agrio road following a trail at least as far as the Río Cascabel.

Río Chalpi hike A trail heads up the east side of the Río Chalpi with good cloudforest. It may be possible to reach Laguna Encantada.

La Bonita to Lumbaqui hike It is possible to walk/canoe from La Bonita on the northern edge of the reserve to Lumbaqui in the Oriente, utilizing a canoe for the lower part of journey. This journey takes 3 to 4 days and passes through Cofán communities.

Bosque Protector Los Cedros It is a 5-hour walk to Bosque Los Cedros from km75 (Guayacan) on the Baeza to Lago Agrio road.

Oyacachi to Hacienda Piemonte hike You can walk north from Oyacachi linking the villages of Gualimburo, Pisarubilla and Sayaro and ending at Hacienda Piemonte on the road to the refuge on Cayambe. This is a several-day hike over the *páramo*.

Laguna Encantada It may be possible to walk from Oyacachi to Laguna Encantada; ask in Oyacaci for directions.

Río Blanco Chico You can walk up several kilometres through good cloudforest to an abandoned water-gauging station. There are tapir tracks and good birding.

CERRO SARA URCO (4,670M)

Maps: IGM 1:50,000 Cangahua and Cerro Saraurco

'With turned out toes we went cautiously along the crisp arête, sharp as a
roof-top, and at 1.30pm stood on the true summit of Sara-Urco; a shattered
ridge of gneiss - wonder of wonders, blue sky above - strewn with fragments
of quartz and micaschist... without a hint of vegetation.'

Edward Whymper, 1892

Sara Urco is one of Ecuador's few
non-volcanic peaks and lies about
15km southeast of Cayambe peak.
Despite its low altitude it is normally
snow capped so many sources and
climbers believe it to be higher than
the given IGM elevation. It is surrounded by jumbled-up
páramo which is either boggy or brushy and difficult to move
through; hence this is not a frequently climbed mountain.
It is technically straightforward and was first climbed in
1880 by Whymper and the Carrels, who seem to have got

everywhere. December and January are the best climbing months; the rest of the year is wet.

Although we haven't climbed this peak we have obtained the following description from various climbers in Ecuador.

Access is the same as for Cayambe (see page 144) as far as the Hacienda Piemonte, after which you turn right (left leads to Cayambe). About 3km beyond the *hacienda* the road peters out. Somewhere around here lives Señor Juan Farinango who is the local guide and can arrange mule hire.

Hiking directions On the first day the guides take you in a generally southeasterly direction past an area known as La Dormida; several small rivers must be forded. The *páramo* in this region is known locally as *pantano* which means 'marsh' or 'swamp'. In realistic hiking terms this means you can expect lots of mud and huge clumps of *ichu* grass. It takes a day to reach the Río Volteado where camp is set up.

The following day you continue in a southeasterly direction to the foot of the southwest ridge which is easy to ascend to the summit. You'll probably need to camp high on the mountain and make the summit on the third day. A small summit glacier will have to be negotiated.

Due to the inhospitable nature of the surroundings it is advisable to hire mules and a guide.

RESERVA ECOLÓGICA ANTISANA

Maps: IGM 1:50,000 Papallacta, Laguna de Mica, Sincholagua, Cotopaxi

Reserva Ecológica Antisana was established in 1994 by INEFAN to protect 120,000ha that include seven ecological zones ranging in elevation from high *páramo* to lowland rainforest. A large portion of the reserve is *páramo*, but like Reserva Ecológica Cayambe-Coca it protects largely untravelled Andean eastern slope terrain including the Cordillera de Los Guacamayos which connects with Parque Nacional Sumaco Napo-Galeras located in the Oriente. The centrepiece of the reserve is Volcán Antisana, a heavily glaciated volcanic peak. Also within the reserve is Laguna Mica, a famous spot for trout fishers.

Coordinating with INEFAN to promote and manage this new reserve is Fundación Antisana (FUNAN), a private non-profit organization based in Quito. They maintain two field offices, one in Píntag for the high elevation region and the other in Borja for the low elevation region, for activity management in the reserve. In addition, FUNAN offers full-service accommodation in a large, well-equipped encampment at 4,000m on the *páramo* of Antisana. It is within a 5-hour hike of the climbers' base camp, and well situated with respect to several points of interest in the reserve. The encampment is available to everyone but is not an open refuge. Stays must be arranged in advance for groups of up to 30. The cost is fixed according to group size and needs. FUNAN can be contacted in Quito at tel: 433849 or 433850; the office is located at Mariana de Jesús and Carvejal, above the San Gabriel church. In Píntag, the contact number is tel: 383 178. There is a US$10 entrance fee to the reserve. (See Antisana map page 160.)

Volcán Antisana

Volcán Antisana (5,758m) is the fourth highest mountain in Ecuador, but is seldom seen by tourists because of its position some 55km southeast of Quito well away from any main road. The broad summit contains four separate peaks which are, in descending order, the main, east, northeast, and south summits. Their elevations are widely disagreed upon. These four summits represent the highest points of a crater rim; the crater itself is totally filled with glacial ice and doesn't appear to be active. For this reason Antisana is popularly supposed to be extinct, but vulcanologists claim that its comparatively recent major eruptions indicate that the volcano is, in fact, still active. The 10km-long lava flow near the Hacienda Pinantura, to the west of the mountain, is attributed to an eruption around 1760, and the 6km-long flow by Laguna Papallacta, to the north of the mountain, dates from 1773. Both these flows originated from fissures in the sides of the volcano, thus a cone is absent. Some fumarolic activity still exists near the highest summit.

The climbing history of this mountain is predictable: another first ascent by Whymper and the Carrels in 1880. Whymper wrote that he could smell sulphurous fumes during the ascent. The lower peaks are more of a challenge and did not see conquests until the 1970s by various Ecuadorian climbers.

The access town of Píntag, with its cobbled streets and tiled roofs, is unusually attractive and the surrounding farmland green and beautiful. The *páramo* near Antisana is more varied than usual. Flowering *puya* plants are plentiful, providing nectar for the many hummingbirds, and there are even some rather subdued looking *frailejones*. The further east or 'around the back' of the mountain you go, the more likely you are to see animals such as the white-tailed deer, mountain tapir, puma and spectacled bear. Lava fields are a fascinating feature of this area. Antisana itself is a splendid sight with its four peaks covered with blue glaciers; to the west is Cotopaxi showing its best profile.

A jeep road runs to the foot of Antisana. Very little traffic uses this track which is in poor condition and ideal for hiking. Many people will choose to return by the same route, but it is possible to hike cross-country to Papallacta on the Quito–Lago Agrio road, or to cross the *páramo* to Cotopaxi via Sincholagua.

Access The approach to the base of Antisana has presented some difficulties in recent years. EMAAP (Quito water utility) has built a new paved road so driving from Píntag is a breeze with a normal car, but you still must obtain permission to pass through the locked gate at the Delgado family's *hacienda* (Hacienda Pintura). The other option is to walk or hitchhike either along the same road from Píntag or on the trail from Papallacta.

The Delgado family will send you back to Quito if you have not paid for permission to enter the reserve. The cost for an entry permit can be anywhere from US$8 to US$25 per vehicle. The number to call is 455 697; the contact person is Mario Palleres. FUNAN will help with access if you are using their facilities and give them several days' advance notice.

Buses leave from Plaza La Marin in Quito several times a day for the hour-long journey to Píntag through lovely scenery and pretty villages. In Píntag, you may decide to hire transport (US$20) to go the 25km to Hacienda El Hato (also known as Hacienda Antisana). The road continues a considerable distance past the *hacienda* to Laguna Micacocha, a popular fishing lake.

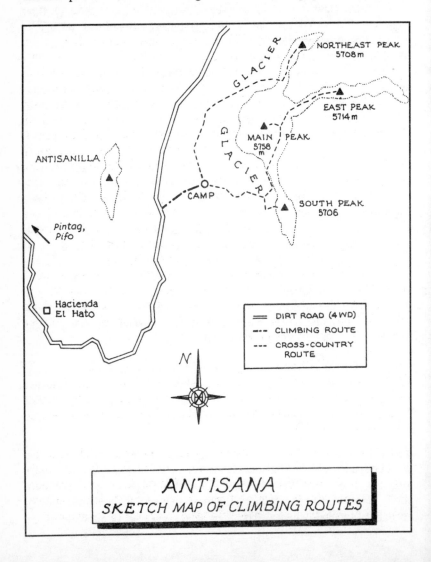

ANTISANA

SKETCH MAP OF CLIMBING ROUTES

On foot from Píntag, head on the paved road to a gravel mine at the toe of the lava flow which is over 200 years old and covered with moss and shrubs. You have the choice of following a path across the lava for a while, or continuing up the new road, or contouring around on the old road to the *hacienda*. If you decide to cross the lava you need to ask for directions to the trail since construction activity has altered the area. Along this trail there are beautiful little rock gardens between the chunks of lava, and all sorts of flowers can be admired. It's worth going out of your way to find a flowering *puya* with its apple-green flowers. After about an hour of lava-leaping you will want to join the road. Look out for an easy access place on your right where the lava cliff is low and no scrambling is involved. Once on the paved road you simply keep walking past a string of beautiful lakes dammed by the lava flows and over several bridges. Continue up the road as it twists and turns through broad fields and *páramo* and look out for short cuts if you're on foot.

About 25km by road after Hacienda Pintura you'll pass the Hacienda El Hato (Hacienda Antisana). Another 3–4km due south is Laguna Micacocha. To reach Antisana turn left, or northwest, on a rapidly deteriorating track. The area is flat pastureland and looks very eerie in low evening sunlight with dozens of cattle skulls dotting the landscape. One route to the base is to follow the track for about 8km where it peters out high in the *páramo* west of the mountain. From here head east for another 2km and make your base camp close to the snowline. Another popular camp is just below the South Peak on a glacial moraine called the South Crespo. To get here, either drive across the Río Antisana, risking getting your vehicle stuck and damaging fragile *páramo* vegetation, or park your car here and continue on foot. Follow the *páramo* up towards the South Peak staying on the south bank of the river. Camp at the toe of the glacier.

The weather is generally wet and cold. If your tent and raingear aren't waterproof you'll probably be miserable – and if you think they're waterproof you'll know for sure by the end of your hike. With Oriente weather conditions prevailing, the driest months are November through February; the wettest months are June through August.

Climbing Antisana

Maps: The IGM 1:100,000 Píntag map gives a good overview of the area and is probably all you need for climbing, but the smaller-scale 1:50,000 maps of Píntag, Papallacta, Laguna Micacocha, Sincholagua and Cotopaxi will be useful for hiking.

Antisana is one of the more difficult peaks in Ecuador to climb and is dangerous because of the many crevasses and bad weather. It is not for the inexperienced. The lengthy access and lack of a mountain refuge compound your problems; this is the highest peak in Ecuador with no hut, and you have to carry complete wet-weather camping gear and food for several days.

Main summit

From the base camp of the South Crespo climb up to the glacier about a ½-hour away. Looking left you'll see the main summit of Antisana, the south peak to the right and a centre ridge separating the two. Head across and up the glacier aiming for the lowest point on this centre ridge. Because of constantly changing snow conditions there's no 'best way' to get there. You'll have to do a bit of route-finding through the snowfields (and crevasses) for the best route up to the ridge. This area should be wanded. Just before you reach the low point on the ridge, a glacier to the left leads to the main summit, ascending just below the ridge. Approaching the summit, stay east (right) of the ice walls on the southeast face. Keep nearer and parallel to the ridgeline, continuing up in a northeast direction as you traverse below the summit. Just as the northeast and east peaks come into view, head left (northwest) up to the main summit. The climb takes 7 to 8 hours in good conditions and without too many route-finding problems.

Another route is to head straight up the glacier; there are numerous crevasses and seracs to negotiate. The route steepens towards the summit with possible vertical ice near the summit plateau.

South Peak

This mixed rock/ice route was first climbed by an American team in the '60s. It's a more difficult climb than the main summit and requires technical equipment, not to mention experience. To climb the south peak follow the route for the main summit to below the same low point on the centre ridge. From here you can see the rocky summit of the south peak to the right. Climb the snowfield which ascends right and leads to a high ridge below the summit. Set up camp at the top of the glacier just below the ridge. It's about a 4 to 6 hour climb from the base camp.

The following day climb to the top of the ridge and follow it up to the rocky base of the summit. At the base, traverse right to a steep snow couloir and ascend it, angling up left to an obvious ramp of volcanic sand. Follow the ramp as it angles up and left. Caution is advised here as no belay is possible and a fall would be disastrous. Continue up the ramp to a rock chimney of 50m, where various sizes of rock protection will be needed for the ascent. Above the chimney there's another 30m of easy climbing to the top of the rock section. Here you'll come to the upper snowfield for the final traverse (right) to the summit. Allow about 6 to 7 hours to reach the summit and another 3 hours back to the snow camp. The following day will get you down to the base camp and breathing easy.

East Peak

This is probably the most difficult of the Antisana summits. You'll need the full regalia of ice gear, including screws and stakes, and even jumars would be helpful. Follow the same route up toward the main peak and set up camp about 50m below the summit. Here you'll find a flat area on the east slope just past the ice walls. A little farther up the snowfield is the ridge which connects the east summit with the main peak. On the second day follow the ridge toward the east summit to a high point called Pico Colgante ('hanging peak') about an hour from camp. Here you'll see that 'hanging peak' gets its name from an extremely deep crevasse which cuts off the approach to the summit. Crossing it involves a rappel down and pendulum across to the lower summit ridge. Set up a fixed rope for the jumar/prussik exercise awaiting you on the return. After all that, begin the ascent of the summit ridge which drastically narrows, provides dramatic views of huge drops on either side, and forces you to sit and scoot along. To wrap up the trip to the summit, climb the 20m ice wall at the end of the ridge – about 60° to 70°.

Northeast Peak

This route was first climbed in 1972 by Santiago Rivadeneira, Leonardo Menses and Hugo Torres. It's not a particularly difficult climb, but some route-finding problems and steep snow/ice make it challenging. From the lower base camp head left along the moraine until you're in line with the main summit. An alternative camp can be set up here as there's plenty of water available. The climb begins by ascending the glacier seen to the left of the main peak. Find the best route up to the ridge which separates the main summit from the northeast peak. Climb this ridge and follow it to the summit. A steep section of snow/ice, about 50° to 60°, will have to be negotiated just below the summit. Allow about 6 to 8 hours to the top.

Antisana to Papallacta hike

Maps: The IGM 1:100,000 Píntag map gives a good overview of the area and is probably all you need for climbing, but the smaller-scale 1:50,000 maps of Píntag, Papallacta, Laguna Micacocha, Sincholagua and Cotopaxi will be useful for hiking.

Hikers and climbers can follow the description (in reverse) to El Tambo to get to the Quito–Lago Agrio road (see *Antisana to Cotopaxi hike*, page 165). Those wishing to continue northwards to Papallacta will have to go cross-country. This is not easy as there are no paths, the countryside is rough, and the vegetation can be extremely dense, especially in the valley bottoms. From the climbers' base camp one heads roughly north to the east of peak 4144. Cross several stream valleys staying well above the cloudforest passing to the east of peak 3857. Continue contouring around several stream valleys until you are directly above an unnamed lake and can see pastures heading down to several huts. Do not be tempted to head down into the cloudforest. From the mouth of the lake (northeast side) follow a faint trail downstream along the Río Tumiguina. This trail soon veers away from the river valley and through the lava flow to a gravel pit. From the gravel pit a road leads to Laguna Papallacta and the Quito–Lago Agrio road. If you

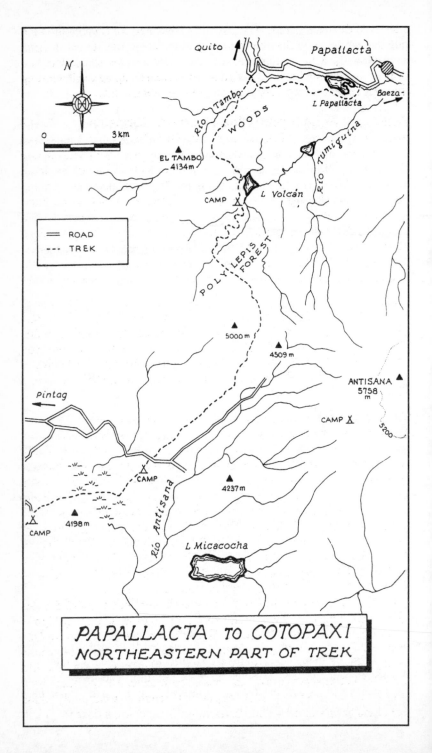

PAPALLACTA TO COTOPAXI
NORTHEASTERN PART OF TREK

wanted to do the hike in reverse, from Papallacta to Antisana, your main problem would be to find the beginning of the rough trail across the lava flow. Once on it, it is straightforward to follow it to the lake where you head up the slope and south to Antisana. This is a challenging and interesting route that requires maps, compass and route-finding ability.

Antisana to Cotopaxi hike (Trek de Cóndor)

Maps: IGM 1:50,000 Papallacta, Laguna de Mica, Sincholagua, Cotopaxi

More than a few seasoned trekkers claim that the walk from Antisana to Cotopaxi is one of the best in Ecuador. It certainly is one of the more challenging, being physically demanding and requiring some route-finding ability. It can also test one's capacity for inclement weather and mud-slogging, depending on the season. The hike takes you over the *páramo* past the peaks of Antisana, Sincholagua and finally Cotopaxi. There is a good chance you will also see a condor, hence the Ecuadorian name for the hike: Trek de Cóndor. The hike takes 4 to 5 days and there is a good chance for rain so come prepared. (See Papallacta to Cotopaxi maps opposite and page 166.)

Access Take a bus from the Terminal Terrestre in Quito to Papallacta (any bus going through Baeza). Cross over a 4,100m pass where there is a shrine to the Virgin and the first impressive views of Antisana (this is the beginning of the Papallacta Pass to Papallacta hike, above). Tell the bus driver you want to get off at El Tambo, a broad river valley where the road makes a sharp bend about 4km before you get to Laguna Papallacta. There are several houses at this bend and a kiosk.

Hiking directions Pick up a faint trail which leads up on the right-hand side of the Río Tambo. After about half an hour, jump across and continue up the left side of the river. There are numerous cattle trails. You'll be heading southwest up the Río Tambo valley for 3km until you reach the base of the long flat-topped hill called El Tambo (4,134m). Here a more defined trail turns south away from the river and angles up through *páramo* and *polylepis* forest to a hummocky pass area on the opposite side of the valley from the peak El Tambo. Continue in a southeasterly direction over boggy countryside for a couple of kilometres until you are within sight of Laguna Tumiguina (or Laguna Vulcán). The trail comes in on the upstream end of the lake where there are some flat camping areas. From the main road it's about 3 to 4 hours to reach Laguna Tumiguina.

Camping early by the lake will give you enough time to make the 1½-hour circuit around it, if you're still keen for a bit of walking. Stay high as you make the round trip. Below the far end of the lake there is a lava field that you can explore. This area offers a variety of interesting vegetation including orchids. To the right you'll see a small hill which can be scaled for some impressive views of Antisana if the weather is clear. There is no trail across the lava and the rocks can be quite rough, so wear sturdy hiking boots and be prepared for a little scrambling. In order to continue the circuit

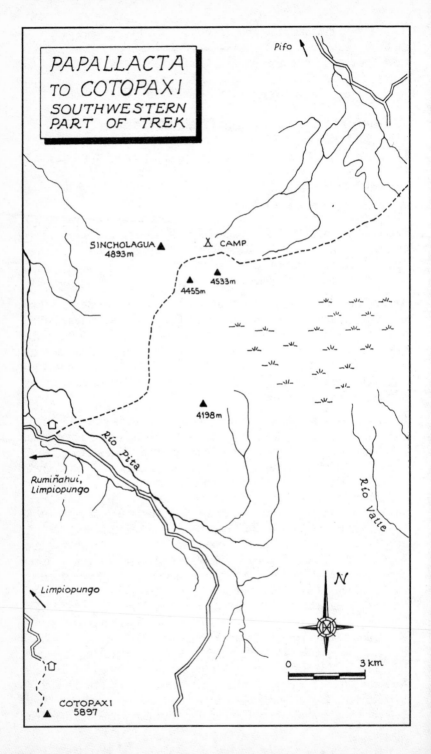

PAPALLACTA
TO COTOPAXI
SOUTHWESTERN
PART OF TREK

Pifo

SINCHOLAGUA ▲
4893m

✗ CAMP

▲ 4533m
▲
4455m

▲
4198m

Río Pita

Rumiñahui,
Limpiopungo

Río Valle

Limpiopungo

N

0   3 km

COTOPAXI
5897

of the lake, you'll have to backtrack across the lava to the main trail. Attempting to continue across the lava and pick up the trail on the other end promises difficult scrambling through high grass and fording many small streams and waterfalls. Add about 3 hours and a high level of frustration if you decide to try it.

On the second day the trail ascends from Laguna Tumiguina for some 3 to 4 hours to Laguna Santa Lucia at the base of Antisana. It is important to find the correct trail from the lake; many people get lost. If you try to head directly up slopes to the east of the lake you will be blocked by thick cloudforest. Head upstream (south) from the lake about 300m to the point where three rivers form a confluence. Ascend the well-defined trail between Quebrada Sunfohuaycu and the stream directly to the east. This trail switchbacks up grassy slopes eventually crossing a narrow cloudforest band. Once above this band follow the trail as it climbs to the east side of Antisanilla (shown as Loma Chosalongo Grande on the IGM map). You are also walking on a contour around a large basin to your left. The trail starts to peter out as the grassy vegetation changes to cushion-plants but just head cross-country (a bit boggy) more or less in the direction of Antisana. There are herds of semi-wild horses in this area along with a number of lapwings, Andean gulls and perhaps a condor or two. Below the flanks of Antisana you will once again pick up a trail which ascends an easy uphill section to a plateau. There is a shallow lake called Laguna Santa Lucia between Antisana and the small rocky peaks of Antisanilla on the right. Camping by the lake is recommended for the views of Antisana but is somewhat exposed to the weather. If time allows, scramble up Antisanilla for excellent sunset views.

From the lake follow a faint track over a hill and descend to a stream where an equally pleasant camp can be set up. Allow about 6 to 7 hours from Laguna Tumiguina to this camp.

The next day's hike of about 6 to 8 hours from the stream camp goes from the base of Antisana heading across *páramo* toward Cerro Sincholagua. You will pass Hacienda El Hato then the going will be mostly cross-country, without the benefit of an established trail, on a golf-course-like plain. Because of this, the route described here may not be exactly what you find but you can't go wrong by heading straight for the high peak of Sincholagua.

From camp, looking right across the stream, you'll see a desert-like hill which has been overgrazed by sheep. Climb this hill and continue across the *páramo* where you'll eventually cross another stream and see another overgrazed area to the left. Here and further along there'll be a series of small *páramo* hills on your right and a prominent hill on the left. Skirt the base of the large hill, keeping to the right, and you'll enter a valley of *almohadones*, tussock-like mounds of spongy vegetation – marshy, and awkward for walking.

Cross the valley as best you can, keeping Sincholagua ahead and to the right. Just beyond the valley there will be two streams to cross in succession. Look for a good camping place between the two.

The following day, cross the second stream and follow the trail leading up a hill, all the time heading directly for Sincholagua. There may be a few cattle tracks in this area but don't follow anything unless it leads in the direction of the volcano. As you near the base of the peak, you'll see a clump of *polylepis* trees and an area of huge rocks looking like ships. The trail meanders between the two, and leads into a wet, marshy valley of more tussock. Crossing the valley, you'll have the base of Sincholagua on the right and high *páramo* hills on the left. Aim for the low point between the two (it's about 1½ to 2 hours from the *polylepis* trees to this low pass) and look for the best place to set up camp as soon as you're out of the marshy valley. It ought to take about 5 to 7 hours from camp to camp. Water is not dependable here. If you can't find any, you may have to continue on another 2 to 4 hours.

From the camp near the base of Sincholagua the trail continues to skirt along the slopes for about 1 to 2 hours to an obvious pass marked by a few cairns. From this high point, you'll see Cotopaxi straight ahead and Rumiñahui off to the right. Descend the slope from the pass, keeping left and making a direct line with Cotopaxi for the easiest way down. It's about 2 to 4 hours down to a river and jeep track where you can camp.

From the jeep track there are several possibilities to finish the trek. If you follow the road going right it's a half day's walk to Laguna Limpiopungo. Heading cross-country will get you to the Cotopaxi refuge in about 3 to 4 hours, or you can pick up the trail to Mulaló which is described in the *Hiking around Cotopaxi* section page 172.

PARQUE NACIONAL COTOPAXI AND SURROUNDINGS

'Cotopaxi's shape is the most beautiful and regular of all the colossal peaks in the high Andes. It is a perfect cone covered by a thick blanket of snow which shines so brilliantly at sunset it seems detached from the azure of the sky.'

Alexander von Humboldt, 1802

The Galápagos islands excepted, this is without a doubt Ecuador's showpiece national park. There are picnic areas, camping sites, huts and a mountain refuge, making it somewhat similar to the national parks in North America and Europe.

The centrepiece of the park is Volcán Cotopaxi (5,897m) which lies about 55km south of Quito and whose symmetrical cone can often be seen from the capital on a clear day. This active volcano is Ecuador's second highest mountain and it has long been considered the highest active volcano in the world (although recent claims in favour of Tupungato on the Argentine-Chilean border cannot be discounted).

The history of Cotopaxi's activity is the most dramatic in Ecuador.

Although other volcanoes may be more active geologically, Cotopaxi has caused the most death and destruction. Records of its eruptions date back to 1534 though it was undoubtedly active long before then. After a long period of dormancy Cotopaxi erupted three times in 1742, destroying the town of Latacunga and killing hundreds of people and livestock. More eruptions followed in 1743, 1744 and 1766. A major eruption in 1768 again destroyed Latacunga, which had been rebuilt, with much loss of life and property. Almost a century of inactivity followed, but in 1853 Cotopaxi again began to display its awesome power and erupted frequently for several years. Four separate eruptions occurred in 1877 and that of June 26 produced catastrophic lahars (avalanches of ice, snow, water, mud and rocks), one of which reached Esmeraldas on the Pacific coast; another swept down on ill-fated Latacunga, wiping out the greater part of it yet again. This lahar was recorded as having reached the town in 30 minutes. Latacunga lies 35km southwest of Cotopaxi as the crow flies but the lahar would have followed the lie of the land by a more circuitous route – the concept of a huge wall of volcanic and glacial debris sweeping toward one at some 90km per hour, or 25m per second, is impossible to comprehend. As Michael Andrews remarks in *The Flight of the Condor*, 'I find it very curious that Latacunga has been rebuilt repeatedly on its old site.' Frequent but minor eruptions continued for eight years after this catastrophe. Since 1885 eruptions have been limited to two minor ones in 1903 and 1904, and a disputed one in 1942. Fumarolic activity continues in Cotopaxi's crater at present, as anyone who has climbed the volcano will know.

Cotopaxi was first climbed in 1872 from the southwest by the German geologist Wilhelm Reiss, accompanied by Angel M Escobar, a Colombian. A few months later the German, Stübel, accompanied by four Ecuadorians (Jantui, Páez, Ramón and Rodriguez), logged the first Ecuadorian ascent. Edward Whymper with the Carrel cousins spent a night on the summit in 1880, a somewhat hazardous exercise bearing in mind the restless nature of the volcano at that time. Since then many successful ascents have been made and today the mountain is a popular destination for weekend mountaineers and tourists from Quito as well as foreign climbers. Despite its relative simplicity this is not a climb for the inexperienced, and beginners should avail themselves of professional guides.

The national park surrounding the volcano offers excellent hiking and camping opportunities as well as lesser peaks to climb. Rumiñahui (4,712m) and Morurco (c4,840m) lie within the park boundaries and the peaks of Sincholagua (4,893m) and Quilindaña (4,878m) are found just outside the park. There is talk of extending the park boundaries. Hiking a complete circuit around the base of Cotopaxi is a good 6–7-day trip and all the above peaks can be seen or climbed. (See Cotopaxi map page 170.)

Access You can reach the museum and administration centre of the park from the El Boliche (closed to vehicles) or Lasso entrances on the Pan-

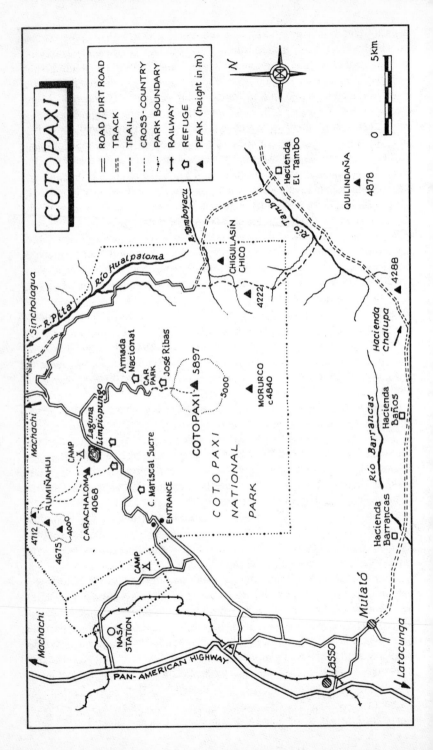

COTOPAXI

Legend:
- ROAD / DIRT ROAD
- TRACK
- TRAIL
- CROSS-COUNTRY
- PARK BOUNDARY
- RAILWAY
- REFUGE
- PEAK (height in m)

N

5km

0

Río Tamboyacu

Hacienda El Tambo

QUILINDAÑA ▲ 4878

Río Hualpaloma

Río Tambo

CHIGUILASÍN CHICO ▲

▲ 4222

▲ 4288

Sincholagua

R. Pita

Machachi

Armada Nacional
CAR PARK
José Ribas

COTOPAXI ▲ 5897

5000

MORURCO ▲ c4840

Laguna Limpiopungo

CAMP

RUMIÑAHUI ▲

4712 ▲

4675 ▲

4000

CARACHALOMA ▲ 4068

C. Mariscal Sucre

ENTRANCE

COTOPAXI NATIONAL PARK

Hacienda Chalupa

Río Barrancas

Hacienda Baños

Machachi

CAMP

NASA STATION

PAN-AMERICAN HIGHWAY

Mulaló

Hacienda Barrancas

LASSO

Latacunga

American Highway. There is no public transportation into the park but it is easy to get to these turn-offs by taking a southbound bus from Quito. Hiking or climbing routes from the centre are described individually. El Boliche is about 1½ hours south of Quito and is also the turn-off to the Clirsen NASA minitrak station. The satellite tracking station is now owned and operated by IGM to download satellite images. It is still marked with a huge sign and the tracking equipment is plainly visible from below. This entrance road is now closed to vehicles but accessible to hikers and mountain bikers.

To reach the park administration centre head to the main entrance just north of Lasso marked by a wooden 'Parque Nacional Cotopaxi' sign. About a kilometre south on the Pan-American Highway, past the turn-off, is a small, rounded, grassy hill on the left; this useful landmark is reputedly a preconquest mound but no-one seems to know very much about it. Turn left on to the entrance road and immediately cross the railway tracks. The route to the park entrance station is clearly marked by arrows at all intersections. You meet up with the El Boliche entrance road before the park entrance station and continue to the park administration centre. This is about a 15km trip from the Pan-American. The road is open to vehicle traffic and during a weekend there is little difficulty hitchhiking into the park, although midweek there is less traffic. Alternatively you can get off the bus at the railway station in the small village of Lasso and hire a taxi or *camioneta* to take you into the park. Sometimes there are taxis waiting at the park entrance turn-off.

It costs about US$10 to hire a taxi to the park administration centre but many hikers opt to hire a ride to Laguna Limpiopungo. If you're on foot you can arrive anytime but if you're driving remember that the park entrance station is open only from 08.00 to 06.00. At weekends it is open longer; from 07.00 to 18.30. Outside of these hours you must find someone to open the locked gate. You'll need your passport and a small fee is charged.

El Boliche entrance is closed to traffic but makes a pleasant walk. The turn-off is asphalted for the first 2km until it reaches the old tracking station where it becomes a dirt road. There are signs most of the way; but stay right following the railroad tracks for 0.5km. You pass a railway station and then cross the tracks and continue to the Río Daule campsite which is about 7km beyond the tracking station. This campsite has plenty of flat tent spaces, two small picnic shelters (unsuitable for sleeping in), and fireplaces. Drinking water is from the river about 500m past the campsite, beyond a bend in the road. This is a good place to spend your first night.

The dirt road continues climbing gradually and 1–2km beyond Río Daule passes a hairpin bend with a camp by it; there is a stable and a thatched hut, but no water. After a further 1–2km take an unmarked left-hand turn (look for herds of llamas; the animals are being studied in the area) down the main road to the park entrance station (where a fee of US$10 is charged). The Mariscal Sucre administration centre is 5–6km beyond the park entrance station and has a museum with a small collection of flora and fauna and views of the mountain. It is about 15km from the museum to the climbers' refuge.

Hiking around Cotopaxi

Maps: IGM 1:50,000 Machachi, Cotopaxi, Sincholagua and Mulaló
This is a beautiful and not too difficult hike which takes about a week and can be combined with ascents of some of the nearby peaks. A dirt road runs more than halfway around the volcano but some cross-country hiking will be involved to complete the circuit. If you're a beginner and not confident of your abilities to hike without trails, you can do the dirt road sections and return the way you came. During weekends you will be able to hitchhike much of the way but midweek you will probably find the jeep road deserted.

Your first step is to reach the park museum and administration centre by one of the two entrance roads described in *Access* above. If you are on foot your first night's camp will probably be at Río Daule. On the second day you should reach the centre in 4 to 6 hours from Río Daule and can continue to one of the several nearby campsites.

The first campsite is some 2–3km along the road beyond the centre. There is a small sign and a turn-off to the left on to a small plain where there are little picnic shelters, an outhouse, a recently built cabin, and water running from a pipe in the gully behind the campsite. On a clear day there are excellent views of Chimborazo about 100km to the south-southwest. This campsite provides one base for climbing Rumiñahui but don't leave your gear here because it is not safe.

About a kilometre further down the road is a second camping site, also signed, but this time to the right. Again picnic shelters and a small cabin are available, but there is no running water.

Just beyond the turn-off to the second campsite there is a track off to the left of the road across a large plain to Laguna de Limpios (also known as Limpiopungo) at about 3,800 m. Around the lake you should watch for waterfowl and other birds, as well as the black Atelopus toad (see *Natural History* in *Chapter One*). There is a trail around the back of the lake which will be described in *Cerro Rumiñahui*, page 179.

To continue your hike around Cotopaxi go from the campsites, past Laguna Limpiopungo, and along the road as it begins to curve further east around the north side of the mountain. Some 2–3km beyond the lake, the hiker will see a signed road to the right leading up to the Cotopaxi climbers' refuge some 9km away (see *Climbing Volcán Cotopaxi*, page 175).

About 3km after the turn-off for the refuge the road forks. The track going straight on will eventually bring you to Machachi over 20km away to the northwest. Take the right fork and curve northeast, east and southeast until you ford an unnamed river about an hour's walk beyond the fork. This point is about 8km from the lake and you could camp here, although it is rather exposed. It's better to continue southeast a further 8km on the gently climbing road around Cotopaxi to the next running water which is usually at the stream crossing the road just above the area marked Mudadero on the IGM map. If this stream is dry, head left or west across flat pastureland to the Río Hualpaloma which runs all year. This camp gives good views of the northeastern flanks of Cotopaxi. (Note that the bridge mentioned in the above paragraph is the departure point for climbing Sincholagua.)

From this camp continue on the jeep road southeast and then south for about 1km to the point where (on the IGM map) the road stops and becomes a 4WD jeep track heading east. This place is easily identified because the track makes a hairpin bend into a small but steep-walled canyon. There is a locked gate near here that prevents vehicular access to a consortium of *haciendas* that have set up a private nature reserve on the edge of the park. If you are on foot and do not plan to hunt or fish through their land there is no problem with access. Continue down the canyon and you'll soon come to the Río Tamboyacu; good camping is also possible here.

Now you have two choices. You can continue along the jeep road as it curves east, south, and finally back west to Hacienda El Tambo. At about the halfway point there is a fork where you go right. Alternatively, you can forsake the jeep track and head south across somewhat boggy country. With the IGM maps and a compass this is quite easy. Head more or less south and pass a small conical hill (Chiguilasín Chico) to your left. Continue south across a plain (you should find a horse track) over a pass to the left of a flat-topped hill. On the other side of the pass you look down on the valley of the northwest branch of the Río Tambo. Follow the valley on the right-hand side southeast for several kilometres until you come to a large valley on your right (southwest branch of the Rio Tambo). From here and further up the southwest branch of the Río Tambo there are good views of Morurco (c4,840m and named Guagua Cotopaxi on the IGM map), Cotopaxi, Antisana and Quilindaña.

Climber's note: Morurco can be approached from this area using an IGM map; Koerner (1976) writes that Morurco is a minor southern peak of Cotopaxi, has only been climbed once, and is reputed to be easy but interesting, with technical possibilities. Access is from the east and north around Cotopaxi. The snow cover is variable.

Cross the southwest branch of the Río Tambo (it is not difficult to ford). If you are coming from Hacienda El Tambo there is a well-travelled trail to this branch as shown on the map. Further upstream this trail is no more than a meandering animal track, but the Río Tambo valley is easy enough to follow. The area is also used as a base for climbs of Quilindaña (see page 183).

Heading southwest you will see a mountain with a steep rock face (Morro) about 7km away. The trail, or what you can find of it, follows the Río Tambo for 4–5km, and where one branch of the river turns west the trail continues southwest over a pass on the northwest side of Morro. Just before the pass is a large flat area which is the best place for a last camp.

Beyond the pass the trail continues clearly to the southwest for 1–2km and then joins a dirt road. A left turn takes you some 8–10km to Hacienda Chalupa, which can be used as another base camp for Quilindaña. A right turn takes you out to the Pan-American Highway. To get to the Pan-American Highway follow the road for some 7–8km past a white stone block marker for Hacienda Baños. A few hundred metres further on take a left fork and after another few hundred metres go straight at a junction. There are no more major turns for the next 3 to 4 hours. Then you descend into the Río Barrancas valley where you could camp. Otherwise climb up the other side and follow the trail for another 3 to 4 hours into Mulaló, where you will find buses to Latacunga. There are many forks in the trail beyond the Río Barrancas; take the most used looking trail and ask the many inhabitants for the way to Mulaló. It is possible to walk out on the road to Mulaló in one long, hard day; otherwise camp in the flat valley bottom of Río Barrancas. There are no hotels in Mulaló and buses stop running before nightfall.

Climbing Volcán Cotopaxi (5,897m)

Not too long ago a German guidebook came out with a description of climbing Cotopaxi that pointedly said it was not a technical climb, therefore no special equipment was necessary. Trying to convince its readers that they could not climb in running shoes was practically impossible. The climb is not difficult, but is considered technical because of the equipment required for the ascent. Ropes, ice axes, crampons and wands are absolutely necessary. Experienced teams don't usually bother with protection, but less experienced climbers may want to carry along a couple of snow stakes and deadmen.

The Cotopaxi area is blessed with the highest number of clear days per year in the Ecuadorian Andes, thus climbs may be attempted year round. Cotopaxi is further west than Cayambe and Antisana, so it experiences the climate of the central highlands rather than the Oriente. June and July are the driest months, but extremely high winds blowing continuously for days on end are not uncommon. December and January are almost as dry and much less windy. (See Cotopaxi route diagram.)

Access If you are a mountaineering party and want to reach the climbers' refuge quickly you'll need to hire a jeep or pick-up truck. This can be done in Lasso, 3km north of the park entrance (see 'Access' in *Hiking Around Cotopaxi*, above), or in Latacunga's Plaza El Salto where you will find an *estacionamento* where there are various transportation companies. A company which will do the trip for around US$25 per pick-up truck is

Cooperativa de Transportes Riberas del Cutuchi.

If you have your own vehicle or are on foot, follow the directions in the 'Access' and *Hiking Around Cotopaxi* sections until you get to the turn-off for the climbers' refuge. The turn-off is at 3,830m; it is 8.5km to the parking area at 4,600m so you have to climb hard. The road is easy to follow; en route you pass the abandoned Armada Nacional refuge at 4,400m. It's old, small, damaged and rarely used. If you're on foot, the gully behind this refuge offers a short cut to the newer refuge; it takes at least an hour with a pack. From the parking lot a trail leads up the sand to the new refuge. Though it looks close, with a heavy pack it will take at least a ½-hour to walk there.

The José Ribas refuge was built in 1971 and extended in 1977. It has room for about 70 climbers in three dozen bunkbeds and on the floor, electricity, basic food supplies, running water, kitchen facilities, outhouses, a fireplace, and lock-up facilities for your gear when you climb. It costs about US$10 per night to stay here for non-residents and half that for residents.

On Easter Sunday in 1996 there was a tragic avalanche that partially buried the refuge and dozens of tourists. The glacier above the refuge was probably weakened by an earthquake that shook the province of Cotopaxi several days prior to the avalanche. In the warm midday sun a huge portion of the ice wall broke loose. Since it was Easter there were many day trippers visiting the mountain who were buried in the ice and snow. Although many were saved and those trapped in the refuge broke windows on the downhill side to climb to safety, more than ten people died on the slope above the refuge. The refuge itself is located in a valley and consequently particularly vulnerable to avalanches. Modifications are being considered to deflect future snow avalanches.

Normal route

The normal route (other routes are rarely climbed) takes 5 to 9 hours for the ascent and 2 to 4 hours for the descent. The snow becomes unpleasantly wet and soft by early afternoon so you should leave the hut between midnight and 02.00. The first hour of the climb takes you up the right-hand side of a triangular scree slope which is sometimes snow covered. You need to climb on to the glacier to your right at about 5,100m, negotiating several crevasses. Once you are on the glacier you generally head south and up, but usually the 'trail' meanders. Although the mountain is well crevassed, for the most part the crevasses are spectacularly large and open and thus easy to avoid. A route is usually well marked around the crevasses with wands and footprints – remember this is the most popular high climb in Ecuador. Above about 5,400m the crevasses are less pervasive and you begin a rather featureless and mainly snow plod towards a huge rock face called Yanasacha (literally 'large black rock' in Quechua). There is a protected spot below a bergschrund just to the right of Yanasacha where you can rest before

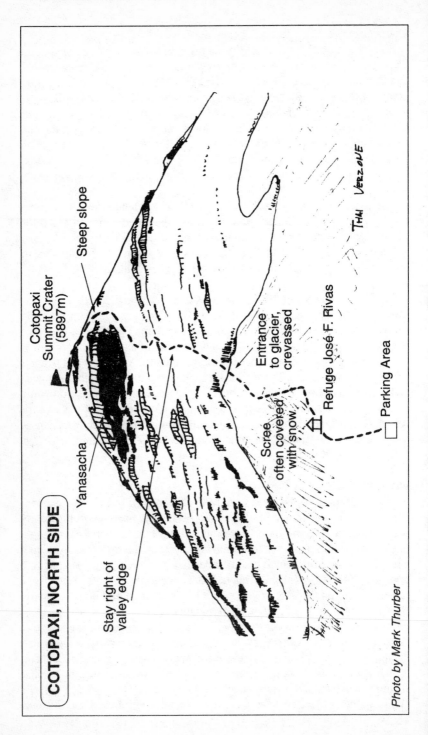

COTOPAXI, NORTH SIDE

Cotopaxi Summit Crater (5897m)

Steep slope

Yanasacha

Stay right of valley edge

Entrance to glacier, crevassed

Scree often covered with snow

Refuge José F. Rivas

Parking Area

THAI VERZOUE

Photo by Mark Thurber

beginning the steep ascent to the crater rim. For the last 250m, angle to the right and up the steep snow then back to the left to the summit. Yanasacha will be to your left.

The classic round crater is over 0.5km wide and a circuit is possible. Steam can be seen escaping from vents in the centre and from the walls. Expeditions into the crater have been undertaken; the first was in 1972 when a Polish-Czech expedition spent 6 hours in the crater and since then several Ecuadorians have repeated the venture.

An alternative route follows the standard climb up the glacier, but then traverses left to below Yanasacha. Here it turns right just below the rock face and climbs a long snow ramp to the summit. Several years ago this was the more commonly used route but a huge crevasse has since made it impassable.

Southern route and Morurco
Damaris Carlisle

This is another non-technical route to the summit and an approach to the southern spur of Morurco (called Guagua Cotopaxi on IGM map). A tent is necessary. Wands are recommended since almost no-one climbs this route. The climb takes 2 to 3 days including the approach or approximately 8 hours from base camp to the summit.

Turn left on to a dirt road, just south of Lasso on the Pan-American Highway at the right turn-off for La Cienaga Hosteria, heading towards the small village of San Ramon. At the first junction turn left, pass several *haciendas*, then take a left at the next junction. In about 200m take a right turn and arrive in San Ramon. Continue through town; you should see a football field on the right. Follow a dry riverbed then turn left. The road becomes rather rocky and looks as though it will fizzle out. Eventually you will come to a church. Take a very sharp right through some low gates. Stick to this road to Rancho María. The gates to the ranch are usually locked but there is a track to the left. Follow this up to the *páramo*. The vehicle should reach 3,400m, where there is a wide place to park. A driveable track continues a bit higher (1 hour).

Start hiking following the track that peters out to a path up a valley. Halfway up the valley you come to a small dammed section where there is a natural spring and the last place to get water. Fill up!

Continue up the valley where it opens out to the *páramo*. From here you should have a view of Cotopaxi to the left and Morurco to the right. There is a small ridge in front of these two peaks with a distinctive big rock on the top. To get to Morurco you head straight for the distinctive big rock then over and down the ridge to the south. To head for Cotopaxi head to the left of the rock, skirting the ridge lower down. Once you come about level with the rock you will see a deep valley. Slide down sandy scree slope, cross and gain the valley on the other side. You can camp in this gully (4,400m). Three glacial tongues of Cotopaxi are visible in front of you.

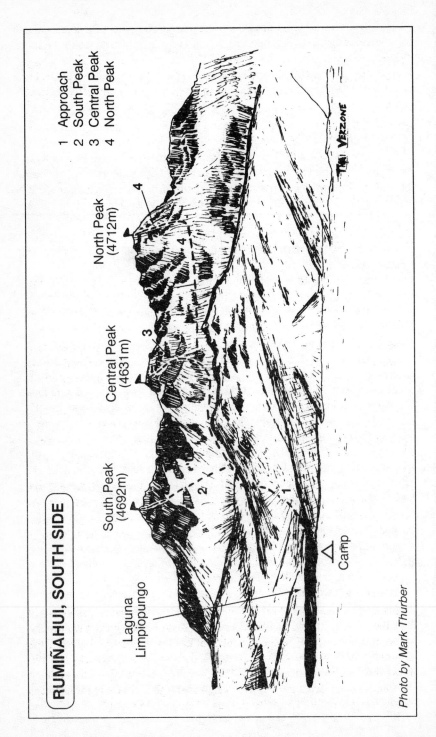

RUMIÑAHUI, SOUTH SIDE

1 Approach
2 South Peak
3 Central Peak
4 North Peak

North Peak
(4712m)

Central Peak
(4631m)

South Peak
(4692m)

Laguna
Limpiopungo

Camp

Photo by Mark Thurber

Gain the ridge to the right of the campsite. The ridge becomes quite narrow, climbing between two tongues of the glacier. Cross on to the left tongue near the end of the ridge and head up the glacier, eventually reaching a large crevasse; skirt to the west of the crevasse. You should see fumaroles above you near the summit. Once past the crevasse, head north to the crater rim near the south summit.

Cerro Rumiñahui (4,712m)

Maps: IGM 1:50,000 Machachi

A geologist would place Rumiñahui in *Chapter Four, The Central Valley*, but it is included here because it is within the confines of Parque Nacional Cotopaxi. This long-extinct volcano is located 45km south of Quito and only 13km northwest of Cotopaxi. It is an easy ascent and has often been climbed although, surprisingly, I could find no records of ascents prior to the 1950s. Although occasionally sprinkled with snow, it is normally a walk up with a rocky scramble at the top.

Rumiñahui is named after one of Atahualpa's famous generals and means 'face of stone'. Despite the name, the stone is heavily laced with metal, so you should descend if an electric storm threatens. (See Rumiñahui route diagram opposite.)

Access The most well-known route begins from Laguna Limpiopungo (see *Hiking around Cotopaxi*, page 172). The lake is quite shallow, and during the dry months may be a bit scummy or even completely dry, but you'll find a path going around its east side and past a boggy area to the north. About 1km northwest of the lake you'll find possible camping spots with clean running water. This is not an officially designated campsite and has no facilities. The closest official camping spot is north of the road below Caracha Loma.

Central Peak (4,631m)

From the campsite head west up a small steep-sided valley, following the stream around to the northwest to a boggy plain below the mountain. Skirt this plain to the northeast and ascend the grassy ridge coming off the Central Peak. Once on the ridge swing west and head for the Central Peak: there is a bit of class 3 scrambling at the top. From the camp it should take 2 to 3 hours to get to the summit.

North Peak (4,712m)

To get to the main north summit, a traverse across the summit ridge is not possible. You'll have to descend about halfway down back towards the grassy ridge where you'll see a number of narrow arêtes running up to the summit of the North Peak. Traverse below these arêtes across rocky *páramo* until you come to the last major gully of reddish sand which is the route to the summit ridge. This gully is just before the large rockface at the northern end of the mountain. Climb to the top of the summit ridge, cross it, and

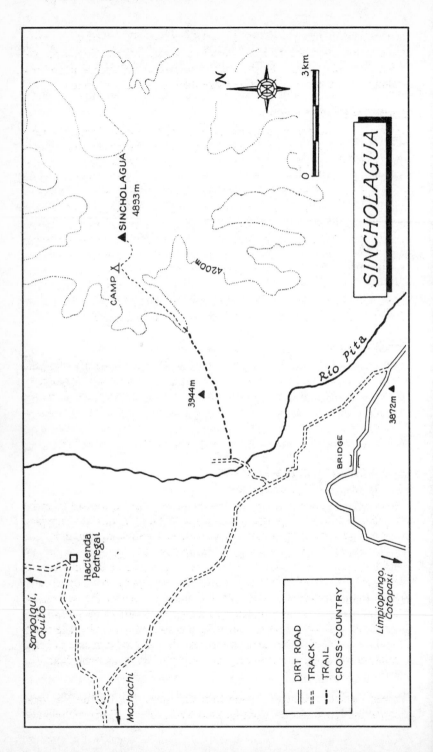

then drop down the western side. From here you should be able to scramble to the summit. Ascents from the eastern side are difficult. Except for the last few metres, which are the usual rotten rock, the ascent is an easy scramble. Even if you don't quite make the top the view is great.

South Peak (4,696m)

Climbing the south peak involves some moderate technical rock climbing (class 5.5) and the proper technical equipment. The climb takes 4 to 6 hours depending on how well you've acclimatized. Walk to the north end of the boggy plain, mentioned in 'Access' above, to Central Peak and begin a scramble up the flanks below the South Peak. There are a number of routes up the centre of the summit pyramid though the rock isn't all that great. For an excellent view into the crater, traverse right from the south summit base and head for the saddle on the ridge that separates the South and Central Peaks. There is an obvious grey sand slope leading up to this saddle. Up to here only a bit of careful scrambling is necessary. However, the rocky traverse across the ridge to either the South or the Central Peak will require some technical rock climbing. It is best to bring rope and some protection if planning the traverse: not for the inexperienced.

Other routes

Other approaches and routes are possible but less frequently climbed. Approaches are made from the northeast over the Filo Santo Domingo to the bottom of the last sandy gully described in the standard route. The rock face just north of this gully offers a technical rock route first climbed in 1972 by the Ecuadorian climbers Cruz, Reinoso and Berge. Ascents from the Machachi side (from the northwest) are reported to be possible.

Cerro Sincholagua (4,893m)

Map: IGM 1:50,000 Sincholagua

Sincholagua is an extinct volcano located 45km south-southeast of Quito and 17km northeast of Cotopaxi, just outside of the national park boundary. It is one of the many mountains first ascended by Edward Whymper and the Carrels in 1880. They climbed the northwest ridge and this is still considered the normal route. It used to be a well-glaciated mountain and the old IGM 1:50,000 Sincholagua map showed a permanent icecap over 1.5km long. In common with other Ecuadorian peaks the permanent snowline has receded over recent decades and today there is no permanent glacier, although after a heavy storm there is some snow cover. The climb is mainly a scramble but the scree below the summit pinnacle is loose except after a good snowfall and cold night when the gravel should be solidly frozen together.

Access is most frequently made from the south via Parque Nacional Cotopaxi although access from Quito is also possible. Enter the national park as usual and continue around Cotopaxi on the dirt road described in *Hiking around Cotopaxi*, page 172. Go to the point on the road when you cross an unnamed river on a small bridge. If in a jeep continue beyond the bridge about 3km until you pass a perfectly cone-shaped hill on your right and a hillock to your left. Look for an unmarked jeep trail which goes hard left and northwest. Follow this track for about 4–5km, then turn right on to a side track which fords the Río Pita. If on foot you can go north cross-country from the bridge and meet the track just before the right turn about 2km north of the bridge.

This point can be reached by 4WD jeep from Quito. Head south on the Valle de los Chillos freeway to Sangolquí and continue to the village of Selva Alegre. Head south towards Hacienda Patichupamba and continue south towards the Río Pita and Sincholagua. The road is difficult and unsigned so ask everyone you meet for directions. It's 50–60km by bad road from Selva Alegre.

Once you've crossed the Río Pita head northeast up a ridge with vehicle tracks on it, past a survey marker (3,969m), until you meet a ridge running northwest. This will take half a day on foot from the river, but a 4WD vehicle will get some of the way up the hill. Camp is usually made near the junction of the two ridges (shown as Parquedero on map) in order to make an early start the next day, whilst the rocks are still frozen together. Water is difficult to find along this ridge.

It is also possible to access the mountain from a road in Quebrada Yagüil on the north side of the mountain that leads to a gravel pit. You will need to do your own route-finding in a 4WD vehicle and on the mountain to intersect with the route described below. (See Sincholagua map, page 180.)

Main Peak (4,893m)

From the Parquedero continue up along the flatter ridge to the base of rocks. Traverse left around and up the rocky peak to the northwest side of the mountain: the route should be cairned. Drop down to a scree- or snow-filled basin and contour up on rocky shelves to a scree saddle below the summit pyramid. After a cold or snowy night the scree is usually frozen together; otherwise the approach to the summit pyramid is difficult because of the loose scree. There is a short exposed pitch (25m) to the summit with fairly good rock. Head for the left skyline where there is a gully. The last 5m are not difficult but very exposed. A descent by rappelling off the summit is sometimes made.

Pico Hoeneisen

For the rock climber, Pico Hoeneisen is a prominent 'lower peak' below the southeast peak of Sincholagua. It was first climbed by Miguel Andrade and Hugo Torres in 1972. You'll need a rope, obviously, and an assortment of nuts and chocks for this technical rock climb. The approach begins at the bridge off the Cotopaxi road described previously in the 'Access' section (page 182). From here you'll see the southeast ridge of Sincholagua with the prominent rock outcrop or peak in the centre of the mountain. Cross the *páramo* northeast following a W-shaped *quebrada* as it ascends to the top of the *páramo*. Drop down from here to just below the base of the south ridge where there is good camping with plenty of water. Follow the *páramo* up from the camping area to the scree and continue along the ridgeline to the mountain. You'll come to a prominent wide ledge, highly visible from below, cutting across the south side of the mountain and intersecting the ridge. Follow the ledge around to the right side of the ridge and you'll come to a 15m chimney of good rock. A thin crack in the chimney will take small nuts. Ascending this, you'll next reach an overhanging section which is fairly difficult – 5.10 free, or maybe requiring some aid moves. The rock is loose at the top of this section. Here, the route traverses right to another small chimney of about 10m. At the top, you'll come to a triangular sand/snow slope which leads up to the summit. The route will have to be descended the same way with several rappels/abseils.

This is the twelfth highest peak in Ecuador but is rarely visited because climbers tend to concentrate on the ten peaks over 5,000m. So much the better! As with Rumiñahui and Cotopaxi, the weather is better than average; the driest months are June through August.

CERRO QUILINDAÑA (4,878M)

Map: IGM 1:50,000 Cotopaxi

This extinct volcano lies just outside the park boundaries about 16km southeast of Cotopaxi and 65km south-southeast of Quito. It is an infrequently climbed, difficult, and technical mountain which offers one of the most interesting rock-climbing routes in Ecuador. It was first climbed in 1952 by a large party of Ecuadorians, Colombians, French and Italians.

Access The normal base for the climb is the Hacienda El Tambo. This can be reached on foot or by 4WD vehicle as described in *Hiking around Cotopaxi*, above. The land south of Parque Nacional Cotopaxi is protected by 'Fundacíon Páramo' that prohibits hunting and fishing. The road is gated at the headwaters of the Río Tamboyacu. You may decide to camp near the *hacienda* the first night. There is a good site just beyond the *hacienda* near the river or you can continue south toward several prominent *páramo* hills, hiking for about an hour. There is no trail, but just after dropping down slightly past the hills there will be a flat area with water, good for camping and with excellent views of Quilindaña. From here you could attempt the summit by leaving at about 05.00 to allow enough time for the return trip. (Hide any gear left behind.) Otherwise, you can continue the following day across the *páramo* to the obvious central (north) ridge which leads to the base of the mountain. At the top of the ridge on the northwest flank is a small lake near the saddle with suitable camping. It's about 1½ to 2 hours up the ridge from the suggested *páramo* camp. The climb from the lake to the summit will take about 3 to 5 hours.

Alternative access is from the Hacienda Chalupas, which can also be reached by 4WD vehicle. The dirt road from Mulaló to the *hacienda* is not marked on the IGM maps so you have to get directions from everyone you meet along the way. From this *hacienda* hike north for about half a day to the lake mentioned above.

The normal route departs from the lake, traversing left to an obvious couloir (which may be either snow or sand depending on the recent weather). The couloir is the only access to the prominent left (northwest) ridge. Begin rock climbing directly up the ridge, slightly difficult at 5.6/5.7. It's easy to pick out the line on the good, solid rock. The technical part ends where the ridge flattens and from here it's only another 150m of easy scrambling to the summit. Keep slightly to the right on the ridge as you approach the peak.

A slightly easier rock route would be to cross the ridge rather than climb directly up, traversing to below the north rockface. The line up the face to the flat part of the ridge is straightforward – easy 5th class.

Koerner describes three routes that I can't comment on, other than to quote him directly: 'On the north face you will see two large and rather triangular rock faces. Somewhere, there exists an aid route which ascends here. To the left is a couloir in which runs another route that is roughly class five, but requires only four to eight pitons.

'The west face may be climbed also. From the ridge to the south of the lakes, go up any one of a number of small snow gullies to a bit of a snow field. Climb this to the saddle and then go left up the summit ridge to the summit.'

Note: Remember that changing snow conditions in Ecuador mean that most of the snow described above has disappeared.

PARQUE NACIONAL LLANGANATES

Maps: IGM 1:50,000 San José de Poala, Río Mulatos, Sucre and Río Negro

If you've heard of the Llanganates you've probably heard of treasure. From the time of the conquistadors it has been believed that treasure was buried here. The story is that when the last Inca, Atahualpa, was murdered by Pizarro, Atahualpa's general, Rumiñahui, hid the treasure from the Spaniards. Many eminent people have been convinced of its existence or have gone to look for it; they include the botanist Richard Spruce, the scientist and evolutionist Alfred Russel Wallace, George Dyott – the man who looked for Colonel Fawcett – and the British climbers Joe Brown and Hamish MacInnes. No-one has found the treasure yet but a Swiss-German resident of Quito, Eugene Brunner, had looked for it for almost half a century. He was convinced that he had found its location but at the time of his death, the treasure, estimated at 750 tons of gold, had yet to be recovered.

In 1996 the area was made a national park though at present there is very little infrastructure or administration. Since it is such an inhospitable place there are practically no development threats except a proposed road from Salcedo to Tena which would be extremely difficult to construct.

If you want to look for the treasure yourself, you'll probably find it the most difficult trip of your life. The following description by Koerner in his (out of print) *The Fool's Climbing Guide to Ecuador* (which the author freely admits to being a work of fiction and plagiarism!) explains why. I like the succinctness of his description so much that I reprint it here:

'The Llanganates are a mysterious and almost impenetrable range to the northeast of Baños. Part of Atahualpa's gold is said to be hidden there, and people occasionally go off to look for it. You can too if your interest is to get hideously and hopelessly lost in 15 foot high, razor sharp pampas grass and continuous rain.

'The Llanganates also contain El Hermoso, 4571m, an occasional snow peak, the identity of which will baffle you when first you see it from some other peak.'

One route into the Llanganates is to follow in the footsteps of Valverde, a Spanish gentleman who claimed on his deathbed to know the location of the treasure and drew a treasure map for the King of Spain. The map is vague but he may have followed the route below. Please remember it is really easy to get lost. The topography is confusing since there are many features that are less than 40m high and do not appear on topographical maps with 40m contour lines. Also it is mostly foggy or raining so often impossible to get a view of where you are located. Avoid flat areas since they may contain 'quaking bogs' where you will sink up to your knees or waist in muck. The Llanganates is the most difficult area in Ecuador to hike – people get lost and die. Wear only rubber boots as hiking boots will get hopelessly wet and muddy. Bring a machete. The best months are December and January when you might get a few days of sunny weather.

A road heads up from Píllaro to Embalse Pisayambo (a large reservoir) where you can walk into the Llanganates more or less following way trails for several days. After that you are on your own. Hire a taxi in Píllaro up to the INEFAN control point at Laguna del Tambo (US$25) where you may be asked to pay a park entrance fee. Continue by car to a bridge over Río Millin and find the trail shown on the map heading south. Head up the ridge and contour around to La Puerta. Below is 'the maze' where two English explorers once became hopelessly lost. Your goal is to get to Laguna Aucacocha and not drop down into the cloudforests of the Río El Golpe. Keep your compass in hand and contour around the southern side of this flat quaking bog. It is easy to miss the lake completely; as it is behind a hill. There is a trail on the hill on the north side of lake. Continue up ridges to Laguna El Cable. This is a good place to camp, a mere 8km from the road, but a long day in the Llanganates. There is a black peak to the east – you need to find a trail that contours on the north side of the peak. Follow the narrow and exposed ridge on the trail to the horseshoe basin that contains Laguna Sogillas: another hard day and a good place to camp. From here you can contour on a way trail to Páramos de Soguillas and cut a trail through cloudforest down steep slopes to an interesting valley northwest of peak 4257. Note the river in this valley has no outlet and probably drops into a cave. We have not gone any farther than this but there is a wild wilderness to the east with rocky peaks and lakes. Again be careful; the difficulty of travel in this area cannot be overestimated.

THE BAÑOS AREA

This resort town is popular for its thermal springs, splendid scenery and pleasant climate. Several day hikes can be made and the town is a good base for climbing Volcán Tungurahua and El Altar, as well as being the beginning of one of Ecuador's principal roads into the jungle.

The town's tourist attractions include several thermal baths (*piscinas*), a small museum, a zoo of Ecuadorian animals, and restaurants serving the typical Andean delicacy *cuy,* or roast guinea pig. Your hotel manager can direct you to all of these. By strolling down the main street in the morning you'll see the shopkeepers busy making taffy. A glob of the soft mixture is slung on to a wooden hook on the wall, then pulled repeatedly until it hardens. Although you can buy it in bars, it's much nicer to pay a few sucres for a wispy piece of still warm taffy.

One hotel can be especially recommended to climbers and hikers on a budget. Pensión Patty at Eloy Alfaro 554 (less than two blocks from the market) is simple but clean, friendly, family-run and inexpensive. Cooking facilities are available and many *gringos* looking for hiking or climbing partners stay here. The landlady's sons, Carlos and José, are both climbers and will give advice and sometimes act as guides. Baños has a broad selection of lodging in most price ranges. Finding something to meet your needs will present no problem.

Day hikes from Baños

Baños lies at 1,800m in the valley of Río Pastaza which flows from west to east. Good day hikes may be made in the mountains to the north and in the foothills of Tungurahua to the south of Baños, as well as down the river valley to the east.

To reach the steep hills on the north side of town you must cross the Río Pastaza on one of two bridges, the Puente San Francisco or the Puente San Martín. Once on the other side, however, directions become meaningless. There are so many paths to choose from, it's up to you how high and far you climb. Just plan to cross one bridge going and the other coming back for variety. The trail to Puente San Francisco leaves from behind the sugarcane stalls by the main bus station, and after crossing the bridge becomes very steep. You can climb to the top of the hill but the trails peter out near the summit. On a clear day you are rewarded with marvellous views of Tungurahua and Chimborazo, as well as of green cultivated fields, passion flowers, waterfalls and the turbulent Río Pastaza.

The Puente San Martin lies over 1km west of town. Walk out on the main westbound road, then cross a bridge. Keep going until you reach a right-hand fork by a blue religious shrine just before the police checkpoint. Take this fork and walk less than 1km to the bridge. It crosses an impressive gorge and a few hundred metres to the right is the waterfall known as Cascada Inés María, which can be seen if you take a rough trail to the right soon after the bridge. The dirt road continues a few kilometres to the village of Lligua and at several points trails climb the hill to the right of the road, so you can take your pick.

There is a small zoo near the Cascada Inés María that houses an interesting collection of Ecuadorian species, including the rare harpy eagle and a free-range, ridiculously tame tapir. The zoo keeper is interested in his job and will give you plenty of information and perhaps let you into some of the cages for photography.

If you prefer a day hike with clearer directions and well defined trails then head for the hills south of town. The hike to Pondoa on the slopes of Volcán Tungurahua is one idea (see *Tungurahua* page 189). Another possibility is the hike to the village of Runtun, which consists of half-a-dozen buildings, one of which is a bar with a pool table! There are two trails to Runtun; the shorter of the two will take about 2 hours from Baños. Leave town by heading south on Calle Tomás Haiflans which soon passes Escuela Vicente Maldonado. Just beyond the school the road becomes a footpath which climbs diagonally left up the hill towards a house with a huge cross plainly visible on the skyline. It's the only good trail so you can't miss it. It will take about an hour to reach the cross with excellent views of Baños. The trail now doubles back to the right and towards the top of the hill until it reaches Runtun. Immediately before the village there is a fork; the left goes to the village (50m) and the right goes down to Baños. This alternative descent is rather longer than returning the way you came. On a clear day the views of Tungurahua from near Runtun are magnificent.

Finally, if you've had enough of running up and down steep mountainsides, you can walk, hitch or take a bus (marked Agoyan) about 6km to the once-famous Agoyan Falls (where the bus terminates). A new hydroelectric plant above the falls has altered their lovely character, though at times they will still be visible from the road. At the bus terminus you can continue through the tunnel (take the one on the right), walking or hitching a further 10km to the Río Verde Falls. There are many different cascades along the road, but the ones at Río Verde are the most impressive. The views along the road are wonderful as the steep-walled Río Pastaza canyon slowly opens up into

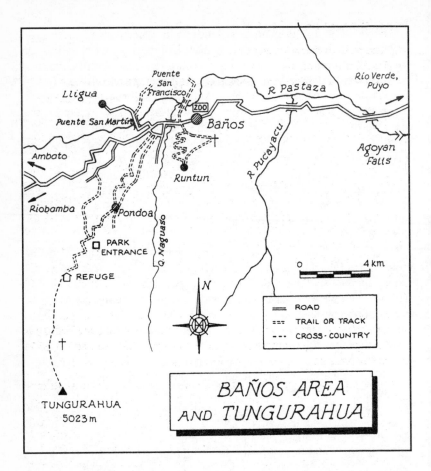

the Oriente. Once at the little village of Río Verde, walk through the village and over the road bridge until you find a trail to your right, just by the last house. The trail leads steeply down to the Río Pastaza which is crossed by a suspension footbridge from where you can view the falls. Better still scramble right up to them on the steep and narrow path immediately before the footbridge. It is an exciting place; the constricted gorge reverberates with power and it is difficult to make yourself heard above the roar. This point is 20km from Baños and about as far as you can easily reach in a day and hitch back to Baños – further trips into the jungle are included in the *Oriente* chapter.

Rock climbing

Just below the zoo in Baños along the river are about eight new bolted routes on columnar andesite ranging in difficulty from 5.9 to 5.12. The rock is reasonably solid and the bolt spacing is close enough to make leading safe. Many of the climbs crest out on overhangs. This new rock-climbing area is a good destination for sport climbing.

Tungurahua (5,023m)

'The paths feather-lined and steep.
Overhead a sky of mud.
Then all of a sudden in the air the purest white lily of a tall volcano.'

Henri Michaux

Tungurahua is a beautiful and active snow-capped volcano situated about 10km south of Baños, and now part of Parque Nacional Sangay. An eruption in 1711 destroyed several towns and a major eruption was recorded early this century. Present activity is limited to a few fumaroles and steam vents, and is responsible for the natural hot springs found in Baños. The volcano was first climbed in 1873 by the Germans, Wilhelm Reiss and Alfons Stübel.

From a climber's point of view, Tungurahua is rather an anomaly. It has been described both as 'easy to access and to climb' and as 'one of the hardest climbs in Ecuador'. Both descriptions are correct because, although the climb is straightforward and easy from a technical viewpoint, it is physically demanding as it involves 3,200m of vertical ascent from Baños at 1,800m.

Access To get to the refuge you can either go on foot or hire transport up to the park entrance where you'll pay $10 park entrance fee and the US$4 per night refuge fee. A morning milk truck leaves from Pensión Patty (US$2) or you can arrange for a *camioneta* to make the trip (about US$10).

Hiking directions If going on foot, start your climb at the western entrance to Baños at a police checkpoint. Across the highway you'll see a dirt road bearing up and to the right. Walk up this road about 100m and turn right at a sign for Refugio Nicolás Martínez where you'll pick up the trail which is very steep and narrow. It follows a ridge with fine views of Baños and 1 or 2 hours' walking are needed to reach the small village of Pondoa. Stop at the Pondoa store and chat with the owner; he will tell you how to reach the hut and can introduce you to the local guide, Sr Angel Perez, who has climbed the volcano dozens of times and is very experienced. He doesn't have much equipment to rent but can arrange mule hire and can guide you if you wish. Only very basic supplies (beer, sardines, and crackers) are available at the store.

It takes 1 to 2 hours to climb from Pondoa to the park entrance. If arriving by local transport, this is the end of the road, and the start of the final approach to the refuge. Often there are mules and horses available to help carry gear up to the refuge (about US$6 per animal), but don't rely on it. If you definitely want to go with pack animals, then arrange it ahead of time.

Follow the cobbled road out of Pondoa, about 30 minutes' walking, to an obvious sharp left which puts you on a well-worn dirt track leading to the park entrance. The trail up to the refuge begins about 100m past the entrance station to the left. It's quite steep in places and often muddy. At several points the trail goes through 'tunnels' of bamboo and other tropical vegetation. Expect to take from 3 to 5 hours getting to the refuge.

When you reach the refuge (built in the late 1970s) you will find floor space for about 18 people and a propane cooking stove. Water is obtained from a spring about 200m beyond the hut. It tends to fill to capacity on Friday afternoons as weekend climbers filter in. There is no secure lock-up for packs, etc; many choose to carry their gear with them to the summit and avoid the risk of leaving it behind unattended. The altitude here is about 3,800m and the view of Chimborazo's east face is impressive.

The climb from the hut to the top is best attempted in the early morning before the summit snow becomes soft and slushy. A dawn start is adequate; a pre-dawn start often better. Head south-southeast to a survey marker at about 4,000m. About 1 to 2 hours above the hut a rockband is reached through which you can easily scramble, and soon after you pass an aluminium cross. Here bear a little to the right (south) towards the craters which will take about 2 to 3 more hours to reach.

There are two craters but only the smaller one is presently active. Climbers sometimes camp in here because it is well sheltered, but don't get too close to the steam vents. The inactive south crater is larger and has a more typical crater shape with beautifully coloured rock walls.

About 45 minutes are needed to climb from the craters to the highest point. Walk straight up the snowfield between the craters. Crampons and ice axe are all that are needed as there is no major crevasse danger and the slope is gentle. Indeed, experienced climbers have reached the top merely by kicking snowsteps with their boots. The top is rather featureless, so if there is any hint of fog take compass bearings.

The descent from the summit back to Baños in one day is not easy, especially with heavy packs. It can be hot, depending on the season, and the steep trail makes it hard on the knees. It is, after all, downhill for 3,200m!

Warning: This is perhaps the easiest snow climb in Ecuador and it is very tempting for beginning climbers to attempt this 5,000m peak. Enough time must be spent acclimatizing in Quito before the climb, as the low altitude of Baños is not sufficient for acclimatization. The apparent simplicity of this climb can fool you; remember climbers have died on Tungurahua.

PARQUE NACIONAL SANGAY

Parque Nacional Sangay, almost doubled in size in 1992 with the addition of 245,000ha to the south, includes vast tracts of high altitude *páramo* and lush lower-level cloudforest. Its original, northern section is listed as a World Heritage site. Within the park, and more specifically around the area of the Sangay volcano, there exists one of the last sizeable refuges for the mountain or woolly mountain tapir. This species is listed as endangered and until the last two decades the area supported a healthy population. Hunting is the major cause in the population decline, despite the laws prohibiting it. Many areas of the park are beginning to open up for hikers with the implementation of new guidelines and services by the parks department. For now, Volcán Sangay, Tungurahua (described in the Baños section) and El Altar, all in the western zone of the park, remain the primary attractions for park visitors.

Although information can be obtained about the park in Quito at the INEFAN offices or at Fundación Natura, the main office for the park is located in Aloa. There should also be guard stations in Aloa (Volcán Sangay, El Placer), Atillo (Guamote–Macas Trail), Candelaría (El Altar), Pondoa (Tungurahua) and Río Negro (Cloudforest).

El Altar (5,320m)

Maps: IGM 1:50,000 Volcán El Altar and Palitahua. For more detail 1:25,000 Cerros Negros and Laguna Pintada are useful. There are some map errors near Laguna Mandur.

This, the fifth highest mountain in Ecuador, undoubtedly involves the most technical climbing and has one of the longest approaches. Situated some 170km south of Quito, El Altar is an extinct volcano which at one time was probably higher than Cotopaxi, but a huge ancient eruption almost totally destroyed the cone leaving a steep-sided and jagged crater 3km in diameter. The west wall was destroyed, allowing easy access into the crater, but the volcano had never been climbed from within until 1984. Despite repeated attempts by many climbers, including Whymper, the icy ramparts of El Altar withstood all assaults until July 7 1963, when an Italian expedition led by Marino Tremonti conquered the last unclimbed 5,000m mountain in Ecuador.

Indigenous legend dates the mountain's huge final explosion to 1460, but vulcanologists agree that it must have been far more ancient. Today, the volcano is inactive. Nine separate sub-summits are recognized on its reversed C-shaped crater. They have now all been climbed, although one of the Frailes was only conquered in 1979 by a team of six Ecuadorian climbers led by Luis Naranjo.

El Altar needs no translation into English and its various peaks all bear church-related names. The highest is El Obispo ('the bishop'), 5,320m, but its height is much in dispute, with some authorities suggesting as much as 5,465m. This was the first peak to be climbed. The Italians, led by Tremonti, played an important part in the conquest of El Altar's peaks. They returned in 1965 to conquer the second peak, El Canonigo ('the canon'), 5,260m, and in 1972 achieved the first ascent of El Fraile Grande ('the great friar'). The three other Fraile peaks were all climbed for the first time by Ecuadorian teams. Bernado Beate, Jacinto Carrasco and Rafael Terán were the summit climbers in two of those first ascents. La Monja Grande ('the great nun'), the third highest peak at 5,160m, was climbed by a US/Japanese team in 1968 and the remaining two peaks, La Monja Chica ('the little nun') and El Tabernáculo ('the tabernacle') fell to a German

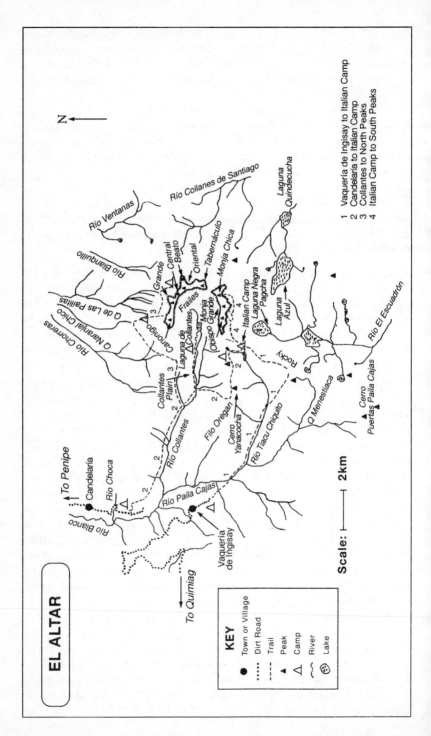

EL ALTAR

KEY

● Town or Village
⋯ Dirt Road
--- Trail
▲ Peak
△ Camp
〜 River
Lake

Scale: ⊢——⊣ 2km

N ←

1 Vaqueria de Ingisay to Italian Camp
2 Candelaria to Italian Camp
3 Collantes to North Peaks
4 Italian Camp to South Peaks

To Penipe
To Quimiag

Candelaria
Río Choca
Río Blanco
Río Chorreras
Río Naranjal Chico
Q de Las Paillas
Río Blanquillo
Río Ventanas
Río Collanes de Santiago

Laguna Quindecucha
Laguna Negra
Laguna Azul
Pacha
Río El Escuadrón

Central
Beato
Oriental
Tabernáculo
Monja Chica
Grande
Frailes
Monja
Obispo Grande
Cañón
Laguna de Collantes
Collantes Plain
Río Collantes
Filo Oregan
Cerro Yanacocha
Río Tiacu Chiquito
Italian Camp
Rocky
Q. Menestiaca
Cerro Puertas Paila Cajas

Río Paila Cajas
Vaqueria de Ingisay

team in 1972. The extremely difficult north face of Obispo was climbed from within the crater by a French/Ecuadorian team in 1984. The ascent of this grade VI rockface took six days to complete.

In October 1995, the nine summits of El Altar were climbed for the first time in one expedition. The team consisted of four Ecuadorian mountaineers: Osvaldo Freile and Gabriel Llano climbed all nine summits. They started at the Italian camp and climbed counter-clockwise for 23 days, ending in Collantes Plain. The loads were carried across the glaciers on sleds. This difficult feat is a watermark in Ecuadorian mountaineering and awaits a repeat.

This volcano is obviously not a jaunt for the beginning climber, but a backpacking trip is very rewarding. There is a grey-green crater lake called, curiously, Laguna Amarilla ('yellow lake'), and from the edge of the crater backpackers can listen to the hanging glaciers crack and rumble and catch glimpses of enormous ice slides. Condors are also seen around here. El Altar is protected as part of Parque Nacional Sangay.

It is rainy most of the year, June and July being the wettest months. The best times to go are from late November through early February, with the majority of successful ascents being made around Christmas and New Year. I have seen one report published in Ecuador which claims that the El Altar region receives 14,600mm (that's about 48ft!) of precipitation annually. Although I find this hard to believe, it does indicate that the region is wet... very wet. (See El Altar maps.)

Access From Quito's Terminal Terrestre, take a bus via Ambato to Baños, and continue on to Penipe, about halfway to Riobamba. From Penipe you must make your way to Candelaría, about 15km away up the Río Blanco valley. It's quite a steep climb.

If you decide to go on foot, and your bus goes into Penipe (rather than passing along the highway), tell the driver you want to go to Candelaría. You will then be let off on the edge of Penipe at the turn-off for Candelaría. The hike takes about 5 hours and is not bad as far as 5-hour hikes go.

The most reliable transport along this route is the *lechera*, or milk truck, departing Penipe at about 06.00. On Thursday, Saturday and Sunday there is a mid-morning truck. The Penipe market is on Sunday, so all day there are various vehicles bound for Candelaría. There is also a driver who will take you in his pick-up truck from Penipe to Candelaría and Hacienda Releche. Ask around the main plaza for Ernesto Haro. He charges about US$5 and will pick you up for the return trip at a pre-arranged time if you wish.

For the return from Candelaría to Penipe you can catch the *lechera* between 06.00 and 07.00, or ask the teachers for a lift when they leave at about noon.

In Candelaría there is a small store with very basic food supplies and they may be able to suggest somewhere you can sleep. There are also mules available to transport your gear up to the base of the mountain. Return pick-up times can be arranged.

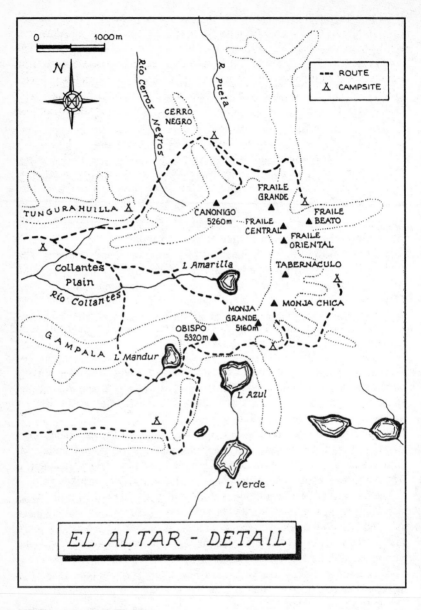

EL ALTAR - DETAIL

Hiking around El Altar

From Candelaría continue along the road for about 2km until you come to a light green building with a Parque Nacional Sangay sign; this is the ranger station. For a modest charge, you can overnight in the ranger cabin with toilets and cooking facilities before continuing on. Pay your park fee (US$10) and follow this road to the right up a steep hill, across a stream and past the Hacienda Releche. After about 45 minutes the correct trail branches off to the left. This is the only confusing part since there are now only cowpaths running up through the meadows. The trail to El Altar goes high on the west-facing hillside just below a waterfall but above the cultivated fields. The trail is just behind the trees and is not visible from below, but if you follow the cowpaths uphill through the fields you will come to it – major intersections are now signed. Once you connect with the main trail, turn right and stride out. There are no other paths to confuse you.

The trail heads east, passing through scrubby woodlands, going gently uphill before rounding a corner and giving you your first views of El Altar and its river valley. A marvellous sight. From there it's a gentle 3 hours of nearly level walking until you arrive at the broad pasture called Collantes (also known as Collanes). This is normally as far as the mules will take you (unless you're going northeast towards Canonigo) and it is often used as a campsite. Too often, in fact, judging by the amount of trash there. This section takes 5 to 8 hours from Candelaría. You can cross the Collantes plain to the trees at the base of the crater to camp out of the wind. Edward Whymper did just that in 1880.

From the Collantes Plain there are three basic choices, assuming, that is, you wish to do anything at all. You can go east and visit the crater; you can go south to climb the southern peaks (including Obispo, the highest) or do some backpacking in a beautifully wild and trackless area with many lakes; or you can go north to climb the northern peaks (including Canonigo, the second highest) and do some backpacking in this area which is little explored. A challenging and adventurous hike would be all the way around the back of the mountain – it is rarely done.

The best route from Collantes to the rim of the crater is up along the wooded ridge on the left of the river (follow cowpaths), heading toward the deeply incised rockface. Although you can go around the hill at the left of the ridge, the shortest route up is the gully just to the right of the knob at the end of the wooded ridge. The first 5m are very steep, but not difficult as there is tussock grass to hang on to and flat places where you can regain your breath. If it has been raining you might feel safer (and drier) taking the long route around and up the left ridge, but you'll have to climb much higher. The reward for going this way is that the views are better. It takes about 3 to 4 hours for the round trip.

For the return trip, consider hiking to Hacienda Puelazo via Vaquería de Ingisay (see below).

Climbing Obispo and the southern peaks

The best approach is via the *hacienda* of Vaquería Ingisay and the Cordillera de Mandur. From the end of the road it is a mere 4 hours with mules plus 2 hours carrying packs to the Italian Camp. From Riobamba or Baños get a bus to Cubijiés or Químiag. In Cubijíes you can hire a taxi (4WD not necessary) to transport you up to the *hacienda* of Vaquería Ingisay or to the

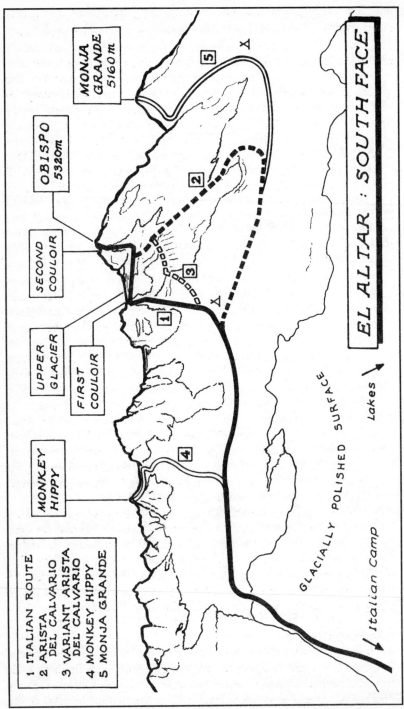

EL ALTAR : SOUTH FACE

MONJA GRANDE 5160 m

OBISPO 5320m

SECOND COULOIR

UPPER GLACIER

FIRST COULOIR

MONKEY HIPPY

1 ITALIAN ROUTE
2 ARISTA DEL CALVARIO
3 VARIANT ARISTA DEL CALVARIO
4 MONKEY HIPPY
5 MONJA GRANDE

GLACIALLY POLISHED SURFACE

Lakes

Italian Camp

end of the road where there is a water diversion project. Expect to pay about US$10 for the vehicle – it is about an hour's drive on a gravel road. You can hire mules near the *hacienda*; ask for José Colcha Mandsanda. It may take a few hours to organize so it is best to plan an overnight stay here so that you are assured of making it to the Italian Camp the next day. The mules can take you to within 2–3km of the camp. The route is muddy so rubber boots are recommended. Try to get the mule driver to take horses up the Cordillera de Mandur as far as they can get before encountering rocky terrain. The best route is to cross to the east side of the Río Paila Cajas (also called Río Blanco) and head straight up to a way trail that contours above cloudforest and into the Río Tiacu Chiquito valley. Head across tussocky terrain to the head of the valley, cross to the south side of Río Tiacu Chiquito and climb the steep grassy slopes to the ridge crest of Cordillera de Mandur. On ascent avoid the cliffs near the waterfall, and stay far right where there are no cliffs. Walk up the rocky ridge to the Italian Camp (4,550m) with obvious tent platforms in a notch with a 5m-high spire. The camp is sometimes buried in snow. Laguna de Mandur is located west and Laguna Negra Pagcha is southeast of the camp. The Italian Camp has an inordinate amount of trash around the tent platform; please help clean up this once pristine spot. A small spring can be found about 100m down the ridge on the west side of the ridge, or you can melt snow.

An alternative and more arduous route is from Collantes Plain. From the plain head south and climb up to Filo de Oregan. The cliffs of Cerro Yanacocha look impenetrable but there is a gully marked with cairns between the peaks marked as 4548 and 4685. An easier route is to head right from the beginning of Collantes Plain and climb the steep grass to a ridge where you will find a trail. There are spectacular views of Altar, Tungurahua, Carihuairazo and Chimborazo. Contour on the north side of Cerro Yanacocha and the south side of peak 4685 until you get to a green lake with an ice fall above. For some reason this lake is not shown on the map, perhaps because old aerial photos where used when glacial ice was present. There are some nice camp spots above this lake.

Follow the outlet stream of this lake downstream towards Laguna Mandur, but before arriving at the lakeshore contour below and eventually up some gravelly ledges and gullies to the Cordillera de Mandur where the Italian Camp is located in a notch. This route is cairned but may be difficult to follow; the tricky part is the finding the right gully up to the ridge. Be careful of rockfall. Realistically with heavy packs it is 2 days to the Italian Camp following this approach. (See El Altar route diagram.)

Climbing Obispo

There are three main routes up Obispo, all of which are described below. Snow conditions are changing on Obispo thus making route finding on this technical peak necessary. It should be noted that the Italian route is rarely climbed because of poor snow conditions in the first couloir. When the

Italians climbed it the gullies were full of snow; now it is a mixed route with rotten rock.

For all routes continue up the ridge from the Italian Camp for about 30 minutes until you get to a gully of rotten rock (there are a couple of tent platforms here) that heads right and down to a glacially polished plain covered with gravel debris. Continue north to the lower glacier, ascend and contour right to the base of Obispo. You can also make a camp here, though the peak can be done in one long day. Any route from the Italian Camp will take at least 12 hours round-trip.

The rock on Obispo is a poorly consolidated volcanic breccia: boulders and cobbles in a mud matrix. Consequently it is easy to pull blocks out and difficult to protect rock pitches. Slinging large protruding boulders is often the best you can do. Climbing without a helmet is stupid.

Italian route The Italian route climbs the wide and obvious couloir in the rock to the left of the main peak. This couloir is now a mixed rock and ice climb (or should we say mixed dirt and snow climb?). With heavy snow covering it is easier. It passes through a rockband to the upper glacier to the left of Obispo and the upper glacier. Once through the first couloir, traverse the upper glacier to the right until you reach the base of a second couloir (rock or snow, depending on conditions), much steeper and narrower than the first. This gully brings you to the summit ridge. From the ridge, head right and you'll be faced with a moderate 30m-high rock wall which is the final barrier to the summit. This final pitch is class 5.5 or 5.6, but the rotten rock makes it much more difficult. It is exposed above the crater, very airy.

Arista de Calvario route To avoid the first couloir of the Italian route, continue around the base of the rock below the upper glacier to the west side of an obvious ridge. Follow up a snow gully to get on the arista or ridge. You may need to negotiate a moat to get on to the rock (low class 5) and follow the ridge to the upper glacier. There may be some crevasses to negotiate on the upper glacier in order to reach the second couloir. From here follow the Italian route.

Variant of Arista de Carvario route or Hidden Couloir From the base of the first couloir on the Italian route find a white dike forming a diagonal couloir heading to the right. This scramble and low class 5 route joins the Arista de Calvario route near the base of the upper glacier. This route is perhaps the most straightforward and fastest access to the upper glacier.

Monkey Hippy
To the left of Obispo is a pyramid-shaped peak on the ridge affectionately named Monkey Hippy after a famous Ecuadorian brand of peanuts. This is a good warm-up climb from the Italian camp. Head straight up the glacier to the ridge to the right of Monkey Hippy; you may need to negotiate some 60° plus slopes to avoid crevasses. It is also possible to climb the rock but

it looks difficult to protect. You can do this climb in about 5 hours round-trip from the Italian camp.

Climbing Monja Grande, Monja Chica and Tabernáculo

To climb the other southern peaks you have to continue from the base of Obispo around the south side of the mountain along the foot of the glacier. Ecuadorian climbers are now using an upper route that traverses across the glaciers. The routes involve technical ice climbing and are more difficult than the routes up Obispo.

Climbing Canonigo and the northern peaks

From the Collantes plain head northeast over the Tungurahuilla ridge where there are possible campsites. Continue to the next ridge, Cerro Negro, where a base camp is made. Mules from Candelaría can reach this point in 2 days, or perhaps one long hard one.

From the base camp on Cerro Negro ridge, traverse the glacier which lies to the northeast of Canonigo, the second highest peak of Altar. Head towards the base of a small ridge which leads to a minor eastern summit of Canonigo. Difficult mixed climbing takes you up the western side of this small ridge and you then curve around the crater towards the summit west of you. A bivouac is often necessary. Canonigo is less frequently climbed than Obispo and is more difficult.

To climb the other northern peaks, the four Frailes, continue around the bottom of the northern glaciers to a camp in the cirque of the Frailes. These peaks have had very few ascents.

Volcán Sangay (5,230m)

Maps: IGM 1:50,000 Volcán Sangay, Alao Llagtapamba and Guamote. You might also try tracking down the 1:25,000 IGM topo for the zone around the volcano, CT-NIV Río Culebrillas.

In many ways Sangay is the most difficult and dangerous mountain to climb in Ecuador. It is said to be the most continuously active volcano in South America and the constant shower of red-hot rocks and ash makes all attempts to climb it an exceedingly hazardous venture. Furthermore it is situated in a very remote region and several days of hard travel are required to reach its base. The volcano is found in the southern central part of the largely inaccessible Parque Nacional Sangay, some 200km south of Quito.

The height of Sangay is usually given as 5,230m but constant activity periodically alters this. The shape of the cone and the number of craters are also constantly changing. The vulcanologist Minard L Hall recorded three main craters and several smaller ones during investigations in 1976.

The first recorded eruption was in 1628 but Sangay was doubtless active before that date. The next 100 years were apparently quiet but since 1728 the volcano has been erupting almost continuously. In 1849 the Frenchman,

Sebastian Wisse, explored the area and counted 267 strong explosions within one hour. A short spell of inactivity occurred from 1916 to 1934 and it was during this time that the volcano was first ascended. The US climbers Robert T and Terris Moore, Paul Austin and Lewis Thorne reached the summit on August 4 1929. Attempts since then have claimed the lives of several climbers, including two British mountaineers who died in 1976 as recorded by Richard Snailham in the book *Sangay Survived*. Despite the constant eruptions and danger, several successful ascents by Ecuadorian climbers have been reported in the 1970s and '80s. On September 16 1982, Helena Landázuri of the Fundación Natura became the first woman to reach the summit. Since then, the volcano has seen quite a few successful attempts, both by expeditions and by individual climbers. (See Sangay map.)

Approach and climb Hiring a guide is essential. You could probably get into the base camp at La Playa with no problem, but finding your way across the lower flanks of the volcano at 02.30 presents some real time-consuming considerations. The route-finding descent is no less difficult. Few guides will accompany you to the summit (each will adamantly declare he has a wife and children to think about!) but a guide will get you to the start of the climb and wait there for your return. There are about 25 guides in an association based in San Antonio across the river from Aloa. The core of this group are Roberto and Carlos Cas. Another well-recommended fellow is José Baño Masa who lives in Alao on the south side of the river; ask anyone in the village for directions to his house, where you can also stay the night. He charges about US$10 a day, depending on the size of the group. Food must be provided for the guide and any porters that may be hired in addition to the wages paid. Be sure to bring enough for everyone.

It is reported that, recently, locals with knowledge of the area are setting themselves up as guides but they are ill-equipped, stand rigidly on a US$10 a day fee for guiding and speak no English. This may be in reaction to INEFAN beefing up the park headquarters, adding more staff, and infusing the system with improvements (with much credit due to Fundación Natura and the US Peace Corps), making it appear as if charging more is justified. Most of them do know the route and can get you in, but be prepared to bargain fiercely.

The initial stages of the approach are simple: take one of many buses from Quito's Terminal Terrestre to Riobamba. On M/W/F/Sa, vegetable trucks depart around 12.30–14.00 for the 2–4-hour trip to Alao from Riobamba's Parque Libertad. At other times, several buses a day go to Licto or Pungala, about 20km south-southeast of Riobamba. From Licto or Pungala occasional trucks go into Alao, which is the starting point for any attempt on Sangay. Taxis can be hired to make the Riobamba–Alao trip for about US$20. There is occasional transport from Licto to Aloa; the walk is 4 hours.

Departing Alao for the return trip to Riobamba is easier. There is an

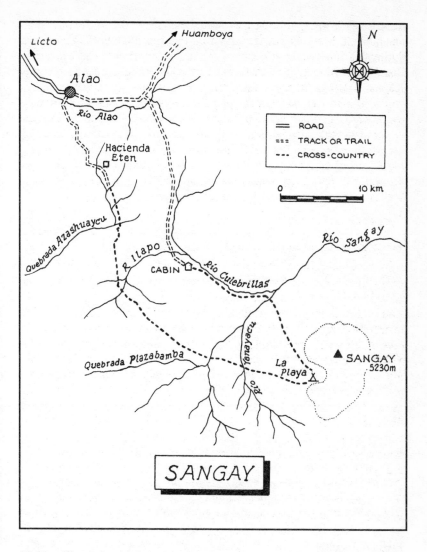

SANGAY

08.00 milk truck which makes the trip daily in addition to other irregular transport.

Alao is a very small village which nevertheless boasts a few small shops where basic last-minute supplies may be purchased. There is also a national park station and two park wardens who will let you sleep in the station for a nominal fee. The park entrance fee is a more-than-nominal US$10.

There are two established routes into La Playa at the base of Sangay. The Eten/Plazapamba route is 3 to 4 days and mules can travel most of the way to mountain. The shorter Culebrillas route takes 3 days but you can only use pack animals on the first day.

Eten/Plazapamba route

It may require some time in Aloa to arrange pack animals. This route begins from Hacienda Eten which is almost a day's hike from Alao. From Eten you head more or less south along the Quebrada Azashuaycu and camp in an area known as Escaleras, continuing the next day in a roughly southeast direction to Plazabamba. The going is very up and down as you constantly climb rises and cross rivers. In one day 14 river fordings were reported. The vegetation here is not too thick. Plazabamba is a large, flat, low area which can be seen from quite a distance. There is a simple shelter which is easy to find in the flat plain. This is as far as the mules will be taken unless the trail is dry (December/January). From here the mule-driver/guide will help you carry your gear to the base camp at La Playa, but the going is difficult.

From Plazabamba, there is more vegetation and the terrain becomes increasingly ridged and difficult. There are many streams and small rivers to ford. La Playa base camp is approximately east-southeast of Plazabamba. Although you are now close to the mountain, almost constant cloud makes a sighting infrequent.

Culebrillas route

This shorter route requires you to carry in your own gear. Pack animals can go part of the way in, but not far enough to justify using them. Because this route is shorter – only 2 to 3 days to base camp – hiring porters to carry extra gear might be more practical than dealing with mules. From Alao the first day's hike goes to the river junction of the Culebrillas, taking anywhere from 8 to 12 hours depending on the trail conditions. The track crosses a watershed which means an ascent (and descent) of almost 1,000 m. There are a couple of grass huts for shelter if you don't feel like setting up a tent. If the weather is good, you'll see magnificent views of Sangay.

From Culebrillas the following day gets you to the Yanayacu river camp in about 4 to 6 hours. If the weather conditions were perfect, and your physical condition nearly that, you could probably make it to La Playa base camp in one very long day. However, it's more realistic to plan on camping at Yanayacu after a day of wading through streams and crossing numerous bogs. From here to La Playa, the route goes up and down constantly, through thick, rough vegetation that can cut the hands. A pair of light gloves will provide some protection. The La Playa area, at 3,600m, is reached after about 4 to 6 hours from Yanayacu. On the southwest side of the mountain, this base camp is an obvious red lava flow flanked by streams. There is a flattish platform of several hundred square metres in size which is used for the camp. Set up tents as close to the mountain as possible. There are signs of previous camps.

In 1995, with the aid of Fundación Natura, the World Wide Fund for Nature and the US Peace Corps, a refuge was constructed at La Playa. It measures 3x5m, with no sleeping pads, but can accommodate 8 to 10 people.

There is a wood stove (but not much wood around the refuge) and a nearby latrine.

At the base camp you may hear numerous explosions but the activity in the last few years has lessened. Clouds often obscure the volcano during the day making night-time viewing the best. Although it is hard work to reach this point you are still not in danger from falling rocks. The ascent to the summit can be done in some 8 hours but changing conditions make it impossible to give a standard route. For quite some time there have been three craters on the summit with all three active at different times and to different degrees. One friend who went in to climb was told by an experienced Ecuadorian climber that the north crater was inactive and that rocks only fell down the western face. When he got there, all three craters were active and, though there were a considerable number of rocks being blown down the west side, he found that debris was coming down all visible faces at one time or another. Another couple of friends who climbed the peak reported that red-hot rocks the size of Volkswagen Beetles were being blasted out of the volcano on the north and west sides of the cone. To the south and east, only small rocks were coming down and most of these were loosened by the vibration of the eruptions and thawing by the sun. The moral of the story is that it is difficult to predict the conditions. Any descriptions will be out of date by the time you get to Sangay and inaccurate information is more dangerous than none at all. However a few general points can make a summit attempt less risky:

- Find out from your guide where the majority of rocks have been falling lately and take some time to observe for yourself.
- Most recent successful attempts have gone up the southeast face which is smooth and virtually featureless. There is no glacier, only firm, compacted snow in places.
- Remember that all routes to the summit can be dangerous. Some climbers have made it to the top without any rocks falling around them, but the risk is real.
- Move as quickly up and back down the slopes as possible and keep your head up, always looking for missiles coming your way.
- An early start, about 02.30, is essential to minimize the danger from rockfall and to make the going quicker on firm snow.

Your guide will take you to the highest point on the base above a *páramo* ridge. Be sure to have him wait for you there. Carry a compass so as not to get lost on the way down in the invariable morning fog. Crampons and an ice axe may or may not be necessary, but it's best to bring them. The climb is not technical but quite steep in parts and it's difficult to avoid falling on your backside on the way down. Wearing two pairs of old trousers will protect you from the sharp lava rock which rips clothes, and skin, easily. A helmet and sturdy work-type gloves are also advised for safety. A rope is not recommended as it would severely limit your ability to dodge falling rocks. There are no good maps covering the region.

Even if you're not planning to climb, a hike to the base camp can be a tremendous experience, especially if the weather is good. For both hiking and climbing, a good selection of waterproofs is a must, including rubber boots for the muddier sections of trail. Attempts on the summit and hikes into the area can be made year round but December to February are the driest months as a rule. July and August are the wettest but other months are also very rainy.

Other routes have been reported as well. Chris Bonington was there in 1966 and records his experiences in his book *The Last Horizon*. He climbed up from the southeast via the Río Upano and Río Volcán. It took him 9 days and he wrote '... every foot of the way had to be hacked from the impenetrable entanglement presented by the undergrowth'. Doesn't sound like much fun! He also reports his ice axe turning a dull yellow-green because of the sulphurous fumes.

El Placer

Maps: IGM 1:50,000 Alao Llagtapamba and Guamote
One of the recent developments in Parque Nacional Sangay is a site named El Placer in the western part of the park about 25km from Alao. A 10-person refuge has been constructed with cooking facilities, toilets and running water. A wood grill exists but a small stove is recommended since there is no wood cache and wood around the refuge is usually wet. The area offers natural hot springs perfect for bathing, excellent trout fishing and superb birdwatching. Spectacled bear and mountain tapir are at home in the dense vegetation.

It's a 2-day trip from Alao, following the old jeep trail to Huambaya, a former community in the centre of the park which was expelled after the area received park status. Take this road out of Alao (locals can point it out) and follow along the clearly defined track for about 5 hours to the site of Cusniparcha where you'll see a small herder's hut and find good camping. If you have access to a 4WD vehicle you can actually drive this far in the dry season; the distance is about 15km of gradual uphill going. Continue along the track 4.5km up to Laguna Negra (3,900m) and then onwards almost 6km to El Placer. You can rent horses in Alao to take you as far as the site known as Magnalena, about 2 hours and 3km above El Placer (3,000m).

Be cautious of leaving your gear at the refuge because a lot of locals use the area for fishing and have been known to take a few things. It is best to leave your gear in the bushes if you plan an extended visit to fish or to explore the hot springs.

From the refuge you can walk 300m (20 minutes) on a very muddy trail to a river where trout fishing can be had. The hot springs are 100m back on the trail that you came down to reach the refuge. About 10m beyond a waterfall is a trail on the right; follow this 350m to a large waist-deep pool with pleasant temperatures ranging between 102° and 105° F. The pool has a sandy bottom with cement walls on one side and there is a changing enclosure.

The best months for hiking in the area are November through January, though raingear and mud boots should be packed even during this 'dry' season. Abundant rain and cloudy conditions make the rest of the year predictably miserable for visitors.

Beyond El Placer

It is possible to continue from El Placer, crossing the park from Aloa to the town of Palora in the Amazon basin. We quote Shane McCarthy, former Peace Corps volunteer working in the park:

> 'Below El Placer, for those hikers liberally endowed with energy, determination, time and a fairly high threshold of pain and misery, there is a great bushwhack route that crosses the park longitudinally, exiting in the Amazon basin and connecting into the Puyo–Macas road. This route provides the opportunity to take in all of the existing life zones in the park, enjoy the thermal pool at El Placer, observe an incredible array of wildlife, and explore ground and historic sites such as ghost town of Huamboya, rarely seen by human eyes.'

With this said, the hike takes 7 to 10 days depending on how many *macheteros* you have in the group. Shane says most definitely you should hire a guide or he recommends 'updating your will and insurance policy'. The only time it makes sense to do the hike is December–February when the rivers are low.

THE ATILLO AREA

The two hikes described in this section originate in the Atillo area yet are completely different in character. One goes across rough *páramo* past high lakes; the other is a hardy hike to the jungles of the Oriente. Take your pick or invent one of your own using the IGM maps for the area. The region is wide open for adventure and exploration.

This is an area for experienced campers, hikers and mountaineers who want to get as far off the beaten track as possible.

Access The following access information covers the various possible routes to Atillo, which is approached from the main city of Riobamba.

To get to Riobamba take one of several buses which leave daily from Quito's Terminal Terrestre. From Riobamba you can either take the Cebadas–El Tingo route to Atillo, or go via the new direct Guamote–Atillo road. Transport is scarce beyond both Cebadas and Guamote, but the road from Guamote is more direct and in better condition.

Head for Guamote which is situated just off the Pan-American Highway, about an hour south of Riobamba. You can take a bus direct from Riobamba, or any heading south (to Alausí or Cuenca), and have the driver let you off at the village entrance. The best place to stay in Guamote is Residencial Turismo Guamote – about US$3 per night. There are several basic restaurants in town. Not many visitors come to Guamote so the locals are very friendly. If you bump into Milton Arguello Rivera, the director of the high school, he may invite you to share some rum and songs with his friends.

The newly constructed road to Atillo has regular transport on Thursday mornings but very few vehicles make the trip on other days. You could hire a truck in Guamote (contact Gonzalo Leon on 916 133 and expect to pay about US$35 for the trip), or walk for 1½ days (about 45km) to Atillo. Thursday is market day in Guamote, and transport in general is much easier to come by then, either up the new road toward Atillo, or along the alternative route through Cebadas to El Tingo.

Alternatively, to get to Cebadas, make your way to the Barrio El Dolorosa section of Riobamba (a taxi will take you there cheaply) to catch the Cooperativa de Transportes Unidos (CTU) bus. It leaves daily at 15.00 from the intersection two blocks away from El Dolorosa bus terminal. There is an extra bus on Wednesdays and three additional ones on Saturdays going to Cebadas. There are no places to stay in the village but plenty of options for camping. From here you'll need to make your way to El Tingo. A milk truck leaves every morning at 04.00 (except holidays) for the trip up to El Tingo. If going on foot, it's about 6 to 7 hours of pleasant road walking. Other options for getting to El Tingo are to hire a *camioneta* in Riobamba, or to catch a market-day truck from Guamote (detailed above). The trip from El Tingo to Atillo is covered in the first day's hike in El Tingo to Macas; see 'Hiking directions' on page 208.

The following two hikes tell you what to do once you've managed to get into this area.

From Andes to jungle: El Tingo to Macas
Maps: IGM 1:50,000 Guamote, Palmira, Totoras, Río Upano, Macas 207 (planometric)

> 'In the course of a day, the nakedness of the Interior changed to the luxuriousness of the tropics;... we passed through forest trees rising 150 feet high, mast-like, without a branch, laden with parasitic growth.'
> Edward Whymper, 1892

Walking through windswept *páramo*, passing remote thatched huts and bundled-up indigenous people herding sheep, crossing a high Andean pass and then dropping down through lush high mountain forest into the jungles of the Oriente – this is an adventurous hike which shows a remarkable cross section of Ecuador's scenery, vegetation and wildlife.

The locals walk this trail in 3 long days, but we recommend twice this if you are to enjoy the scenery and observe some of the wildlife. The hike begins in the highlands south of the major town of Riobamba, then crosses a pass in the Eastern Cordillera some 30km southwest of the continuously active volcano, Sangay, before dropping steeply into the huge wilderness area of the almost trackless Parque Nacional Sangay. You finally emerge at the small but important town of Macas, about 1,000m above sea level, situated on the Río Upano on the edge of Ecuadorian Amazonia.

Macas was first settled by the Spaniards nearly 400 years ago and the trail follows the old communication and trading route joining the lowlands with the highlands. Thus the hike is of historical as well as geographical and ecological interest. Today Macas is at the end of an unasphalted road running north–south along the banks of the Río Upano. The northbound road to Puyo is now completed. Transportes San Francisco has buses which depart daily from Macas; the southbound road goes through Sucua and then on to Cuenca, the nearest major city, some 12 hours away. A road is projected westwards over the highlands to Guamote and the first section to the Río Abanico, some 20km west of Macas, has been completed. On the Andes side a road has now been put in past Atillo, and should be completed all the way to Macas by the year 2000. For now, however, little transport uses the new sections of road, so the hike is still a pleasing one. (See Andes to Jungle Hike map, page 209.)

Weather and times to go In the highland section, you are just west enough to experience the weather pattern of the central highlands. The typical dry season is from June through September, with a short dry season in late December and early January and wet otherwise. The lowlands are always wet but the least rainy months are late September through December. We went during the first week in October and more or less avoided rain, but it seems as if most other periods (with the exception of December) will have rain during one part of the hike or another.

Equipment By following this route description carefully, you'll find a shelter for every night except one. You may decide to take the risk of one night's wet bivvy and leave the tent behind. But a tent is useful for complete independence, so good campsites are also mentioned. The difficulty, of course, is that the warm clothing needed for the highlands will be unnecessary weight in the lowlands. I partially solved the problem by bringing a very light sleeping bag and sleeping in my clothes in the highlands. (In December/January temperatures in both highlands and lowlands may be cool enough to warrant a medium-weight sleeping bag.) Raingear is essential.

I found ex-army jungle boots the best footwear because regular boots soon became hopelessly waterlogged and heavy in the deep mud of the lowland section. I made a point of keeping a dry shirt, pair of trousers and sneakers in a plastic bag. This way I always had warm, dry clothes to put on in the evenings, even if I'd spent hours sloshing through calf-deep mud and bogs during the day. (This system only works if you're prepared to dress in your wet and muddy hiking outfit every morning.) Insect repellent is useful, although the bugs are not bad. Very little food is available en route and you should bring enough for 5 to 6 days.

Access Refer to the access directions on page 205.

Hiking directions A suitable distance for the first hiking day is from El Tingo to Atillo. You will be following a newly constructed, yet deserted, dirt road the entire way, but don't let this put you off. This is an extremely pleasant and not difficult 5 to 7-hour walk through gently rising pastureland with starkly beautiful rather than spectacular views. You'll see herds of sheep, cattle and perhaps semi-wild horses. The people are politely friendly but rather reserved and obviously not used to backpackers. The vegetation is grassy. You are within sight of the river all the way and there is plenty of water.

The road follows along Río Cebadas until the river divides in two, forming Río Osogoche which falls away to the southwest, and Río Atillo which now runs alongside the road. It passes through the straggling community of Colay (a few houses and a schoolhouse) and continues south and southeast through the wide river valley to the village of Atillo, some 7–8km beyond Colay. En route you will change from the Palmira to the Totoras map. Atillo is distinguished by a church, a cemetery and a schoolhouse in which you can sleep. There are plenty of good camping spots in the area before Atillo, or you can continue for about an hour beyond the village to campsites near the lakes.

Past Atillo the road soon curves around to the east and heads along the northern shores of the Laguna de Atillo. There are good campsites with fine views of the lakes and the occasional snow peaks of Cerros Achipungo (4,630m), Yanaurco and Sasquín beyond the lakes to the south. Don't camp too close to the lakes as the banks are boggy; it's best to camp on the hillocks just north of the first lake. There are streams for drinking water.

The second day is in many ways the most spectacular of the whole hike as you cross a pass in the Eastern Cordillera and start dropping down into the Amazonian rainforest. The change in vegetation is remarkable. Standing on the pass, you see the stark grassy *páramo* stretching away behind you, while in front huge cloud masses build up from the lowlands as the highlands fall away into incredibly lush cloudforest full of bromeliads and birdsong. Stands of huge trees rear out of the dense carpet of lower foliage and everywhere you look is covered with seemingly impenetrable vegetation. The change from bleak *páramo* to tropical cloudforest is so sudden it stuns your credibility – it has to be seen to be believed.

The road follows along the north sides of Lagunas de Atillo and the third lake Laguna Negra and continues over the pass. Since the road is under construction it is best to ask how to get on to the trail at wherever the road ends. The steep trail down through the jungle is unmistakable and there are no forks where you could get lost, but it is sometimes used by pack animals and is usually churned up with thick mud. Occasional slippery logs are a psychological aid, although when you slide off them and end up in the muck you may not feel that they are all that helpful. After an hour of very

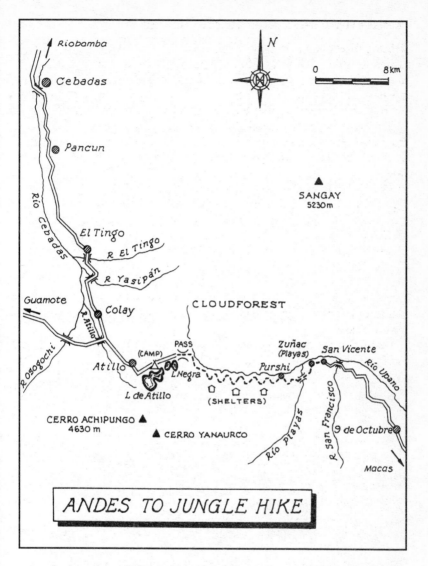

ANDES TO JUNGLE HIKE

steep descent the trail flattens out and follows the south side of the deeply cut Río Upano valley. About 2 to 3 hours beyond the divide you'll cross a small stream (with possible but stony camping spots on either side). It's better to continue for an hour to a flat, grassy camping area with the remains (four poles) of a small shelter on the right of the trail. The stream just mentioned is your best water source, but there are also smaller trickles every few hundred metres.

The following day will be an extremely muddy one. Sloshing along the trail isn't really much fun; what we did was make this a half day's walk and then spent the afternoon at the next campsite which boasts good views and the chance to admire the flowers, trees, bromeliads and thick vegetation and to observe colourful insects and various bird species such as hummingbirds and parrots. Why rush? Relax and enjoy your unusual surroundings – easier to do from a dry camp than along the trail.

From the remains of the first shelter continue about 2 hours to a second one in similar condition. Another 2 hours will bring you to an actual hut with a tin roof and wooden floor which is suitable for passing the afternoon and spending the night. You can't get lost on the trail.

The fourth day will see you continuing eastwards following the slowly dropping Río Upano valley through lush vegetation and ending up at an unusual campsite... From the hut about 3 hours of hiking will bring you to the settlement of Purshi which is marked on the map with ten squares and a Parque Nacional Sangay sign. You could camp here if you wanted, though there are some rather wild-looking cattle which would probably love to rub themselves up against your tent, but about 1 hour beyond Purshi you come to a covered bridge crossing the Río Playas. This bridge, some 10m long and 2m wide and with a tin roof, provided us with a unique campsite where we were lulled to sleep by the rushing rapids below. Be careful not to drop anything though; you certainly wouldn't see it again.

If you don't like the idea of sleeping on the bridge then you could continue for about an hour to the friendly village marked as Zuñac on the map but known locally as Playas after the nearby river. The village consists of about two dozen buildings scattered around a large grass square, and there is a church and a schoolhouse where you can sleep. This is the first settlement after Atillo. Although the distance from Atillo to Zuñac looks relatively short on the map, the extremely winding trail makes it a much longer hike than the map indicates.

On the fifth day you will be walking through more cultivated countryside with plenty of signs of settlement. You'll probably meet a few people driving mules up the trail, or a woodcutter or smallholder. They'll usually stop for a chat and are good sources of information about the trail ahead. The trail beyond Zuñac is blessedly firmer and less muddy. From Zuñac 1½ hours of steep climbing will bring you to two or three huts marking the community of San Vicente. Here is where the hard-packed dirt road picks up once again (or ends if one is travelling from Macas). Follow the road for about 4 to 5 hours until you reach Nueve de Octubre which is the largest community on the hike but unmarked on the maps. You could spend the night in a schoolhouse here, or in the Parque Nacional Sangay hut which is staffed by a friendly warden. Buses leave for Macas on Wednesdays and Sundays, or you can hire a truck (US$10) for the 1½-hour trip.

Macas is a gateway town into the jungle. Views of the nearby active volcano Sangay are good on clear days (rare) and it is a useful centre for day hikes into the surrounding countryside (see *The Macas Area* in *Chapter Seven*). There are some mid-priced hotels with private baths as well as the cheap and basic variety and plenty of restaurants. You're back in the 20th century.

Atillo to Achupallas

Maps: From Atillo, two 1:50,000 topographical maps cover the route - Totoras and Alausí. If coming from Cebadas, you'll also need the 1:50,000 maps of Guamote and Palmira.

Very few established hikes in Ecuador combine cross-country navigating across high *páramo* and around remote lakes with isolated villages where simple footpaths provide the only means of access. This 3- to 5-day hike goes into an area rarely visited by any outsider, let alone *gringo* trekkers. For this reason, it is a unique and spectacular area to explore. On the other hand, it sets up a fragile situation which demands a level of responsibility from the intruder. Practising sound environmental and ecological techniques means not only preserving the natural beauty around you by treading lightly, but treating those cultures with whom you come into contact with equal care. Sweets and loose change tossed out liberally serve no purpose other than to corrupt. As an old-time American hiker once said, 'Take only photographs and leave only footprints', and even taking photographs (of people) should be avoided. There is a lot of wet ground so bring rubber boots for hiking. (See Atillo to Achupallas map page 212.)

Access Refer to the access directions for *Atillo Area* page 205.

Hiking directions Because of the lengthy approach, you are likely to be arriving in Atillo in the early afternoon. For camping, you can continue past Atillo and look for a suitable spot along Río Atillo. Better still, and time allowing, you could continue another ½-hour to just below Laguna Atillo, or another 2 to 3 hours to Laguna Iguan. Atillo is a spread-out community and the residents are suspicious of visitors. Since the area is part of Parque Nacional Sangay, locals on horseback may ask you for written permission to enter. To avoid this problem you can pay the entrance fee, either at the INEFAN offices in Quito or on the spot.

The route follows the road out of the village for about 5 minutes until Laguna Atillo comes into view. The road will continue up along the north shore, but as soon as you see the lake drop south, crossing a small creek just below the road, and head through a pasture toward Río Atillo about a ½-hour away. From the road you'll spot two prominent hills before Lake Atillo. Head for the right-hand hill and you'll find camping possible between the hill and the river. If continuing on, find the best place to cross the river, and then begin the climb up the middle valley (you'll see three valleys coming down into Laguna Atillo) to Laguna Iguan about 1 hour away. There's no trail, but cattle tracks are everywhere. The going is easy up this steep valley, following the left-hand side of the creek which flows from the lake. Laguna Iguan is beautiful, situated in a big bowl with stunning views looking back northeast to the mountains. There is obvious camping on the southeast side of the lake. A picturesque waterfall at the south end completes the scene. At night the place comes alive with the lights of a million fireflies

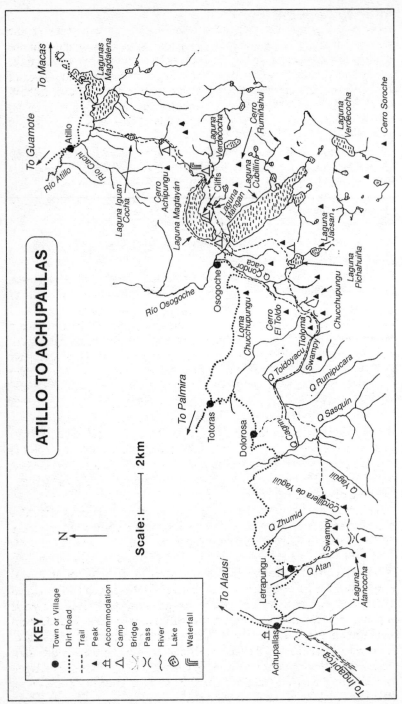

ATILLO TO ACHUPALLAS

Scale: ├──────┤ 2km

N ←

KEY
● Town or Village
⋯⋯ Dirt Road
--- Trail
▲ Peak
⌂ Accommodation
△ Camp
)(Bridge
)(Pass
⌒ River
◯ Lake
▥ Waterfall

and noisy frogs singing in chorus.

The next day is a very rugged stretch, heading cross-country up the *páramo*. The going is wet and awkward across tussocks, or spongy clumps of vegetation, heading up to Laguna Pocacocha 2 hours away. Animal trails will be found occasionally to make the going a little easier, but you can't rely on them. Get a compass bearing before starting out. The route follows a wide valley with a creek from Pocacocha flowing through it; keep far right on the flanks as you climb up to the lake. The area is lovely around Laguna Pocacocha and good for camping.

From Laguna Pocacocha, the route climbs up to a pass at 4,300m about 2 hours away. Again, take a compass bearing before continuing. Stay on the right side of the valley as you skirt Laguna Pocacocha, and follow alongside the creek as the route ascends. About halfway up the valley, the creek begins to branch out and following it will not be reliable. At this point look up toward the only grassy pass and spot a huge rectangular-shaped rock leaning at an angle to the right. Head for this and cross the pass which is about 50m above.

An interesting sidetrip from the pass would be to climb Cerro Achipungo, a mere 360m higher. The climb to the top is easy, following the ridge up to the summit.

From the pass, it's fairly obvious where to go, but it's best to take a compass bearing off the map for the easternmost point of Laguna Magtayán. You can see two smaller lakes from the pass, and could also get a compass bearing on these. The descent follows a narrow creek through a marshy area which funnels down to an obvious notch. Before you get to a notch find a pass to the right and follow a cattle trail down to a large rockfall. In this section you get glimpses of Laguna Magtayán and Osogoche. Follow a stream around to the eastern end of Laguna Magtayá. The last 200m is a little tricky. A steep grassy chute almost literally drops you down to the lake. Hanging on to the tall grass and sliding on your backside is one method that works. It's about 2 hours from the top of the pass down to the lake. Camping near its eastern point is ideal.

The following day you have two options, skirting the right or left sides of the Laguna Magtayán. The trail on the right is straightforward and takes you to the community of Osogoche. The more interesting route on the left side heads up to a pass above a rocky cliff that blocks travel along the lakeshore. Climb high early and contour over to the pass about 1 hour away. From this pass you see two lakes, Laguna Mangan and an unnamed lake. A cowpath skirts to the right of the unnamed lake. This is a good camping spot. It's easy walking across (still more) *páramo*, with the trail becoming more distinct as you continue southwest past the small lake. Cross the outlet stream of the lakes and contour around a grassy ridge until Laguna Cubillín comes into view. Make your way west to the point between the lakes Magtayán and Cubillín. There are spectacular views of the entire area: lots of lakes and small settlements.

(For the truly adventurous, an extra day or two could be set aside for exploring the southwest end of Laguna Cubillín. From the map it would appear to be an incredible area with rocky bluffs and an abundance of small lakes.)

The trail heads for a small settlement at the north point of Cubillín lake, but the villagers here have learned to beg from the few strangers passing through. It may be better to keep a little distance. There are footbridges across both streams but they are also easily waded. Once across the streams, head for the road leading into Osogoche. The villagers here may also be persistent about wanting gifts or money. As with the last community, it might be easier to avoid the village by skirting south, picking up the road leading out of town. You can camp about 15–30 minutes out of Osogoche, near a stream, depending on how long or short a day you choose. There is daily traffic from Osogoche to Totoras in the morning and you can arrange to buy a meal in Osogoche.

You could continue by walking the road to Achupallas but a more interesting route is through the high country. Head up the ridge on the west side of Laguna Cubillín over peak 4008 and Loma Chugchuyacu. The basin to the west does not contain two lakes as shown on the IGM map! Cross the basin and head southwest to Laguna Pichahuiña, a good spot to camp with opportunities to see condors. Walk around the north side of Laguna Pichahuiña and head for Cerro El Toldo, a grassy hill to the west. Reach the pass between Cerro El Toldo and Tioloma, contour around to the pass on the southeast side of Tioloma, then drop down into the grassy U-shaped valley of Quebrada Toldoyacu. This valley is boggy because for most of it there is no stream channel so water flows through the vegetation. Turn left at Quebrada Cagrín. We found a good camping spot next to Quebrada Rumipucará.

It is an easy walk from here on an established track south of Loma Yurac to the Achupallas road. If you have an extra day, heading up the rocky ridge of Cordillera de Yagüil is highly recommended for the views. Go downstream slightly and contour around Loma Santa Ana. Cross Quebrada Sasquin and find a trail on the right-hand side of Quebrada Tiucuhuaycu that eventually crosses the ridge of the same name. Descend to Quebrada Yagüil where there is a colourful community of *chozas*. Find a water pipeline on the other side and follow it uphill to a water tank. Continue to the rocks above. From here are spectacular views of Cerro Soroche, a seldom seen let alone climbed peak 20km to the east. Cerro Soroche is very alpine looking and sometimes covered with snowfields. Head southwest around Cerro Atán on a trail. The walking along the ridge is quite pleasant. We crossed a pass and descended the right side of Quebrada Atán to the village of Letrapunga but you can also continue to Atilla Puga and descend directly into Achupallas avoiding the road altogether. Below the cliffs, Laguna Atancocha is beautiful, but it is too swampy to camp alongside the lake. There are places to camp above 3,920m next to the stream; below this elevation the valley sides are steep. You could also arrange to stay in the village of Letrapungu.

In Achupallas there are no hotels or restaurants, but you can stay in the school. Contact Jorge Merchan or Alonso Zea (both on the main square near the church) for meals or a bed. Transport is available to Alausí about 2 hours away. Trucks leave at 07.00 for Alausí and return around lunchtime. You can also get a truck to Alausí for about US$20. Even better, continue along the Inca road to Ingapirca (see *Chapter Four*).

SARAGURO

Maps: IGM 1:50,000 Saraguro and San José de Yacuambi

Saraguro is home to the Cañari indigenous group who fiercely resisted the Inca conquest and to this day maintain cultural independence and pride. Sunday is market day with a chance to see the distinctive Canãri dress and perhaps buy some pigs, vegetables and handicrafts. The countryside around Saraguro is well worth exploring. You can hike 2km outside of town to the caves of Sinincapa where there are several pools including the Inca's bathtub. Take the road north out of town and ask for directions. A trip to the Virgencaca waterfall located on the Río Huaylashi makes a full day on foot. There are two possible routes, both on jeep tracks: Tuncarta–Tambopamba–Oñacapa or Namarin–Tambopamba–Oñacapa. The falls are about a mile down from Oñacapa and it's best to have someone show you the way. You can climb Puglla from Saraguro or Cerro de Areos from the village of Manu. Not many travellers visit this area and there are more day hikes to be discovered. To reach Saraguro take a bus on the Pan-American Highway from Cuenca (3 hours) or Loja (1 hour). You can easily arrange a homestay with a Cañari family or try the Residencia Armijos in town.

Saraguro to Yacuambi

This is another Andes to Amazon route that was once used frequently to drive cattle from the Oriente until it was supplanted by access from a new road between Loja and Zamora. We have not done this route but it would probably take 3 days and you should carry adequate food. It is a good idea to find someone to guide you on this route. You pass three *páramo* lakes and a rock formation known as the *piedra voladora* ('flying stone').

THE VILCABAMBA VALLEY AND PARQUE NACIONAL PODOCARPUS

The Vilcabamba Valley located in the southern province of Loja is an area of rolling hills and lush vegetation that ranges from tropical montane cloudforest to stark *páramo*. The valley at 1,500m is surrounded by forested mountains nearing an altitude of 3,500m. With the dramatic snow-capped volcanoes attracting the majority of attention in the central and northern parts of the country, this beautiful area is often overlooked by hikers. Access is from the city of Loja which, being the commercial centre of the province, is served by buses from all parts of the country. There is also an airport about an hour away with daily flights (except Sunday) from Quito and Guayaquil. Vilcabamba is about 45 minutes by road south of Loja. Buses leave frequently from Azuay and Guerrero on the west side of Loja across the river.

The Vilcabamba Valley

Vilcabamba has for many years been famous as the 'Valley of Longevity'. Based on a single anthropological study done some years ago, international attention was drawn to the valley inhabitants who supposedly lived to be well over 100 years old. The excellent climate and simple, unhurried lifestyle in this peaceful valley were said to be major contributing factors. Further scientific research has failed to substantiate the initial research but the legend persists and gives the area a certain claim to fame.

The valley is popular with travellers looking for a place to take it easy. Vilcabamba is a small town and horses can be rented for excursions into the countryside. There are some charming places to stay, one of the most popular being the *cabañas* of Madre Tierra. The simple bungalows, rustic sauna (with mud baths), home-cooked, mostly vegetarian meals, and gardens of colourful flowers make it an excellent base for hikes around the area. Owners Jaime Mendoza and his Canadian wife, Durga, are wonderful people and excellent sources of information. About 4km south of town the cheaper and equally friendly Cabañas Río Yambala are run by Charlie and Sarah.

Day hikes and longer excursions are limited only by one's imagination. The IGM 1:50,000 Vilcabamba map shows a number of trails and local *gringos* can suggest many more. One short trip worth making is to visit the local zoo, called Subcomisión Ecuatoriana Centro Recreacional. It's about a 20-minute walk out of the town centre. Follow the road on the north side of the plaza and go east, crossing a bridge and continuing uphill. The road angles to the right (southeast) and you'll follow it until it reaches a junction with a school on the right. Take the smaller dirt road on the right and continue downhill until you see the zoo sign. The collection of animals including monkeys, spectacled bears, ocelots and a variety of large birds is somewhat interesting, but what makes the trip worthwhile is the large greenhouse devoted solely to the cultivation of orchids. There are over 30 varieties, some quite rare, which have been collected from areas throughout the province.

For more demanding excursions, Parque Nacional Podocarpus is a magnificent hiking area with much potential, just north of Vilcabamba. It has seen little tourism so far, but a few hikes are described here.

Parque Nacional Podocarpus

Maps: Along with the rather vague yet functional map of the park available from the INEFAN office, the 1:100,000 IGM map Gonzanamá gives a good overview of the Vilcabamba side of the park, and the 1:50,000 maps of Río Sabinilla and Vilcabamba will serve for hikes. On the Zamora side the 1:50,000 maps of Zamora and Cordillera de Tzunantza cover a fair bit of the area but cannot be purchased at IGM.

Parque Nacional Podocarpus was established by the Ministry of Agriculture on December 15 1982 and now is managed by INEFAN. Podocarpus is the scientific name for a type of conifer tree, the only one native to Ecuador. This huge tree can occasionally be found with trunks 3m in diameter and growing to 40m in height. However, its fine, rose-coloured wood is highly prized and the pressure of logging has resulted in the elimination of this magnificent conifer from much of the Ecuadorian sierra. Today the majority of remaining small forests now exist within the park boundaries.

The park spans an area of 146,280ha, much of which is unspoiled cloudforest between the highland city of Loja and the city of Zamora in the Oriente. Divided by the Cordillera El Nudo de Sabanilla mountain range, the park ranges in altitude from 1,000m to 3,600m. Six distinct life zones from Amazonian rainforest to high Andean *páramo* provide suitable habitats for a wide array of plants and animals. It is one of the few remaining protected areas for the elusive spectacled bear. Other mammals found in the park include the mountain tapir, the sloth, the Andean wolf (which is actually a fox) and the puma. The birdlife is especially noteworthy with such species as guans, toucans, woodpeckers, flycatchers, swifts, tanagers, hummingbirds and parrots.

There are two principal entrances into the park. The Cajanuma Park Station is approached from Loja on the western side of the park, and the Bombuscara Park Station is located on the Zamora side in the Oriente. Both have basic refuges at the park entrance where small groups could probably sleep or set up tents nearby. Plans call for an expansion of these facilities, but progress is slow. Short self-guided trails have been developed by Peace Corps worker Eric Horstman and other volunteers, and ideas for a more detailed information centre are being discussed. A park entrance fee of US$10 for the highlands and US$20 for lowland portions of the park is charged and permission should be obtained from the INEFAN office in either Loja or Zamora. If this proves difficult you could show up at either of the stations and probably pay there. The advantage of going to the INEFAN office is for a map of the area which. though quite basic, is nonetheless useful.

Fundación Ecológica Arco Iris has a strong interest in preserving the forests of Podocarpus and southern Ecuador. They have education programmes for children, assist scientists, and are working to keep mining interests out of the park. They also have several reserves including Tambo Negro, a dry forest near the Peruvian border. Arco Iris is one of the most serious NGOs in Ecuador working for conservation. For more information on hikes in the Loja area contact Fausto Lopez at their offices in Loja: Lauro Guerrero 12-09 y Mercadillo, tel: 572 926, email: fai1@fai.org.ec.

Weather and times to go As the park is so heavily forested, with a broad range of elevations running from the highlands to the edge of the Oriente, the weather within its boundaries is a combination of many climatic zones. This mainly means that when it's raining in the highlands from February through April, it rains in Podocarpus, and when it's raining in the Oriente from

May through August, it rains in Podocarpus. And of course even during the dry season it can rain! The best month for visiting either side of the park is November, with a somewhat dry period of grace between September and January. On the Cajanuma side the rain is a major impediment; due to the altitude it is quite cold and potentially hypothermic. On the Zamora side this is less of a problem. Here the rain is just wet and the trail muddy (it almost always is!), and it is refreshing rather than a major bother.

Equipment If it's not already obvious, good raingear is an essential part of the equipment list, along with the usual tent, stove, sleeping bag, etc. Sturdy, waterproof jungle boots are best, but you can temporarily mistreat your feet and get by with simple rubber boots (*botas para agua*). Bring plenty of plastic bags to keep spare clothes and other items dry.

Cajanuma ranger station park entrance

Access The Loja–Vilcabamba bus passes the Cajanuma park entrance at the top of the pass about 6km south out of Loja. From here it's a 7km, 2–3-hour walk uphill to the ranger station. Alternatively, you can hire a taxi in Loja for about US$6 and, if going only for the day, can arrange with the driver to return and pick you up at a fixed time.

Hikes within the area At the ranger station, there are several short hiking trails, one which takes you up through temperate forests full of mountain tanagers to a prominent ridge for some beautiful views over the valley. A longer hike requiring an overnight camp is to head up to Laguna de Compadre, which is actually several lakes, in a high *páramo* setting. A steep trail with great cloudforest vegetation leads up from the ranger station, crosses the *cordillera* and finally gets you to the lakes at 3,200m in about 6 to 8 hours. The trail may be marked by flagging, but it is important to stay on the spine of the *cordillera* as trails branch off the main trail. There are views of the Vilcabamba valley and the uncut watershed of the Río Sabinilla. It's a beautiful place to stay for a day or two, making short hikes in the area.

Bombuscara ranger station park entrance

Access This entrance is located outside of Zamora on the eastern side of the park. The vegetation is much more tropical here and the climate more tolerable. From Loja you can take a bus; Transportes Viajeros or Transportes Loja both make the 3-hour trip several times a day. The ride across the *cordillera* and the drop down to the Oriente side is spectacular. Zamora has a few simple places to stay, Hostal Seyma (US$3.50) just off the plaza being one of the best. You can also go directly to the park entrance (easiest to hire a taxi) and walk 20 minutes into the refuge to camp there. Before leaving Zamora, however, it would be best to stop at the INEFAN office which is on the main road just as you enter Zamora. Look for a large INEFAN sign on the right. Here you can get a map, pay your entrance fee and talk with the park guardians.

Hiking around the area For birdwatchers, the Bombuscara area is especially exciting. You don't have to wander far from the guard station to see an incredible variety of bird species. There is a day hike (4 hours in) along a good trail following the Río Bombuscara. It wanders through semi-tropical vegetation and cloudforest and is not too demanding. The friendly park guards (Luis Tambo is especially knowledgeable) can suggest other outings in the area.

For a longer and more rugged adventure, I heartily suggest the following 4- to 5-day hike from Romerillos. For cloudforest vegetation, this area is unequalled in all of Ecuador, perhaps even in South America. I must, however, admit that our experience in the area was unique and not likely to be repeated by subsequent hikers.

It started when our plans for hiking into the park from the Cajanuma side were literally washed away. We had set aside the time for an extended hike or two and were not to be swayed in our attempts to get out and do something. We decided that if it was going to rain, we might as well be in an area where it wouldn't matter so we headed for the Zamora side of Parque Nacional Podocarpus. Looking at the maps in the MAG office and talking with the park guards, we discovered there was a loop trek that appeared to take about 3 days. The guard looked a little sceptical, explaining that going in was no problem but the last section out was a *trocha* (barely-hacked trail) of *puro lodo* (pure mud). It was also an area of the park where mining concessions had been granted by another ministry (such is life in South America) and we had to get permission from the mining company to enter this part of the park. Undaunted by the *trocha* of *puro lodo* and with permission in hand, we set off to the settlement of Romerillos for the start of the hike. We discovered the route most of the way was a log trail constructed by RTZ mining company several years ago. Despite the explorative mining operation in the area, this part of the forest is virtually untouched and the birdlife prolific. The mountain tanagers became common after the first day, loads of Amazonas parrots flew overhead and we were lucky enough to see the Andean cock-of-the-rock and an umbrella bird among many other colourful species, which are fairly common at Bombuscara.

Early on the first day we passed a messenger going into one of the mining camps who eyed us incredulously. Evidently three *gringo* women carrying large packs were not a common sight. (We discovered later that we were the first trekkers to have ever gone into that area.) About the time we were ready to stop for the day we arrived at the makeshift mining camp to find they were expecting us. The messenger had done his job admirably. We were given hot coffee, fed dinner and provided with our own dry tent (compliments of the miners) for the night. Talk around the fire after dinner was entertaining with tales of lost cities and other jungle lore. We also discovered that further along the trail two established camps of wooden buildings had been permanently set up for the mining operation. These we could use along the way.

With thanks for the unexpected hospitality, we set out the next day, planning only to hike the 4 hours or so to the first of the wooden structures called Dos Camas. It was an interesting juxtaposition of concepts to be walking along a well-constructed log trail and to realize at the same time that we were deep into a remote area of virgin cloudforest. This was made even clearer when we arrived at Dos Camas and found the two guardians there preparing lunch – for us! Without our knowing, a runner had been sent from the previous camp early that morning with the message that we were on our way and to take good care of us. We were shown to our readied bunkroom, fed lunch and dinner, and breakfast the next morning! It was slightly embarrassing to find ourselves being treated so well on our 'adventurous' trek.

Again we gave thanks for the unexpected hospitality and headed for the second of the mining structures, called La Cumbre, near the top of the *cordillera*. It was an uphill hike, almost 1,000m gain to La Cumbre at 2,450m. The vegetation began to change and the forest opened up from time to time presenting some of the most amazing views I've ever seen – mountain after mountain after mountain of cloudforest. The last hour to La Cumbre was spent in pouring rain, not entirely comfortable at that altitude. However, we were greeted at the top by the camp guardian, Ramiro, who declared, '*Que valiente!*' and admitted he didn't think we'd make it. We should have known we'd be expected. Hot coffee was delivered to our bunkroom only a few minutes after arriving, and we were invited to help ourselves to hot showers whenever we were ready! It turned out that La Cumbre was the operations centre for the mining company, and all was provided for, including flush toilets and a generator for electricity. Needless to say, we had lunch, dinner and breakfast provided, along with some interesting conversation with Ramiro, who knew the area well.

The next morning we gave the accustomed warm thanks and headed up to the top of the mountain and beyond, to the *trocha* and *puro lodo* that awaited us. We were accompanied by Ubaldo, one of the camp guardians, who was leaving for his short vacation. We were hoping to make the 17km to Romerillos in one day, but the *trocha* and *puro lodo* made moving difficult. We came to appreciate fairly quickly the 3 days spent walking along the log trail. This was work – traversing vertical landslide areas with little more than vines to hang on to, picking our way gingerly around pits of thigh-high mud, slipping down through narrow trails as vines and branches snagged bulky backpacks, and crossing raging rivers on thin logs. The day wore on interminably and Romerillos seemed a distant fantasy. So did the last 3 days of easy living. After 12 hours of *pura lucha* (pure struggle), we found an abandoned shelter, shook out our sleeping bags, and laid down our weary bones without so much as a thought about eating. It was just good not to be stumbling any longer.

The following morning we made it back to Romerillos in time for the

08.00 bus to Zamora, on which we suffered the stares of the other passengers who no doubt were wondering how these *gringas* came to be so far from home and so completely covered with *puro lodo*!

The Romerillos Loop

Warning: This area may not be as safe as it once was. Gangs of 'freelance' miners and robbers may be roaming the area due to the lack of supervision once provided by the principal mining company there. Check with the park officials in Zamora first.

It appears that the mining company has pulled out of the area, not having found the 'mother lode', and it will be interesting to see what INEFAN decides to do with this part of the park. The buildings along the way are permanent, so even if things are locked up there's enough covered space to make a suitable shelter.

From Zamora, buses depart from the Terminal Terrestre for Romerillos twice a day, at 06.30 and 14.15, for the 2-hour trip. There is only one IGM map which covers very little of the actual hike – the 1:50,000 Cordillera de Tzunantza – and it's not very useful in the thick forest. Actually you don't really need much more than the INEFAN map. It's pretty difficult to get lost on the trip in. If you're not on the trail, you're in impenetrable cloudforest and not going anywhere.

At the collection of small houses known as Romerillos, the official road ends. There is a park refuge here where you could pass the night. The hike starts at the bridge – cross it and follow the dirt road which continues to run alongside the river for a short way and then angles left. The road eventually peters out and a track picks up. Stay on the main track, which is noticeably wider and more used than any smaller tracks you may cross. It makes a series of short up and downs for about 1½ hours, then begins a serious ascent of a steep hill just past the bridge. This is the last water until ½ an hour past the summit.

The ascent, now along a log trail, takes about 2 to 3 hours, going from 1,450m at Romerillos to 2,400m at the top, and back down to about 1,650m at camp. There are some lovely areas with waterfalls past the summit making a nice lunch stop. Continuing along the trail, you'll eventually cross another bridge and about 45 minutes later will come to some cleared areas suitable for camping. However, it is best to keep on for another hour to the third bridge, where just on the other side there is good camping on a low rise to the right. The river here is also good for a swim. Plan on spending some 6 to 7 hours walking from the roadhead.

From the third bridge camp, the trail continues fairly flatly through splendid vegetation. You'll pass a small farm on the right after about 2 hours. Further on, the trail turns to run alongside a fast-flowing river. Keep an eye out for torrent ducks. Another 2 hours of steady walking will bring you to the wooden buildings of Dos Camas, high on the right as the trail angles left to cross a bridge. La Cumbre camp is only another 3 hours of steady hiking from here, but it seems much nicer to finish walking early in order to enjoy the incredible environment of cloudforest. You'll find Dos Camas a suitable shelter for the night.

The next day is 6km of steady uphill to La Cumbre at 2,465m and 33km from Romerillos. Here you'll find quite a set-up of several buildings. They may be locked, but there will be suitable shelter for camping. You may

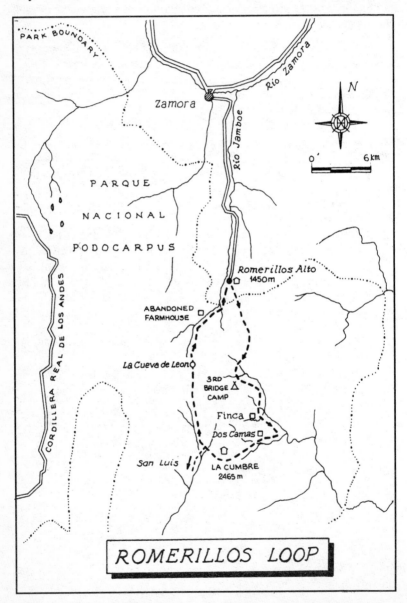

ROMERILLOS LOOP

even find that the permanent flush toilets are still working! This is a great area to spend an extra day if you have the time. Leading off to the right behind the lower building is a trail originally constructed by the Incas. It leads down to an old Incan mine which has seen present-day mining. The round-trip from camp would take about 3 hours. For some marvellous views of the whole region, follow the main trail up past La Cumbre for about 5 minutes to a cleared area. This was the heliport area for the miners. In fact, if the weather's good and the platform is still there, it would make a good place to camp.

For the trip back to Romerillos there are two choices. Take the easy way out and go back the way you came in. There's still plenty to see and you'll be able to avoid the struggle of the other choice. That is to continue the loop and find your way along a hacked-out trail that is barely manageable. To do this, follow the trail up past La Cumbre to the true summit about 45 minutes away. Along here you'll have to cross three very flimsy bridges which get you from one side of a landslide area to the other. Unfortunately, if these are gone, you'll get no further. After the third bridge, the trail descends to the river following the debris of another landslide. It is a little tricky here as the trail is somewhat lost in the rubble. At the river's edge you'll see the obvious trail continuing on the other side. It ascends and in a short while you come to a mining sign 'San Luis' and a very faint trail heading downhill. Continue past and up through wet, *páramo* vegetation, climbing up through a gully as the trail seems to disappear.

About 1½ hours from La Cumbre you'll come to a small shelter called Las Dantas camp. The trail continues up from here to El Mirador (the lookout) about 2 hours away. This is the beginning of the area called 'El Piñal' after the tundra-like vegetation resembling pineapple tops. Here you are at the watershed: Río Nagantza flows west and the Río San Luis flows eastward. The area is extremely boggy and it gets worse a little further up. Keep to the sides of the trail, watching for any vegetation which will support your weight and keep you from sinking in the deep mud. Fortunately the worst is over in about ½ an hour, and when the mud resumes it's a manageable, ankle-deep level. After an hour, you'll come to the Cueva de Leon, a huge overhanging boulder which provides some shelter at its base. Just past this is another basic shelter high on the right; beyond it the trail begins a steep, difficult descent of about 2 to 3 hours to the river. Picking your way through this area is a little confusing as the trail gets lost from time to time as it wanders in and out of several stream crossings. The thing to remember is that the trail will always end up on the right-hand side of the river. If you lose it, head downstream as best you can until you see it on the right bank. You'll eventually come to an open pasture area where the trail leaves the river and cuts across the pasture heading right. There is an abandoned shelter here, suitable for spending the night. The next shelter is another 2 to 3 hours up the trail on the left side of the trail. Romerillos is a thankful 1 hour from this last shelter.

Chapter Seven

The Oriente

'If you are wise and know the art of travel, let yourself go on the stream of the unknown and accept whatever comes in the spirit in which the gods may offer it.'

Freya Stark

The Oriente is the name given to Ecuador's Amazonia, a huge lowland area east of the Andes and comprising 36% of Ecuador's total territory. Popularly known as 'the jungle', the region is properly referred to as 'tropical rainforest'. Dense, hot and wet, just as one would expect it to be, the Oriente was largely unexplored and untravelled until the oil boom of the 1960s. Now four roads penetrate the region and access is relatively straightforward.

Without a doubt, the most fascinating aspect of the Oriente is its incredible variety of flora and fauna. This is partly due to the so-called edge effect. This means that any region where two different ecological zones are in sharp juxtaposition will have a greater variety of species than a region where two ecological zones gradually merge. The dramatic drop of the Andes to the Oriente is sudden enough to produce this effect. Over 700, or half, of Ecuador's bird species have been recorded in the Oriente; this is roughly equivalent to all the species found in the United States. About 3,000 species of butterfly are known in Ecuador; this represents an incredible 15% of the world's butterflies. Sloths, armadillos and anteaters are present, members of the strange Edentate family which is found only in the Americas. On a single 10-day trip into the Oriente (admittedly to a remote region) I saw six different species of monkey. And, of course, there are countless insects, many of which still prove to be new to science when classified. The trees and plants are no less varied and interesting; the giant buttressed ceibal tree, the chonta palm covered with thousands of needle-sharp thorns over its trunk, and the blossoms muskily scenting the forest all contribute to this fascinating natural wilderness.

Ecuador, land of volcanoes, even manages to produce a couple of volcanoes perched on the very edge of the lowlands. Rearing out of the rainforest, they are the active Reventador (3,562m) and the presently dormant Sumaco (3,732m). Both mountains have slopes dropping within 25km to high Amazonian forests at 1,200m.

Although roads now penetrate the lowlands, and airstrips occasionally puncture the rainforest, some of the most satisfying journeys into the jungle will be by dugout canoe and on foot. This section describes a variety of trips to different areas with an emphasis on hiking and dugouts.

THE MISAHUALLÍ AREA

For the traveller with a limited amount of time, a trip to the small river port of Misahuallí on the Río Napo will give a good glimpse of the Oriente.

The journey begins at Baños, the prettily situated gateway town to the Oriente (see *The Baños Area* in *Chapter Six*). From here you take a bus to Puyo which is the capital of the lowland province of Pastaza. Only 66km away from Baños, it lies just 950m above sea level. The winding gravel road follows the Río Pastaza valley and, as it drops, you can appreciate the rapidly changing vegetation and the many waterfalls (one of which cascades from an overhanging cliff on to the road – a damp experience in a pick-up truck). From the narrow confines of the Río Pastaza gorge, the first sudden sighting of the Amazonian plains is breathtaking. There is an obligatory passport control in Shell-Mera, some 15km before Puyo.

From Puyo, if the weather is clear, you can view various snow-capped peaks rising over 4,000m above you and only 50km distant. Sangay is sometimes visible, exploding away some 65km to the southwest. Several buses a day leave Puyo for Tena. Get off the bus at Puerto Napo, some 75km beyond Puyo and 7km before Tena. From Puerto Napo, frequent pick-up trucks act as a bus service to Puerto Misahuallí, 11km away at the end of the road.

Now you're in the tropical lowlands, just 600m above sea level. It's amazing to realize that only 80km away to the northwest Antisana towers over 5,000m above you, whilst the mouth of the Amazon at Belém lies over 3,000km to the east, with no higher ground in between.

Just 20 years ago Puerto Misahuallí was no more than a huddle of a few huts, but the oil boom, the new road and tourism have enlarged it to over 1,000 inhabitants. It is still a very sleepy little port, with only very basic hotels and restaurants. Sometimes gaily painted dugout canoes powered by modern outboard motors arrive at Misahuallí's sandy beach loaded down with cargoes varying from bananas to parrots. Most produce now goes by way of the new Tena–Coca road, however, and river traffic has slowed to a trickle. Nevertheless, occasional gold panners come into town to sell gold dust and hardy colonists may arrive in the port trying to sell their corn, papayas and other produce.

Just a generation ago, the region east of here was the territory of the indigenous people known as the Aucas, which in Quechua means 'savage'. The term Auca is considered derogatory and has been discarded for the more favoured term, Huaorani (also spelled Waorani), which means 'the people' in their native language. In 1956 five missionaries were killed by the Huaorani. Oil was discovered about ten years later and the outpost of Coca began to grow into an important oil town. Killings by both settlers and indigenous people continued into the 1960s but by the '70s the situation had stabilized with the Huaorani withdrawing to remote regions of the jungle, as they have done for centuries to avoid genocidal conflicts. In 1983 a reservation of 66,570ha was set aside for them in a remote region where, for the time being, they are able to continue life in a relatively traditional manner. Nevertheless, some Huaorani are now undergoing the painful change from their simple livelihoods to a 20th century society, a process which is so rapid that it proves very traumatic and often fatal to many primitive peoples.

Some 2 to 3 days' walk away from Misahuallí is an Huaorani indigenous village. Local guides used to take groups of tourists there to gawk. The indigenous people sat around miserably with little interest in their surroundings or in the visitors who had come to see them. Seeing the parade of goods which to us seem basic – shoes, backpacks, sunglasses, cameras, penknives, matches, etc – is a disorientating experience for these people. For the visitors, it is sad to visit a group of bewildered-looking indigenous people who are losing their traditional values and abilities. What promised to be an exciting adventure to see 'real' primitive Indians turned out to be a long, uncomfortable trek with a somewhat shaming conclusion.

The Huaorani are now governed by an organization called ONHAE, which requires all guides entering their territory to have a permit. They are attempting to develop tourism as a sustainable alternative to entering the labourforce of the Oriente as low-paid workers. A highly motivated Canadian, Randy Smith, has helped them in this effort and recently published a manual for ecotourism for the Huaorani and other indigenous groups. The title of this book is *Manual de Ecotourism, Para Guías y Comunidades Indigenas de La Amazonia Ecuatoriana*. The book is also useful for travellers since it has an excellent appendix on Huaorani, Quechua, Shuar, English, Spanish and Latin names for species found in the jungle.

Even if you don't normally take organized tours, some of those offered in Misahuallí are both inexpensive and worthwhile. Many outfitters are available (too many to list here); the SAEC office in Quito or other travellers can make recommendations. Tours range from 1-day walks in the nearby jungles to 10-day trips reaching close to the Peruvian border. Usually a minimum of five people are needed (more for longer trips) but there are plenty of *gringos* in Misahuallí looking for companions. Food, transport and accommodation are provided for US$25-40 a day depending on the difficulty and duration of the trip. It must be remembered that the immediate area has been colonized so you won't see much in the way of monkeys, peccaries and so on. Local wildlife is limited to birds and insects which are varied and colourful. A trip along the river near Misahuallí often produces sightings of egrets, vultures, toucans, anis, tanagers, caciques and oropendulas.

On guided trips, keep your eyes open for well-camouflaged stick insects, fist-sized toads, armies of ants, and hosts of colourful butterflies. Ask to be shown the *achiote* (*Bixa orellana*), a plant which is crushed to produce a red paint for body decorations, and a vine containing water fit to drink. A good guide will be able to show you much you would have missed on your own, particularly if you ask questions and convey your interest and enthusiasm.

If you can get a group together and take a longer tour you will see more wildlife. These tours are not for the soft traveller, but you'll certainly see monkeys, caiman, macaws, and parrots; and with any luck pacas, capybaras, anteaters, armadillos, peccaries and – who knows? – a tapir or a jaguar.

CONTINUING INTO THE ORIENTE

Maps: IGM 1:50,000 for most of the area; some maps are restricted.

The best-preserved rainforest is downstream of Coca on the Río Napo and downstream of Lago Agrio on the Rio Aguarico but it requires time and expense to visit. There are two reserves in this area: Reserva Produccíon Faunística Cuyabeno and Parque Nacional Yasuní. Both of these reserves harbour some of the most diverse ecosystems in the world but are currently being degraded by oil development and illegal colonization. Outside the reserves are lands that are owned by colonists, indigenous groups and about a dozen private reserves usually associated with tourism. Much lip service is given to ecotourism in the Oriente and many communities have decided to follow a path of development that incorporates elements of ecotourism in their land-use planning and hunting practices. This is particularly true of indigenous communities who have a tradition of living in balance with the rainforest ecosystem. Efforts to conserve lands outside the reserves are evidence that tourism has a positive impact on these once isolated areas, providing an alternative to oil development, deforestation and cultural genocide. As you travel through the boom towns of Coca, Shushufindi and Lago Agrio you will be reminded of the American West in the last century – roaming the streets are outlaws, oil workers, hard-working colonists, confused indigenous people and a few tourists. Your visit to indigenous villages organized for tourism or to a jungle lodge strengthens the conservation ethic in the Oriente.

Access One interesting way to get to Coca from Misahuallí is to continue downriver by motorized dugout canoe for the 6-hour journey to the town of Coca and beyond; but, with the new Tena–Coca road, regular river transportation has been reduced. It can be costly to hire an unscheduled canoe to make the trip. This part of the Río Napo has long been travelled and settled, so don't expect to see monkeys and 'wild Indians', but you will see dramatic views of the forest and many birds including parrots. Easier and less expensive is to take the bus from Misahuallí to Coca. With the new Loreto road, transport is cheaper and faster to this ramshackle town and many guides have begun to operate trips into the jungle from here.

From Coca, daily buses head north to Lago Agrio, another jungle town produced by the oil boom. It is the most eastern town of any size in Ecuador and the capital of the new province of Sucumbíos. The Sunday market brings in members of the local Cofán tribe, with the men often wearing their typical *kushma*, or knee-length smock, and perhaps a headband of porcupine quills around their short hair. They often bring necklaces of feathers, seeds, teeth and even insect wings to sell to tourists.

From Lago Agrio a gravel road follows the oil line to Quito, some 265km and 10 hours away by bus. The road passes the active volcano Reventador (3,562m) and the village of Baeza, both described later in this chapter, and continues past Volcán Antisana (5,758m) and the village of Papallacta (see *Chapter Six*) before reaching Quito.

Regular flights from both Lago Agrio and Coca return to Quito, or you can return from Puerto Misahuallí to Quito by bus via Tena, capital of Napo province (several a day from Misahuallí). Good views are often had of the dormant volcano Sumaco (3,732m) about 50km north-northeast. From Tena buses continue on the new dirt road north which runs parallel to the Andes, passing through Archidona and on to Baeza nearly 100km away. Archidona is famous as the centre from which you can visit the large cave complex of Jumandi. Unfortunately, the stalactite hunter and phantom spray painter have reached the caves before you, and they are now a rather sorry sight.

Jungle trips For any jungle trip you will need to travel by canoe downriver. You have the choice of arranging a stay with an indigenous family, travelling with a guide on an extended canoe trip, or visiting a lodge. Although from the air much of this area appears to be wild country, the forest is criss-crossed by numerous trails. If you are not accustomed to travelling in the rainforest it is best to arrange trips through the SAEC in Quito with guides from Quito, Coca or Lago Agrio. Two native guides well-recommended for trips on the Napo and Aguarico are Wymper Torres and Luis García. Randy Smith works closely with the Huaorani as a guide. Diego Llori is excellent with motorized canoes and knows the Napo like the back of his hand; he can be contacted at the Hotel Cotopaxi in Coca.

There are a dozen established lodges from which you can explore the forest by canoe and on day hikes, accompanied by native guides and, usually, English-speaking translators. The advantage of a lodge is that after a day of walking you come back to a shower, clean bed and good food. Some of the best lodges on the Ríos Napo and Aguarico are Yachana Lodge, La Selva, Sacha Lodge, Primavera, Yuturi and Paradise Huts. It is best to book trips to these lodges in Quito; information can be obtained at the SAEC in Quito. An excellent source of written information on the Napo region is

The Ecotourist Guide to the Ecuadorian Amazon edited by Rolf Wesche, available at the IGM (3rd floor) or at the SAEC.

Some interesting areas to visit along the wide Río Napo are Lagunas Limoncocha, Pañacocha, Challuacocha, Añangucocha and Yuturi. These oxbow lakes have very high bird, fish and mammal diversity. Most of the people living on the Napo downstream of Coca are Quechuas and are accustomed to tourism. It is also possible to travel down the Ríos Tiputini and Curaray from the Vía Auca which heads south from Coca. These narrow rivers offer a good glimpse of primary rainforest but require more than a week of sometimes uncomfortable travel in a canoe and camping.

The Aguarico is a smaller river than the Napo, so travelling on it you are closer to the shore and have better chances to see wildlife. You will travel from Lago Agrio to Poza Honda or Chiritza to catch a canoe downstream. Some of the Secoya (eg: San Pablo) and Cofán communities welcome visitors. The Quechua, Siona, Shuar and colonial communities are more reserved and generally should not be visited unless they are set up for tourism.

There is one Quechua community that will cater to hikers, Pucapeña. From this community there is a tough 2-day hike that crosses from the Río Aguarico to the Río Napo that gets you into primary forest. Bring rubber boots as you will be wading through streams and mucking around in the mud. It begins in the Quechua community of Pucapeña on the Río Aguarico and ends in the small settlement of Pañacocha on the Río Napo. You will pass through the Bosque Protector Pañacocha. Contact Franklin Grefa in Pucapeña – he has guided a few people on this *pica* (ill-defined trail through the forest). Once in the town of Pañacocha try to get up to the Lagunas de Pañacocha for a chance to see freshwater dolphins and caiman.

The Río Aguarico eventually cuts through the centre of Reserva Producción Faunística Cuyabeno. Both rivers meet at the international border near the town of Rocafuerte though passing on to Peru is not possible because of the ongoing border conflict.

A final note about the weather. It can rain year round but June through August seem to be the wettest around Misahuallí. November and December have the least rain. During these times the Río Napo could be either too high or too low to make a boat trip.

REVENTADOR (3,562M)

Maps: IGM 1:50,000 Volcán El Reventador. An IGM aerial photo of the peak, which is extremely detailed and useful, can also be purchased.

Reventador is a unique geologic and ecological landscape to visit. The recent eruptive history and its location on the edge of the Oriente have created interesting landforms and habitats that are changing extremely rapidly. It would be intriguing to come back in 20 years and compare your notes and impressions of your initial climb – they are likely to be radically different.

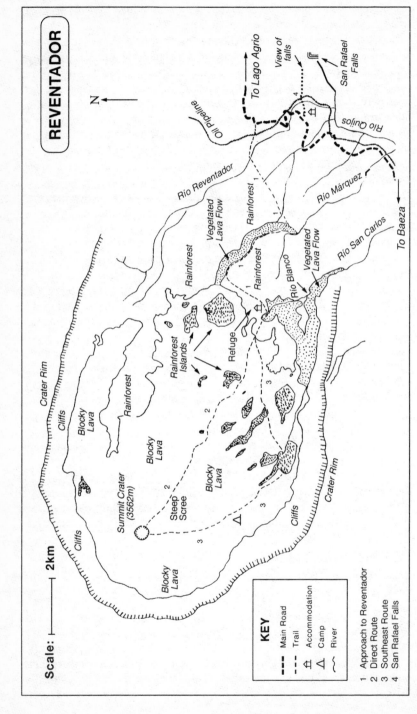

Reventador lies 90km east northeast of Quito. Its name means 'exploder' and this volcano has been frequently active as far back as records go; the first recorded eruption was in 1541. For many years little was known about the area and it was not until 1931 that an Ecuadorian, L Paz y Miño, visited the area to study it and map it for the first time. It remained relatively inaccessible until the building of the trans-Ecuadorian oil pipeline began in the late 1960s. This in turn prompted the construction of a road from Baeza to the new oil boom town of Lago Agrio and it is from this all-weather road that access to Reventador is made.

Reventador consists of an outer crater 2–3km across within which is an imposing 1,000m-tall resurgent volcanic cone. This andesitic strato-volcano erupted catastrophically, blowing away much of the summit and leaving only the flanks of a volcano that once rivalled Chimborazo in height. Since Reventador lies to the east of the main crest of the Andes on the edge of the Oriente it must have been a truly awesome sight, a glaciated peak towering over the rainforest.

The south rim of the volcano is missing, which indicates that large-scale debris flows broke the rim, depositing material in the Río Quijos valley. Outcrops of unconsolidated lahars (random mixtures of boulders, gravel and volcanic sand) can be observed from the road and on the approach to the peak. This material is not stable so landsliding has created a chaotic landscape of steep ridges. The opening on the south rim also provides an outlet for lava flows from the active cone, some of which have reached to within 1.5km of the road.

The central cone is in the process of rebuilding the volcanic edifice but has been relatively dormant since the late 1970s. This kind of lava was extremely viscous when it was erupting and broke into large blocks as it cooled, forming large fields of boulders with ankle-breaking crevices. This makes walking to the summit an extremely slow and difficult process of hopping from one mossy boulder to the next.

The recent lava flows are revegetating with mosses and shrubs. As a soil develops the cloudforest will eventually cover these lava flows, at least until another hot lava flow restarts the process. Remnant islands of cloudforest vegetation can be observed where lava did not cover the old soil surface. It is interesting to compare the quietness on the relatively barren lava flows to the familiar sounds of birds and insects within these small ecologically isolated islands. Also when you are on the summit of the cone the roots of the volcano can be seen in the layers exposed in the cliffs on the inside of the old crater rim – there are alternating strata of andesite flows and lahars representing previous eruptions.

The danger of eruption at the time of writing is not great, but conditions may change. The top of the cone has a small crater, approximately 100m across, with significant fumarole activity. The hydrogen sulphide fumes are toxic and the superheated stream can scald. It is not recommended to camp on the summit, especially within the crater, since fumarole activity may increase unexpectedly and gas you in your sleep. It is advisable to check with locals or the SAEC in Quito for current conditions before attempting this climb. (See Reventador map, page 230.)

Weather and times to go A friend who lives in the Lago Agrio area claims to have driven the Lago Agrio–Quito road dozens of times but has only seen Reventador twice, although it is only 8km from the road as the crow flies. The area is very wet and usually cloudy. The wettest months are June and July, and the best are September through December – but you can still expect daily showers.

Equipment The trail to the lava flows quickly becomes overgrown so a machete is necessary. During the 'dry' season, insects aren't a major problem but repellent should be brought during the wetter months. A waterproof tent is a must. My preferred clothing is raingear (Gore-Tex) over T-shirt and shorts, with a dry shirt and pair of trousers kept in plastic bags for camp and tent wear. It does not get too cold so a sweater and light sleeping bag or blanket are sufficient for the evening. The trail is muddy in places. Sturdy leather boots for ankle-twisting lava blocks are a must. The Ecuadorian knee-high rubber boots (*botas para agua*) are quite suitable for the approach, though not entirely comfortable. A spare pair of sneakers for camp and tent wear mean your feet can dry out occasionally. A large selection of plastic bags is a must. A compass and topographic map are absolutely necessary. If you are leaving gear at the refuge bring a padlock to secure your things in a locker. Bring extra water bottles because if you camp high on the peak you will be waterless. Lastly, be responsible and carry out all of your litter.

Access Catch a bus from Quito's Terminal Terrestre through Baeza to Lago Agrio. Although you will only be going two-thirds of the way to Lago Agrio you may be charged the full fare at the bus station. Tell the bus driver you are going to Cascada San Rafael (San Rafael Waterfall). The bus journey is very interesting and worth a description.

The road descends from Quito through several growing suburbs and is paved for 70km until just before Papallacta on the other side of the crest of the Andes. The ascent to the Andean crest takes you up a broad valley with cliffs above which condors are very occasionally spotted. Also about halfway, the remnants of an Inca Trail can be seen if you know what you are looking for. The pass at the top of the Eastern Cordillera is 4,100m and is marked by an altar to the Virgin Mary. The road then drops to the lake of Papallacta, formed when a lava flow from Antisana dammed the Río Papallacta. The hike from Papallacta to Cotopaxi begins here.

Just before the village of Papallacta, over 60km from Quito, is the turn-off to the left with a sign for a hostel and thermal baths which are some of the best in the country. The road continues to drop through enchantingly beautiful cloudforest with many strange plants and colourful birds.

Approximately 100km from Quito the road forks; follow the left fork and proceed through the villages of Borja and El Chaco, from where you may get your first views of Reventador. There are frequent views of the Río Quijos on your right. About 150km from Quito you cross the Río Salado which is a major landmark. Ten kilometres further you cross the Río Malo (starting point for the route used when Reventador was active). Another 10km on, or 170km from Quito, you arrive at a little cement block hut with an INECEL sign at a turn-off to your right which leads to Cascada San Rafael. Down this road 500m there is a complex of buildings originally constructed for a planned hydroelectric diversion around the falls. The complex is now run nominally as a tourist hotel by Hotel Quito, but hardly anyone uses it. Since the bus ride from Quito is 5 to 6 hours, you can stay here and get information on where the trail starts from the guard. Cheaper options are several basic hotels in the town of El Chaco 45km before Cascada San Rafael and the Hotel Amazonas 13kms beyond the Cascada San Rafael in the village of El Reventador.

Climbing Reventador
The climb takes 3 to 5 days round-trip and is physically demanding but not technically difficult. If you decide to hire a guide for the climb, there are some local guides available. Guillermo Vasquez was involved in chopping the original trail and knows the area well. He lives close by the school in the Pampas area, 2 to 3km before Cascada San Rafael. Luis 'Lucho' Viteri can be found in Baeza, and Edgar Ortiz in the Hotel Amazonas in the village of Reventador.

Finding the beginning of the hike is a little tricky and colonization in the area results in new trails that lead to pastures, so it is always good to ask locals. On the main road, continue 5 minutes beyond the turn-off to the INECEL camp to the bridge over Río Reventador. From here continue 15 minutes uphill until the pipeline crosses the road. Here you can turn left next to the pipeline up a steep hill, or continue 5 minutes up the road to the next stream (1,520m) and follow a trail west up a pasture to the pipeline on the hill crest. I recommend following the trail: it has steps. Whichever route you take, the important thing is to find a wooden ladder over the pipeline just before it heads up a very steep incline. Cross over the ladder and head northwest, staying to the right of a wooden shack in a flat field. There is a vague trail in the grass that soon enters forest where it becomes more defined. You should be heading towards a grove of palm trees on a ridge in the distance. Soon you reach a small stream choked with cobbles; jump across and look for the trail several metres upstream. A few minutes later the trail forks; stay left, as the right fork heads up to new pastureland. If the trail gets steep you are on the wrong branch. Soon descend to Río Reventador with great bedrock pools for bathing. Wade across this stream and find the trail slightly upstream marked by a cairn. The trail skirts the right-hand side of a pasture and re-enters forest. You come to an overlook which has been constructed for views of the Río Quijos.

Now the trail is relatively easy to follow. It ascends over two ridges with well-constructed steps and views crossing several small streams and then ascends to the toe of a vegetated lava flow. Here the surface changes from mud to awkward boulders. The trail works its way northwest up the southwest side of this lava flow and then heads southwest across the forest to Río Blanco (not named on IGM map) where the refuge is located (2,050m). If you do not get lost count on 3 to 4 hours from the road to the refuge.

The refuge was built in 1994 and is a great place to spend the first night since it is free. On a clear day the peak can be seen from the kitchen window. It also looks out over a flat, thinly vegetated lava flow with great birding. There are a total of eight basic bunks in two rooms (no mattresses) and plenty of floor space if your group is large; a basic cooking/dining area with fireplace but no running water, gas stove or cooking utensils; and storage lockers to secure the things you leave behind while climbing. There is no guardian but as the refuge is rarely visited your belongings are probably safe in the lockers.

You can attempt the peak from here in one long day or set up a high camp at the base of the cone. It is 9 to 12 hours of walking round-trip depending how comfortable you are at hopping the mossy boulders. Remember, once it gets dark, finding your way on the lava flows is nearly impossible. The problem with camping at the base of the cone is that there is no water on the lava flows, so you need to carry all your water with you from the refuge. You should have a minimum of 5 litres of water per day.

In front of the refuge, wade across the 3m-wide stream known as the Río Blanco (slightly white from dissolved solids in the groundwater leaving the volcano) and head generally northwest on a trail across a swampy area and up a steep vegetated hill. About 40 minutes from the refuge you reach the edge of the blocky lava flow (2,150m) with an open view of the cone 4km in the distance. There is an obvious and abrupt change in vegetation to moss and shrubs and the spot should be marked by wooden poles. Here you have two alternatives.

Direct route Head directly for the summit cone across the lava blocks. If the summit cannot be seen head northwest. There is a vague trail that can be followed to the base of the cone, which is distinguished by crushed moss and occasional cut shrubs. Orientation on a clear day is easy but in fog or at night you could easily spend hours or even days wandering around the lava flows. Mark your ascent route for easy return. After cresting over several low ridges pass to the left of an island of cloudforest. Follow a 30m-high ridge to the left of a dry streambed to the base of the cone, head up a silver (mossy) slope to the left of another small cloudforest island, then traverse right into a dry streambed. It takes 2 to 3 hours to reach this point from the toe of the lava flow. This is a reasonable place to camp (2,630m) though you may need to flatten a spot for your tent. From here the trail steepens but the footing is easier and after another 2 to 3 hours of following a rocky gully you reach the summit rim (3,500m). Watch out for rockfall. Near the crater rim are steaming fumaroles and the soil is warm. The actual summit (3,560m) requires a short jaunt around to the west side of the rim. The total time from the refuge to the summit is 6 to 8 hours. The descent to the wooden poles takes 3 to 4 hours.

Southeast route From the edge of the lava flow head west across several ridges of rough blocky terrain – this is slow going. After about an hour reach a smooth lava flow covered with spongy moss. Continue up the flow, crossing below a thick forest on to blocky lava again. Cross the lava and find a streambed heading west, then follow it upstream to the saddle between the old rim and the cone. This is a good place to camp. It takes 3 to 4 hours to reach the saddle from the poles. The summit is easily reached by following the stream northwest and then north to the south side of the crater rim: 1 to 2 hours of hiking. The descent to the wooden poles takes 3 to 4 hours.

The view from the top of the desolate, steaming crater is worth the muddy, slippery effort; it is a beautiful, empty, chaotic place which few visit. When you arrive back at the San Rafael camp it is worth the ½-hour hike down to an overlook of the San Rafael falls on the Río Quijos.

PARQUE NACIONAL SUMACO-GALERAS

Maps: IGM 1:50,000 Volcán Sumaco and Pavayacu

The wilderness surrounding Volcán Sumaco has so far mostly escaped the impact of colonization and oil development and now is protected in Parque Nacional Sumaco-Galeras. The park is rarely visited by foreigners and Ecuadorians alike so the area is mostly untrailed and difficult to travel through. Several scientific expeditions have visited the area and discovered endemic species. The wildlife does not appear to be frightened by people which indicates it is not often hunted. A difficult but rewarding adventure would be to cross this park over a period of several weeks, perhaps climbing Cerro Negro or Cerro Pan de Azucar, two peaks that have no record of being visited. There are also plans to put in a trail to the top of Galeras, a limestone mountain just north of the Río Napo with many endemic species and caves.

Volcán Sumaco (3,732m)

The jewel of the park is the recently active Volcán Sumaco. This anomalous volcano rises from the jungle 60km east of the main crest of the Andes. The route to the summit passes through an intact elevation gradient of vegetation from 1,300m to 3,700m with undisturbed lowland rainforest, cloudforest and, close to the summit, *páramo* vegetation. On a clear day from the summit crater you can see several of the major glaciated peaks of the Andes, including El Altar, Tungurahua and Chimborazo, as well as the

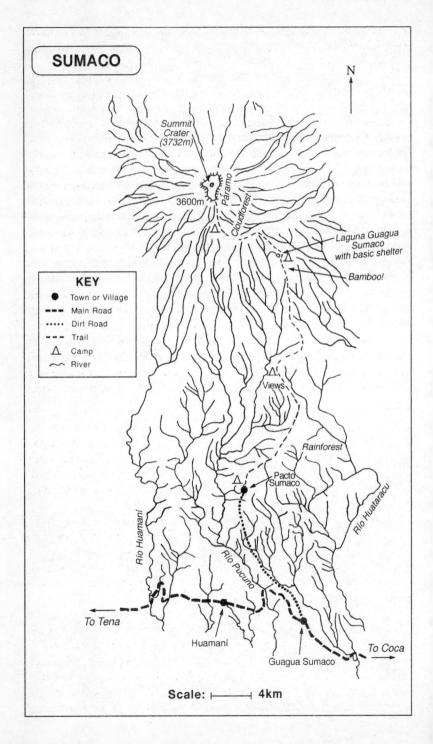

SUMACO

N

Summit
Crater
(3732m)

Páramo

3600m

Cloudforest

Laguna Guagua
Sumaco
with basic shelter

Bamboo!

KEY

● Town or Village
▬ ▬ Main Road
••••• Dirt Road
- - - Trail
△ Camp
~ River

Views

Rainforest

Pacto
Sumaco

Río Huamaní

Río Pucuno

Río Huataracu

← To Tena

Huamaní

Guagua Sumaco

To Coca →

Scale: ⊢——⊣ 4km

Río Napo snaking through the lowland rainforest. The non-technical route takes 4 to 6 days round-trip and involves much machete work and route finding. We do not know anyone who has climbed it without a guide.

The volcano has been known to Europeans since the Spanish conquest when Francisco de Orellana recorded its presence in 1541 after he saw it from the Río Napo during the first stages of his historic first descent of the Amazon. However, its isolated, forest-bound position and generally wet weather have made it one of Ecuador's least-known volcanoes.

Although some sources consider Sumaco to be extinct, the few records we have of it indicate that it is an active volcano. Jiménez de la Espada, who made the first ascent in 1865, found a gullied, 100m-wide crater blown open to the south. In 1925, the British climber George M Dyott climbed Sumaco and recorded that the crater was 210m wide with no signs of cracks or gullies. This indicates that an eruption must have occurred between the years 1865 and 1925, but the volcano's isolated position prevented this phenomenon from being recorded by any observer. This theory is supported by the fact that Sumaco has a conical shape which, in an environment promoting severe erosion, indicates that activity must have occurred within the last few hundred years. At present there appears to be no activity whatsoever but vulcanologists still consider Sumaco to be potentially active. Dyott also collected several rock samples that he sent to Columbia University for analysis. They proved to be geochemically distinct from all other volcanoes in Ecuador, indicating that the lavas of Sumaco have a different origin from those of other Ecuadorian volcanoes. (See Sumaco map.)

Access Take a bus from Quito's Terminal Terrestre to Coca along the relatively new Loreto road, getting off in the small village of Huamani. As the trip takes 6 to 7 hours, it is best to leave early in the morning so that you have time to arrange a guide for the following day. You can also take a bus to Tena, getting off at the 'Y' at the roadside village of Narupa. From here buses pass on their way to Coca every 1 to 2 hours. Huamani is 1½ hours from Narupa.

Huamani is a prospering little village with several stores offering basic supplies. You can begin your hike in Huamani, but most people continue 15 minutes down the road by bus to the town of Guagua Sumaco where a new spur road leads to the colonial town of Pacto Sumaco. You can arrange a truck to take you to Pacto Sumaco (½ hour) for about US$5, saving 3 hours of walking.

The reason for stopping in Huamani is to contact the best-known guide in the area, Don Francisco Chimbo, a Quechua in his sixties who has the body of a 40-year-old. He has guided many groups to the summit but is getting older and should not be asked to carry much weight. He will charge US$7–10 a day. He doesn't have camping gear so you need to provide him with tent space, a rain poncho and food. Since he has accompanied several scientific expeditions he no longer hunts in the park and is very interested in the flora and fauna. If you cannot contact Don Francisco there are others in Huamani and Pacto Sumaco who know the route. The topographical maps are not much use since you are under the canopy most of the time and the trail is obscure in places, so again we recommend using a guide.

Equipment Try to travel light and expect to get wet. You need to be prepared for humid warm weather and close to freezing weather on the summit (see *Reventador,* page 232).

Climbing Sumaco From Pacto Sumaco you follow a trail constructed of cut logs for about 2 hours, crossing pasture and second-growth forest with several intersections. In another hour you reach a lean-to (1,600m) with room for three people; here you are in primary forest. The trail climbs gently, passing a viewpoint and arriving at the second camp 1½ hours from the lean-to. From here the trail soon enters thick bamboo and if you don't have to do much cutting you should reach the third camp (2,100m) 7 to 8 hours from Pacto. On the following day, or that afternoon if you are feeling ambitious, you can climb to the small lake of Guagua Sumaco (unnamed lake near peak 2525 on map), which fills a parasitic cone on the flanks of Sumaco. There is a wooden platform and usually plastic rain tarps (sheets) to construct a shelter. The views and birding are great from this camp. The lake is said to be home to a large serpent so don't ask your guide to go for a swim!

Sumaco seems close from the lake, but you must climb over several ridges before you reach the base of the peak. You eventually drop down to a saddle between peak 2870 and Volcán Sumaco. The next camp (just a few cleared areas on a steep slope) is at 3,150m about 6 to 7 hours of hard hiking from the lake. The following day you break out of the forest on to *páramo* (3,250m) and climb grassy slopes to the summit ridge (2 to 3 hours with a daypack). You need to drop off the ridge to the right to a small saddle and make a short climb of the cone. There is a small lake at the bottom of the crater and an orange communication hut below the northeast side of the cone. The return trip to Pacto Sumaco along the newly cut trail takes 2 days.

THE BAEZA AREA

Map: IGM 1:50,000 Baeza

Baeza is a small but historical town in the eastern foothills at 1,400 m. It was on an ancient trade route even before the conquest. The coming of the Spaniards elevated it to the position of a mission settlement but nowadays no vestige remains of its past. It is a very quiet place with one basic hotel and a couple of cheap restaurants. It is surrounded by steep hills which could provide days of hiking and exploration. I describe one day hike here, but armed with the IGM 1:50,000 Baeza map you could have several to choose from.

Access Buses pass through Baeza several times a day to and from Tena. If you are on the Quito–Lago Agrio route you have to walk about 1.5km up the road from the Baeza turn-off. Baeza is about 100km by road from Quito.

Hiking directions Leave the town plaza on the road going uphill to the right of the church. In a few minutes you will pass the hospital to your left and the cemetery to your right. The trail becomes a stony path. After 15 minutes the trail forks at a footbridge. You can go left over the bridge up a steep trail which peters out in fields after about an hour with nice views of Baeza in the valley below. Or you can head straight up the trail (don't cross the river) which takes you through beautiful low mountain pastureland surrounded by trees laden with epiphytes. The birdlife is prolific. I saw hawks and hummingbirds, wrens and woodpeckers, tanagers and thrushes, so bring your binoculars. About 10 minutes past the bridge the trail forks again. Take the right one uphill leaving the stream to your left. A further 10 minutes brings you to a flattish area showing signs of logging. From here the trail becomes increasingly muddy, although stony sections offer relief from the squelch. The trail follows the fence line and then steeply zigzags over and around a hill. About an hour beyond the logged area it is crossed by a fence and stops suddenly in high pasture on top of a hill. This is a good place for a rest and picnic.

THE MACAS AREA

Though a small town, Macas is the capital of one of the largest provinces in Ecuador, Morona-Santiago. Its history goes back at least four centuries; it was an important Spanish missionary and trading settlement linked with the highlands by a trail still in existence and described in *Chapter Six, From the Andes to the Jungle*. Despite its provincial capital status, Macas had remained a very isolated town until recently. It now has an airport with daily flights to/from Quito, and the recently constructed road north to Puyo now gives this jungle city two means of access to the sierra. At one time its only link with the rest of Ecuador was the southbound road through Sucua to Cuenca, some 10 hours away by bus.

The Oriente east of Macas is perhaps the least explored region in the entire country. It is the home of the Jívaros, famous for their expertise (no longer practised) at shrinking the heads of their enemies. Today the Jívaros prefer to call themselves Shuar and are integrating quite rapidly into Ecuadorian society. There is a major Shuar centre in Sucua which is partially run by indigenous people and plays an important part both in recording and encouraging traditional lifestyles and in aiding the Shuar people in the difficult process of entering 20th century life, which they seem to be doing with more success than many groups. Nevertheless, some semi-wild groups still exist deep in the forests.

From Macas, trails are marked on the maps which penetrate deeply into the Oriente reaching extremely remote villages. The trails are not often used as small aircraft are the main means of communication with Macas, and river travel is used between the villages. I did find, however, one trail which can easily be walked in a day from Macas.

Hiking directions From Macas, cross the Río Upano by a simple bridge to Sevilla Don Bosco, a Salesian mission. From here, head south along the road, roughly following the eastern riverbank. This dirt road slowly deteriorates into a side track impassable to vehicles. You will pass cultivated areas and indigenous huts and perhaps be invited to try some of their yucca *chicha*. This drink is made by the women masticating the yucca and then spitting the contents into a bowl of water which is left to ferment, the process started by the ptyalin in saliva. It takes some time (and a lack of imagination) to develop a taste for this sour, gruel-like drink which is served cold in large gourds. One is normally expected to drink the whole gourd in one or two gulps.

Some 4 hours from Sevilla Don Bosco you come to the small indigenous centre of San Luis where you can buy soft drinks if you're not up to *chicha*. San Luis is almost the halfway point to Sucua but when I was there a bridge had washed out further along the trail so I returned the way I came. Either way it is a good day hike. If you do get all the way to Sucua you could return to Macas by one of the frequent buses joining the two towns.

Chapter Eight

The Western Lowlands and Pacific Coast

'Here I am, safely returned over those peaks from a journey far more beautiful and strange than anything I had hoped for or imagined – how is it that this safe return brings such regret?'

Peter Matthiessen

West of the Andes and stretching to the Pacific Ocean lies some of Ecuador's most valuable agricultural land. Although this is good for the Ecuadorian economy, it means also that much of the lowland forest has been destroyed, along with the accompanying wildlife. The best places to see the western forests are the slopes of the Andes; here the terrain is too rough for agriculture. Few trails have been cut and the area is not really conducive to backpacking trips, being hot, humid, thickly covered with vegetation, and lacking the interest of volcanoes to climb. It is, however, excellent for birdwatching. The village of Mindo, 3 or 4 hours west of Quito, has a few basic hotels and is a good centre for birding.

A good variety of sea- and shore-birds is found on the coast. The southern coast has mangrove swamps but is nevertheless rather scrubby and dry, as is the Santa Elena peninsula west of Guayaquil. Rainfall here is comparatively low and falls mainly from January to April. Further north there is more rainfall, more vegetation, and a longer rainy season, from January to June; and on the far northern coast it sometimes rains during the 'dry' season. Good areas for birdwatching in the south are found at Jambelí, which is a low-lying island off Puerto Bolívar, near Machala, the capital of the province of El Oro. From Machala frequent buses do the short trip to Puerto Bolívar, where motor boats can be hired to cruise among the swamps, estuaries and islands of the area where you can see large flocks of pelicans and other seabirds. In the Santa Elena peninsula are found many fishing villages and tourist resorts, such as Playas and Salinas. These are often used as bases for walks along the beach although overnight backpacking trips aren't normally done.

The northern coast is perhaps richest in coastal birdlife because of the heavier rainfall and vegetation. I did a hike along part of the coast here. There are also various resort towns you can use as a base.

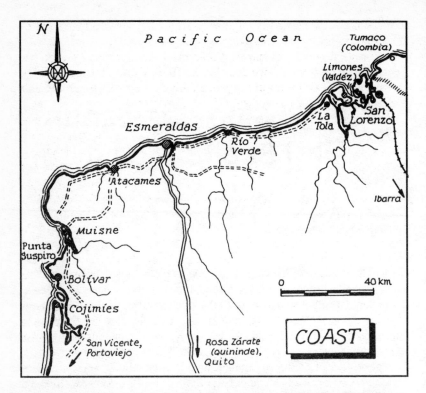

ANDES TO COAST: BY TRAIN, CANOE, BUS, ON FOOT

The most popular route to the coast is probably by bus via Santa Domingo to either Esmeraldas or Bahía de Caraquez, but the train is much more fun and passes through remote areas unaffected by a constant stream of traffic. There are two lines: one from Quito via Riobamba to Guayaquil and a shorter one linking Ibarra with San Lorenzo on the northern coast. The 464km Quito–Guayaquil line is now run in two sections. The Andes section runs from Quito to Riobamba, and the coastal section goes from Alausí. It reaches a height of 3,609m and is a marvel of railway engineering. At one point it climbs nearly 300m in less than 80km and includes complex loops and switchbacks – a must for a railway enthusiast. Both the *South American Handbook* and *Ecuador, a travel survival kit* have excellent descriptions of the ride. I personally prefer the 293km Ibarra–San Lorenzo line because you detrain in a sleepy coastal port with only boat and train connections, rather than in the huge bustling port of Guayaquil. Trains have been running in 1996 between Riobamba and Alausí as well, but the schedule is erratic.

The train is known locally as *autoferro* and is little more than a converted schoolbus mounted on a railway chassis. When I took it from Ibarra to San Lorenzo the journey, which usually takes 7 hours, lasted 12. We were stopped by two minor landslides, which, by all accounts, was par for the course.

The train is accompanied throughout much of its memorable descent by the Río Mira which provides exciting whitewater views.

In late 1996, a new but unpaved road from Ibarra to San Lorenzo had been built and there were two daily buses linking the two towns. It may be that the railway journey will become a thing of the past, though the train was still running as of early 1997.

Once in San Lorenzo (where there are only basic hotels and restaurants) you continue down the coast by dugout canoe through Limones (officially known as Valdéz) to La Tola, some 2 hours away. This is a fascinating trip past mangrove swamps with opportunities to see pelicans galore, as well as ospreys and frigate birds. The Cayapa Indians live in the area and sometimes come into Limones, particularly at weekends. Unfortunately, they have recently been swept by an epidemic which has affected 60% of the population and leads to blindness. Attempts to halt the spread of the disease have not been very successful because of lack of funds, the isolation of the villages, and lack of medical knowledge about the causes of the illness.

Occasionally boats go from San Lorenzo directly to Esmeraldas, but normally you have to catch a bus from La Tola for the 4-hour journey on to Esmeraldas. This takes you through lush coastal pastureland with good viewing of egrets, herons and wading birds. I persuaded the driver to let me sit on the roof which made the hot trip very pleasant, but be careful of sunburn.

Once in Esmeraldas most people continue by bus to Atacames, a popular seaside resort with good beaches and many hotels. A further 30km by rough dirt road brings you to Muisne, a very quiet resort with cabins on the beach and fewer tourists; it is located on an island with a frequent ferry service. From Muisne you can continue south on foot along the beach to Cojimíes; this is a good coastal walk. At low tide, curious open-sided buses or pick-up trucks speed up and down the hard-packed sand every hour or so.

Warning: In recent years the beaches in these areas have deteriorated in terms of safety. Robberies and even rape, unfortunately, have become rather commonplace. The complete hike as described below is no longer recommended for security reasons, unless you go in a group and stick together. However, we have left it intact for the descriptions of the particular areas and the possibility of day hikes. If the idea of doing the complete trip is appealing, we suggest you use the local transport available.

Muisne to Cojimíes

Maps: There are two IGM maps of this area. The 1:50,000 Muisne topographical map covers from Muisne to just before Mompiche and the 1:50,000 Cojimíes planometric map shows from Mompiche to Cojimíes.

From the cabins on the Muisne seafront walk back to the river behind the island to the main pier, where you can get a boat to ferry you across the Río Muisne for a few sucres. On the other side of the river go upstream to the tiny settlement of Los Manchas, less than 1km away, where there is a huddle of houses and a very small store. Walk through the village and continue along a track on the other side which leads to the coast less than 1km away. (If you want to avoid Los Manchas you can just follow the coast.) About 7km of walking will bring you to the tiny coastal village of Mompiche where there is a poorly stocked store which is often closed. A headland (Punta Suspiro) blocks the beach walk, but a sandy vehicle track goes over the headland and through coastal pastureland which is absolutely teeming with birdlife. You arrive at the Portete Estuary about 4km away where there will again be a dugout canoe waiting to ferry you across for a few sucres.

Now you have to get to the next town of Bolívar. Dugout canoes will take you there up the Portete Estuary, or you can just cross the river and walk through a few hundred metres of streams and mangroves to the village of Portete where there is the usual ill-stocked, rarely open store. From here you can walk 6km along the coast around Punta Bolívar and on to Bolívar. The vegetation is very thick and comes right down to the high-tide mark so this section must be done at low tide.

Getting from Muisne to Bolívar involves about 22km of walking. This can be cut down by taking a boat from Portete to Bolívar or by taking a ride on the occasional vehicles along the beach between Muisne and Portete. Carry plenty of water as the rivers aren't very clean or fresh. Sun protection is essential on the sandy, unshaded beaches. Don't forget problem areas like the backs of your legs.

Once in Bolívar you'll find several small stores where you can buy drinks. I couldn't find a hotel but you could probably persuade someone to give you a place to sleep. The best advice is to leave Muisne at dawn (which gives you a couple of cool walking hours) and arrive in Bolívar in early afternoon. It is then easy to find a boat to Cojimíes, about 8km due south; the trip takes about 30 minutes. (There are passenger boats, but don't charter a boat for yourself unless you are desperate. People will encourage you to do so but it is expensive.) Cojimíes is a fishing village with a few basic *residencias*. There are simple restaurants and friendly people. It is off the beaten tourist track and a good place to spend the night (or two).

From Cojimíes you can continue south to San Vicente by beach bus. The open-sided buses are well ventilated(!), the views are good, and the journey takes about 5 hours. This section is less suited to walking as there are much longer distances between villages and little water. San Vicente is a good beach resort, joined by ferry with Bahía de Caráquez from where you can get buses to anywhere.

Note: Rain during the wet months may cause delays.

Reserva Ecológica Mache-Chindul
The coastal ranges of Mache-Chindul near the city of Esmeraldas have received considerable attention from the conservation community ever since

the late Al Gentry and Ted Parker from Conservation International surveyed the area for the Rapid Assessment Program. This area of coastal premontane wet forest is isolated from the Andes but its rugged topography (300 to 800m) and coastal climate create a dense fog that sustains cloudforest vegetation usually restricted to higher elevations. Because of the isolation of the range there is a high degree of plant endemism which has stimulated botanists from around the world to collect and catalogue these species which one day may have economic value. The reserve also harbours jaguars, the umbrella bird and abundant populations of the threatened mantled howler monkey.

Fundación Jatun Sacha first set up a private reserve (Bilsa) in this area in 1994 and every year adds land to its 2,500ha holding. Unfortunately there are extreme development pressures from logging companies and colonists, primarily from the province of Manabí, who are rapidly deforesting the area. The ex-director of INEFAN, Jorge Barba, declared this area a Reserva Ecológica in July 1996 as he was leaving office, much to the delight of the international and Ecuadorian conservation community. The status of the reserve is controversial with the logging companies and the colonists, however, and it remains to be seen whether the reserve will receive the protection it deserves.

Access The easiest way to visit the area is by arranging a stay at the Jatun Sacha research station located a day's drive and walk from the town of Quinindé. Take a bus towards Esmeraldas and get off in Quinindé (about 4 hours from Quito). There are several cheap hotels in Quinindé, including the Paraíso (US$3 a night) and Hotel Sans (US$9 a night). From Quinindé you can get a truck from the gas station Cinco Esquinas towards the settlement of Herrera, a town about 25km from the reserve. In the wet season (January–June) you can only get as far as 'La Y' by private truck, leaving a 3–4-hour walk to the reserve. As conditions become drier (September–December) you can sometimes drive right through to the reserve, but don't count on it.

The facilities at the research station are mostly set up for volunteers, scientists and students but an interested tourist could make arrangements to stay there. Reservations need to be made through Jatun Sacha in Quito, tel: 593 2 441 592 or 250 976; advance warning is appreciated. There is room for 40 people and non-Ecuadorian visitors pay US$20 a night which covers room and board.

Hiking directions There are numerous day walks from the Bilsa research station. It is possible to join a park guard on his rounds of the forest or perhaps a scientist if you are willing to help with research.

A longer overnight trip is to hike from Bilsa to the coastal village of Muisne, crossing the coastal range. It is best to arrange a guide since the area is isolated and it is easy to get lost. You will pass through primary forest and Chachi communities, one of the few coastal indigenous groups remaining in Ecuador.

From Bilsa walk west to the colonist town of Mono (3–5 hours). The trail is frequently travelled and if you leave early you can usually find someone who will accompany you along the trail. You pass through small farms and secondary-growth forest. It is possible to sleep in the school in Mono or with a family. Although the people of this village do not ask for money it is polite to buy some food for your host.

The next day walk northwest to the Río Sucio drainage and eventually to the Chachi community of San Salvador. This is a long day through primary forest and could be broken into 2 days of walking. You can hire a guide from Mono for this section. In San Salvador you can stay in the Casa Comunal. Since this community is lower in elevation (200m above sea level) you should have a mosquito net.

The last day you walk west to Puerto Nuevo (4–6 hours). You do not really need a guide for this section since there are enough people along the way to ask directions. In Puerto Nuevo there are motor boats to Muisne every few hours. Muisne is a quiet fishing community with a few inexpensive hotels on the beach catering to budget travellers. It is about an hour by bus to Esmeraldas where you can catch a bus or plane to Quito.

Reserva Ecológica Manglares-Churute

Maps: You can probably get by without a map in the mangrove swamps since you will be guided, but IGM 1:50,000 Laguna El Canclón covers most of the Cordillera Churute in the park.

The Reserva Ecológica Manglares-Churute preserves a 35,000ha area of mangrove swamps and the coastal forest of the Cordillera Churutes next door to Guayaquil. The reserve was declared in 1979 since much of the coastal mangrove swamps were and are being converted into shrimp ranches, and coastal forests are heavily logged. The ecosystem of the swamps supports a rich and diverse marine fauna and is an important breeding area for some fish species. The forests of the Cordillera Churute are dry tropical forests as in Parque Nacional Machalilla (see page 257) and contain numerous endemic tree species. The reserve is largely undeveloped but can be accessed from the water (Río Guayaquil) or land (Guayaquil–Machala road).

Access The easiest access is to take a bus south from Guayaquil towards Machala and get off at the settlement of Cooperativa El Mate. Here you can arrange transport to the park guard on the Río Churute who can take you by canoe into the mangrove swamps. Alternatively you can hike through the Cordillera Churute up to Cerro El Mate and on to the lake of El Canclón where there is a population of endangered and endemic ducks. Not many travellers visit this reserve but it would make an interesting day excursion on your way south to Peru.

Parque Nacional Machalilla
Maps: IGM 1:50,000 Puerto López, Jipijapa, Pedro P Gómez and Delicias

Parque Nacional Machalilla is located on the central coast between Jipijapa to the north and Manglaralto to the south. It was established in 1979 to protect 55,000ha of an endangered tropical dry coastal forest ecosystem, unique coastal and island resources, and important pre-Columbian archaeological ruins and artefacts. Much of the year the vegetation seems dead but it springs to life when the January rains arrive. It is very hot and dry most of the year.

The park is expensive, approximately US$20 for a 5-day entrance ticket. Tickets should be purchased in the town of Puerto López. There are also restrictions on hiking because of joint land titles with communities within the park, so you may need to hire a local guide. Having said this, if you are on the coast it is worth a visit for the diversity of birds and the unique dry forest vegetation. Several areas within and near the park are described below.

Los Frailes
Los Frailes are three beautiful beaches and rocky headlands connected by a trail. There is also a short self-guided nature trail. The entrance gate to the beach is about 1km south of the town of Machalilla. The beaches are reached by walking or driving 2km down a dirt road.

Agua Blanca
Agua Blanca is the largest present-day settlement within the park and was built over a pre-Columbian site of the Manta culture. Known as Señorío de Salangomé, this pre-Columbian capital city served as the political and administrative centre for the area. A large part of this ancient settlement has been excavated and an impressive site museum, constructed with traditional materials, is located in the centre of the modern village. In order to visit the museum and archaeological ruins of Agua Blanca an additional fee must be paid to the community (about US$4). There is a rather grungy sulphur spring near the town and trails that take you past the ruins. Several families in Agua Blanca are accustomed to taking in people for overnight stays, especially when they are planning to hike or ride up to the San Sebastián cloudforest area of the park.

San Sebastian
In the heart of the park is an undisturbed example of pre-montane forest near the community of San Sebastian. This dense vegetation, which includes tall trees and palms, supports howler monkeys, white-tailed deer, ant-eaters, iguanas and numerous bird species. In order to visit the area you need to hire a guide and mules from the community of Agua Blanca for the 4-hour trek; you are not allowed to go independently. It is better to make arrangements for the hike in Agua Blanca rather than at one of the agencies

in Puerto Lopez since your money then goes directly to the community and supports the idea of the park. We recommend the guide Enrique Ventura – he seems to have a good knowledge of the fauna and pre-Columbian ruins. In San Sebastian you can camp or stay in a wooden house owned by two brothers who make a living from tourism and collecting Tagua nuts. It may also be possible to do this hike from the town of El Pital.

Isla de La Plata
The Isla de La Plata is a small island (2x4km) located 24km off the coast but still protected within the park. It has been dubbed locally the 'poor folk's Galápagos' since it is much cheaper and easier to visit. It is home to some of the same species found in the Galápagos Islands such as sea lions, sea turtles, red-billed tropic bird, waved albatross, three species of boobies and long-tailed mockingbirds. Between June and October you might spot a migrating humpback whale. Camping is not allowed on the island without special permission. A day tour of Isla de La Plata can be arranged from the waterfront in Puerto Lopez; the boat trip takes about 1½ to 2 hours each way and costs about US$25 (excluding park entrance fee). There are two loop trails on the island that are easily walked in the 4 hours you are on there. It is also possible to snorkel on the coral reefs that surround the island.

Ayampe to Puerto Lopez
This long day hike or more leisurely 2-day walk is outside the park but offers great views of open humid forest with excellent birding opportunities. It also makes a good mountain-bike trip since it is all on dirt tracks. It is best to bring drinking water, as it is usually hot. You will be wading through a shallow river so wear footgear that you don't mind getting wet, such as sandals or sneakers.

Begin the hike in the small community of Ayampe (just south of Alandaluz resort) at the mouth of the Río Ayampe on the main coastal road. The Río Ayampe is the only river that flows year-round from the park and you will notice water trucks filling up for delivery of fresh water to communities along the coast. The track follows the riverbed upstream and in fact sometimes is the riverbed! It tucks through giant bamboo groves and past small wetlands in a lush river valley where there are herons, parakeets and kingfishers. After 3 to 4 hours of walking you reach a turn-off on the left to Cantalopiedra, an organic farm that supplies food to Alandaluz Ecological Resort and a good spot to stop for lunch. About 300m beyond Cantalopiedra you reach a gravel road where a right turn takes you to the village of Guale and eventually the main coastal highway. A left turn takes you on a dirt road to Puerto López. Along the back road to Puerto López you pass through occasional *fincas* and good humid forest. Río Blanco is another 3 to 4 hours, and a good place to sleep if you want to visit a rural village. There is a small store and public water source. Puerto López is about 2 to 2½ hours beyond Río Blanco and there is often traffic on this portion of the hike. You are not in the park on this hike so you do not need to pay an entrance fee or hire a guide.

Guarango to Agua Blanca

Eleven kilometres south of Jipijapa on the main road to Guayaquil is a turn-off for the village of Guarango. Have the bus let you off at the small settlement of San Dimas on the main road. From here it's a short (3 dusty kilometres) walk to the small village of Guarango. Beyond the village (west), along the mostly unused jeep trail, the valley narrows as the track heads north around a steep hill then south again. Two hours after leaving the main road, you'll come to the village of Julcuy. Here there are several examples of pre-Columbian *alvaradas* constructed to catch the infrequent rainwater run-off in this semi-desert area.

The trail runs southeast through the village, leading up toward a notch in the cliffs. About 1km beyond Julcuy, the track drops down to the river valley and enters a deep gorge. Both waterbirds and raptors abound here and the stream has both fish and freshwater shrimp. Once past Julcuy you are in Parque Nacional Machalilla.

After about an hour the trail and the riverbed separate, though they will continue to criss-cross regularly. There are a couple of springs along the way and several small clusters of houses. It is possible to hike through to Agua Blanca in one very long hot day (about 9 to 10 hours from the main road), but much more pleasurable to take 2 leisurely ones looking at the birds and plants. From May to November it's usually dry and this hike can be done without a tent.

The 5km hike from Agua Blanca to the coastal highway can be done in an hour along a gravel road or you can find a dirt track on the left side of the river that takes you through shaded brush and comes out on the highway several hundred metres south of the guard station. Here frequent buses pass going south to the fishing village of Puerto López and north to the village of Machalilla.

Cerro Blanco

Barely 20 minutes out of Guayaquil, west toward Salinas, is the huge cement operation of Cemento Nacional. The name conjures up images of industrialization with all its negative aspects such as habitat destruction, soil erosion, air pollution, constant chugging of machinery and the like. Cemento Nacional, however, has done a contrary thing. It has set aside much of its property as an ecological reserve which may eventually become a national park. The lowland vegetation here ranges from dry forest on the northern flanks to scrub and kapok to the south. Despite being practically a stone's throw from the largest city in Ecuador, Cerro Blanco is home to an amazing variety of wildlife. Puma, jaguar, jaguarundi, ocelots, howler monkeys, coatis and peccaries are representative of some of the mammals. The list of birds in the area is equally impressive: owls, grey hawks, crane hawks, snail kites, chacalacas and a variety of waterfowl to name just a few. You can go in for the day or camp in the reserve.

To get to the Bosque Protector Cerro Blanco catch a bus to Salinas and get off at the entrance marked by a large white sign that says 'Entrada Bosque Protector Cerro Blanco', just before reaching Balrosario cement plant. Taxis from Guyaquil cost between US$7 and US$10. The park is open between 08.30 and 17.00 and the entrance fee is about US$1.

There is a new campground near the visitors' centre with tent pads, tables and cooking grills, as well as toilets with running water. The camping fee is about US$5 per night. The reserve has two trails. The 'Quebrada Canoa' is a short loop trail through a ravine with permanent pools of water and abundant aquatic life. The other trail is the 'Buenavista', a 3–4-hour round-trip hike up to forest and lookouts over the mangrove swamps. A backcountry trail is planned for overnight hikers wishing to visit the core of the reserve. Canoe trips can be arranged through the mangrove swamps.

More information on the area can be obtained from Fundación Natura, D Sucre 401 and Rosendo Avilés in Guayaquil; tel: 441 793.

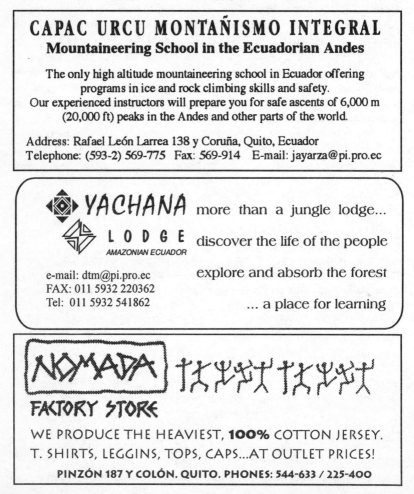

Appendix One

Language

With the exception of a few small, remote, indigenous groups everyone speaks Spanish in Ecuador, including the Andean indigenous people, although for them it is a second language after Quechua. Other European languages are rarely understood except in the major tourist agencies and first-class hotels. Therefore it is essential that you learn some basic Spanish; take heart, it is an easy language to learn.

Quechua, though widely spoken in the highlands, is a difficult language to learn and dialects tend to vary greatly from area to area. So unless you are an avid linguist you're better off learning some Spanish.

The following list of Spanish words and phrases will get you started:

Useful phrases

Where are you going?	¿A dónde va?
Where are you coming from?	¿De dónde viene?
I'm passing through	¿Estoy paseando
Can I camp?	¿Puedo acampar?
Where is the trail to... ?	¿Donde está el camino por.... ?
How are you?	¿Como está?

Greetings

Good morning/day	Buenos días
Good afternoon	Buenas tardes
Good evening/night	Buenas noches
Goodbye	Adiós

Other general vocabulary

Yes	Sí		
No	No	Pick-up truck	Camioneta
Please	Por favor	Bath	Baño
Thank you	Gracias	Bus	Bus, colectivo
Bad	Malo	Road	Carretera
Good	Bueno	Room (in hotel)	Habitación
Baggage	Equipaje	Train	Ferrocarril, tren

Climber's and hiker's vocabulary

			Puente
Above	Arriba	Bridge	Campamento
Altitude	Altura	Camp	Mosquetones
Aqueduct	Acequia	Carabiners	Bajar
Ascent	Subida	Climb (down)	Escalar,
Backpack	Mochila	Climb (up)	Ascender
Below	Abajo	Close (to)	Cerca
Bivouac	Vivac	Cold	Frio
Boots (climbing)	Botas (de andinismo)	Crampons	Grampones

Crevasse	*Grieta*	Mountaineer	*Andinista*
(to) Cross	*Cruzar, Atravesar*	Mule	*Mula*
Distant	*Lejos*	Muleteer	*Arriero*
East	*Este*	Needle	*Aguja*
Face	*Cara*	North	*Norte*
Fixed rope	*Cuerda fija*	Pass	*Paso, Abra, Punta*
Fog	*Niebla*		*Portachuelo,*
Forest	*Bosque*	Peak	*Pico*
Freeze	*Congelar*	Plain (plateau)	*Pampa*
Glacier	*Glaciar*	Point (minor peak)	*Punta*
Hail	*Granizo*	Rain	*Lluvia*
Hammer	*Martillo*	Ravine	*Quebrada*
Highlands	*Sierra*	Right	*Derecha*
Hill	*Loma*	River	*Río*
House	*Casa*	Rock	*Roca*
Hut (climbers')	*Refugio*	Rope	*Cuerda, Soga*
Ice	*Hielo*	Route	*Ruta*
Ice Axe	*Piolet*	Snow	*Nieve*
Ice Screw	*Tornillo*	South	*Sur*
Lake	*Lago, Laguna*	Straight ahead	*Derecho, Recto*
Landslide	*Derrumbe*	Summit	*Cima, Cumbre*
Left	*Izquierda*	Swamp	*Pantano*
Meadow	*Pampa*	Tent	*Carpa*
Moraine	*Morena*	Trail	*Sendero*
Mountain		Valley	*Valle*
(without snow)	*Cerro*	Village	*Pueblo*
Mountain (snow		Waterfall	*Cascada*
peak)	*Nevado*	West	*Oeste*

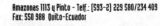

Appendix Two

Elevations

The height of a mountain is a constant source of interest to climbers and non-climbers alike. Upon returning from a climb, one is often asked 'How high is it?' before being questioned about the difficulty, duration or equipment needed for the ascent. In lesser known areas, the question 'How high is it?' is not easily answered. Maps are often sketchy or inaccurate, and different sources come up with various possible heights for the same mountain. Perhaps one of these is correct, perhaps none.

For the sake of consistency, I have used what appears to be the most accurate source for the elevations in this book. These are from the 1979 Instituto Geográfico Militar (IGM) 1:500,000 map of Ecuador. Many other sources are available, and even different maps from the institute give a variety of elevations. The following table lists various given elevations of Ecuador's major peaks – take your pick.

Sources
1 Instituto Geográfico Militar (IGM) 1:500,000 map, 1993
2 IGM 1:1,000,000 map, 1981
3 IGM 1:50,000 series maps 1993
4 Ecuador 1:1,000,000, Kevin Healey, ITMB Publishing, Canada (1993)

	1	2	3		4
Chimborazo	6310	6310	6310	[1991]	6310
Cotopaxi*	5897	5897		[1989]	5897
Cayambe	5790	5790	5790	[1987]	5790
Antisana*	5758	5705	5758	[1983]	5758
El Altar*	5320	5319	5319	[1993]	5319
Iliniza Sur	5248	5263	5245	[1991]	5263
Sangay*	5230	5230	5188	[1993]	5230
Iliniza Norte	5126			[1991]	5126
Tungurahua*	5023	5016	5023	[1989]	5023
Carihuairazo	5020	5020	5018	[1991]	5020
Cotacachi	4944	4937	4944	[1990]	4939
Sincholagua	4893	4899	4873	[1990]	4893
Quilindaña	4878	4878		[1989]	4788
Corazón	4788	4788	4872	[1991]	4788
Guagua Pichincha*	4794	4776	[1990]	4794	
Chiles	4729	4764	4723	[1994]	4723
Rumiñahui	4712	4712	4772	[1991]	4712
Sara Urco		4676	4670	[1988]	4428
Rucu Pichincha			4627	[1990]	4627
Imbabura	4580		4621	[1991]	4609
Hermoso	4571	4571	4571	[1991]	4571

	1	2	3		4
Puntas		4452	**4550**	[1980]	4452
Atacazo	**4463**	4457	4455	[1990]	**4463**
Pasochoa	**4199**	4200	**4199**	[1990]	4200
Sumaco*	**3732**	3900	**3732**	[1988]	**3732**
Reventador*	**3562**	3485	**3562**	[1988]	**3562**

* Active or potentially active volcanoes
All heights are in metres
Elevations used in this book are shown in heavy type.

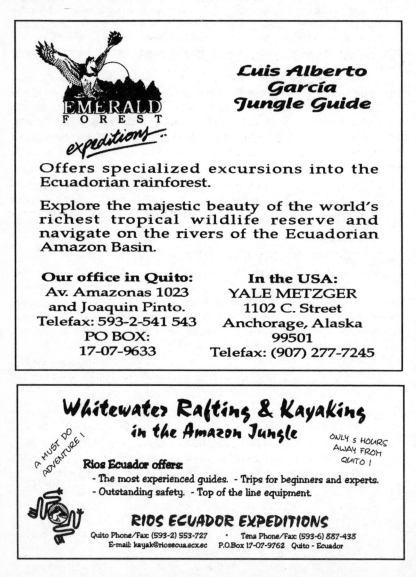

Appendix Three

Further Reading

This section lists all the books we have referred to in preparing this guide and a few more besides, although some are inevitably out of print. I have tried to give as much variety as possible. Books published in Ecuador, and a good selection of English books about Ecuador, are available from Libri Mundi in Quito, tel/fax: 02 504 209.

General South America guidebooks

Ecuador Insight Guides 1996. Beautiful photographs and good background essays.

Ecuador & the Galápagos Islands – a travel survival kit Rachowiecki, Rob. Lonely Planet Publications, Australia, 4th edition 1997 and updated regularly. The best general guide to Ecuador.

South America on a Shoestring Various authors. Lonely Planet Publications, Australia, 6th edition 1997 and updated regularly. A good general guide for the budget traveller, with many city maps.

South American Handbook Box, Ben (ed). Footprint Handbooks, England. Updated annually, this 1,000-plus-page book is the best overall guide to Latin America. Expensive, but worth every penny to anyone planning on spending a long time in Latin America.

Guidebooks for the outdoors

Cardenas, J G and Greiner, K M *Walking the Beaches of Ecuador* Quito, 1988. The authors describe how they walked or jogged the entire Ecuadorian coastline.

Kelsey, Michael R *A Climber's and Hiker's Guide to the World's Mountains* Kelsey Publications, USA, 3rd edition 1990. Includes a section on Ecuador and much more on the rest of the world. A good introductory book for the globetrotting mountaineer.

Plourde, Mark E *Ecuador Volcanoes: An Illustrated Guide To Climbing Selected Peaks of The Northern Andes* This self-published guide is undated (1992?) and difficult to find but covers some of the major Ecuadorian peaks.

Serrano, Rojas and Landazuri *Montañas Del Sol* Campo Abierto, 1994. Spanish-language climbing guide to mountaineering in Ecuador.

Weilbauer, Arthur *Guía Para Excursiones en Automóvil a Través del Ecuador* Quito, 1985. Available in Spanish, German and English. An invaluable guide to all the major and most minor roads in Ecuador. Available only in Ecuador.

Wesche, Rolf (ed) *The Ecotourist's Guide to the Ecuadorian Amazon* University of Ottawa and TR&D, 1995. Excellent guide to ecotourism in Napo Province with some hikes described.

General mountaineering and exploration

Bonington, Chris *The Next Horizon* Victor Gollancz, 1973 (out of print)

Humboldt, Alexander von and Bonpland, Aimé *Personal Narrative of the Travels to the Equinoctial Regions of the New Continent* Various editions. Difficult to find, but fascinating reading for anyone interested in the historical aspects of Latin-American exploration.

Meyer, Hans, translated by Jonás Guerrero, *En Los Altos Andes del Ecuador* Abya-Yala, 1993. Originally published in German as *In den Hoch-Anden von Ecuador*, Berlin, 1907.

Snailham, Richard *Sangay Survived* Hutchinson, 1978 (out of print). The story of a six-man British scientific expedition to the volcano which ended disastrously when an eruption killed or injured most of the members.

Whymper, Edward *Travels Amongst the Great Andes of the Equator* 1891. Describes the 1880 expedition which first climbed Ecuador's highest peak, and made seven other first ascents. Available in several recent reprints by other publishers. Worth getting hold of.

Natural history and vulcanology

Andrews, Michael *The Flight of the Condor* Collins, 1982. Subtitled 'A Wildlife Exploration of the Andes', this well-illustrated book contains an excellent chapter on Ecuador.

Emmons, Louise H *Neotropical Rainforest Mammals – A Field Guide* University of Chicago Press, USA, 1990. A detailed and well-illustrated guide to the mammals of Amazonia and the Central American rainforests. Recommended.

Forsyth, Adrian and Miyata, Ken *Tropical Nature* Scribners, New York, 1984. Sub-titled 'Life and Death in the Rain Forests of Central and South America', this book is a great introduction to the natural history of the rainforest.

Hall, Minard L *El Volcanismo en El Ecuador* IPGH, Quito, 1977. In Spanish, mainly of interest to the vulcanologist. The best work on the subject.

Kricher, John C *A Neotropical Companion* Princeton University Press, USA, 1989. Sub-titled 'An Introduction to the Animals, Plants, and Ecosystems of the New World Tropics', this book is just as good as the one listed above by Forsyth and Miyata. Both are recommended.

Morrison, Tony *The Andes* Time-Life Books, 1975. A beautiful book covering the whole Andean chain; Ecuador's mountains are not forgotten with superb photographs of Cotopaxi and Sangay.

Morrison, Tony *Land Above the Clouds* Deutsch, 1974. This book also deals with the whole Andean chain with an emphasis on its wildlife. Recommended.

Patzelt, Erwin *Fauna del Ecuador* Banco Central del Ecuador, Quito, 1989. In Spanish. Particularly useful for mammals, reptiles and amphibians.

Patzelt, Erwin *Flora del Ecuador* 1985. In Spanish. Out of print but there is talk of a new edition.

Ecuador – in the Shadow of the Volcanoes, Ediciones Libri Mundi, 1981. Available in English, Spanish, German and French. A 'coffee-table' book, with many superb photos.

Ornithology

Crespot, Greenfield & Matheus *Birds of Ecuador* FEPROTUR, Quito, 1990. A locational checklist.

Dunning, John S *South American Birds – A Photographic Aid to Identification* Harrowood Books, PA, USA, 1987. 1,400 birds illustrated and 2,700 described in this book, which covers water as well as land birds.

Green, Clive *Birding Ecuador* 2nd edition 1996. Available from American Birding Association, PO Box 6599, Colorado Springs, CO 80934, USA, tel: (800) 834 7736, fax: (719) 578 9705. Detailed account of birding trips in Ecuador with useful checklists, sketch maps and access details of many birding hotspots in Ecuador.

Hilty, S J and Brown, W L *A Guide to the Birds of Colombia* Princeton University Press, 1986. An excellent field guide which covers most of Ecuador's species.

Ridgely, R and Greenfield, P *A Guide to the Birds of Ecuador* Cornell University Press. The authors have been working on this authoritative two-volume text for over a decade; it is expected to be published in the late 1990s. Meanwhile, use the books above.

For a full list of current natural history books, contact the Natural History Book Service, 2-3 Wills Road, Totnes, Devon TQ9 5XN, England; tel: 01803 865913.

Health

Darvill MD, Fred T *Mountaineering Medicine – A Wilderness Medical Guide* Wilderness Press, USA, 1992. A 100-page booklet worth carrying on hiking and backpacking trips.

Steele, Peter *Medical handbook for mountaineers* Constable, London. Pocket-sized yet detailed.

Wilson-Howarth, Dr Jane *Healthy Travel: Bugs, Bites & Bowels* Cadogan Books, London. For independent travellers.

Wilson-Howarth, Dr Jane and Ellis, Dr Matthew *Your Child's Health Abroad: A manual for travelling parents* Bradt Publications, England, 1998. A comprehensive manual covering all aspects of children's health and safety away from home.

Miscellaneous

Blandin Landivar, Carlos *El Clima y Sus Características en El Ecuador* IPGH, Quito, 1976. A Spanish-language book on the meteorology of Ecuador.

Botting, Douglas *Humboldt and the Cosmos* Sphere Books, London. A biographical account of one of the best-known early explorers of Ecuador and South America.

Corkill, David *Ecuador* World Bibliographical Series, Clio Press, Oxford, England. A complete bibliography of Ecuador.

Corkill, D & Cubitt, D *Ecuador – Fragile Democracy* 1988, Latin American Bureau, UK. A look at historical patterns and current trends in Ecuadorian politics.

Cuvi, Pablo *In the eyes of my people* Dinediciones/Grijalbo, Ecuador, 1988. Difficult to find outside of Ecuador, but highly recommended once you get there. Sub-titled 'Stories and photos of journeys through Ecuador', this book is written by an Ecuadorian who both loves his country and knows how to write. The photos are some of the best I've seen of Ecuador and its people.

Gartelmann, K D *El Mundo Perdido de Los Aucas* (The Lost World of the Aucas) Quito, 1978. A multilingual book with many colour photographs describing one of the least known and least accessible indigenous tribes of Ecuador.

Hemming, John *The Conquest of the Incas* Harcourt Brace, USA, 1970. A thorough and exceptional work on the subject.

Miller, Tom *The Panama Hat Trail* Vintage Departures, NY, USA, 1988. A well-written account of Miller's search for Panama hats in Ecuador, with good descriptions of Ecuadorian life.

Natural Resources Defense Council *Amazon Crude* USA, 1991. A hard-hitting look at the environmental and social problems caused by oil drilling in the Amazon.

Urrutia, Virginia *Two Wheels and a Taxi* The Mountaineers, USA, 1987. Ms Urrutia was 70 when she cycled around Ecuador with a local cab driver for logistical support.

Diez Cuentistas Ecuatorianas (Ten Stories From Ecuador), Libri Mundi, Quito, 1990. Ten short stories by Ecuadorian writers, in Spanish with English translations.

Smith, Randy *Manual de Ecotourism: Para Guías y Comunidades Indigenas de la Amazonia Ecuatoriana* Abya-Yala, Quito, 1996. Good species lists in the appendix in several indigenous languages.

Periodicals

Montaña The magazine of the San Gabriel Climbing Club, Quito. The oldest established mountaineering magazine in Ecuador, appearing at irregular intervals. (No 11, January 1975; No 12, January 1980; No 13, July 1981; No 14, April 1983; No 15, August 1984; No 16, February 1989; No 17, date unknown; No 18, January 1995.) In Spanish with some English mountain descriptions.

Campo Abierto Quito, Ecuador. A more regularly published mountaineering magazine begun in 1982; most recent edition No 16, March 1993. In Spanish.

OTHER BRADT GUIDES TO CENTRAL & SOUTH AMERICA

Guide to Belize (2nd edition)
Alex Bradbury
'An informative guide to help you discover the natural beauty of Belize' *Woman's Journal*
Now updated with additional information on diving areas and wildlife reserves.
336pp   8pp colour   25 maps   £10.95   1 898323 48 8

Guide to Brazil – Pantanal, Amazon and Coastal Regions (2nd edition)
Alex Bradbury et al
'Invaluable' *The Sunday Telegraph*
For those especially interested in the nature and wildlife of Brazil, this guide is the most detailed available.
256pp   8pp colour   16 maps   £11.95   1 898323 59 3

Backpacking in Central America
Tim Burford
Belize, Guatemala, El Salvador, Honduras, Nicaragua, Costa Rica, Panama. This guide emphasises the region's wildlife and protected areas.
336pp   43 maps   £10.95   1 898323 25 9

Central and South America by Road
Pam Ascanio
'Advice about the best vehicle and equipment to take, route-planning, details of border formalities, and country-by-country profiles.' *Geographical Magazine*
256pp   16pp colour   24 maps   £12.95   1 898323 24 0

Backpacking in Chile and Argentina (3rd edition)
Hilary Bradt et al
'This travel guide is a must.' *SA Explorer*
The best and most enjoyable way to see these countries and experience spectacular mountain scenery, well-run national parks, excellent food and wine, good transportation and safe cities.
208pp   45 maps   £10.95   1 898323 04 6

Guide to Cuba (2nd edition)
Stephen Fallon
'Provides virtually everything needed for a first tourist trip to Cuba.' *The Washington Times*
A thorough and sensitive guide to all aspects of Cuba, including history, culture and traditions, with practical listings and advice.
272pp   8pp colour   28 maps   £11.95   1 898323 62 3

Backpacking in Mexico
Tim Burford
A comprehensive and practical guide to Mexico's long- and short-distance hiking trails and volcanoes, covering Yucatán, Chiapas, Baja California and Copper Canyon.
256pp   20 maps   £11.95   1 898323 56 9

Backpacking and Trekking in Peru and Bolivia (6th edition)
Hilary Bradt
'Informative, diverting, encouraging and inspirational' *High Magazine*
Hiking trails aroundInca ruins andthrough maagnificent mountins. Natural history and indian culture, plus advice on low-impact travel.
336pp   32 maps   £10.95   0 946983 86 0

Guide to Venezuela (2nd edition)
Hilary Dunsterville Branch
'Information which is vitalto thenewcomer orprosperctive traveller ... is all here.' *RAC*
Emphasis on the national parks and wild areas, but with plenty of city information too.
400pp   8pp colour   83 maps   £12.95   1 898323 31 3

Bradt Guides are available from bookshops or by mail order from:
Bradt Publications, 41 Nortoft Road, Chalfont St Peter, Bucks SL9 0LA, England.
Tel/fax: 01494 873478. Email: bradtpublications @compuserve.com
Please include your name, address and daytime telephone number with your order and enclose a cheque or postal order, or quote your Visa/Access card number and expiry date. Postage will be charged as follows:
UK: £1.50 for one book; £2.50 for two or more books
Europe (inc. Eire): £2 for one book; £4 for two or more books (airmail printed paper)
Rest of world: £4 for one book; £7 for two or more books (airmail printed paper)

INDEX